The Pittsburgh Penguins

The Pittsburgh Penguins

The First 25 Years

Greg Enright

McFarland & Company, Inc., Publishers

Jefferson, North Carolina

Library of Congress Cataloguing-in-Publication Data

Names: Enright, Greg, 1969– author.
Title: The Pittsburgh Penguins : the first 25 years / Greg Enright.
Description: Jefferson, N.C. : McFarland & Company, Inc.,
    Publishers, 2020. | Includes bibliographical references and index.
Identifiers: LCCN 2020010202 | ISBN 9781476681733
    (paperback : acid free paper) ∞
    ISBN 9781476640013 (ebook)
Subjects: LCSH: Pittsburgh Penguins (Hockey team)—History.
Classification: LCC GV848.P58 E67 2020 | DDC 796.962/640974886—dc23
LC record available at https://lccn.loc.gov/2020010202

British Library cataloguing data are available

ISBN (print) 978-1-4766-8173-3
ISBN (ebook) 978-1-4766-4001-3

Front cover: Mario Lemieux (left) and Jean Pronovost
(photographs courtesy of Doug McLatchy);
the Pittsburgh Civic Arena, nicknamed "The Igloo"
(photograph by Perry Quan)

Printed in the United States of America

McFarland & Company, Inc., Publishers
    Box 611, Jefferson, North Carolina 28640
    www.mcfarlandpub.com

For Trace, Lucas and Melia
and
in memory of my father,
who loved the game

Acknowledgments

Hockey is a team game and so is writing a book. Thank you to everyone who has helped me make this idea a reality, including the many former Penguin players who graciously took the time to speak with me: Dave Burrows, Dave Hannan, Denis Herron, Earl Ingarfield, Rick Kehoe, Troy Loney, Dick Mattiussi, Noel Price, Jean Pronovost, Dan Quinn and Ron Stackhouse; the reporters who shared their insights and memories of their time covering the team: Bill Heufelder, Lou Prato and Bob Smizik; Joe Gordon, who told me what it was like at the very beginning; Cindy Himes at the Penguins Alumni, who connected me with many of the former players with whom I spoke; Pittsburgh mayor Bill Peduto, who took time out of his busy schedule to share his Penguin memories; Mike Hanczar for his photos and for giving me the fan's perspective; Gary Mitchem and the entire team at McFarland for their help and guidance throughout the publishing process; the many friends and family members who showed their enthusiastic support; Doug McLatchy and Ron Kerrigan for providing photos; Nicholas Hartley and the staff at the Office of the City Clerk in Pittsburgh for collecting images of the Civic Arena; Brian Jamieson for his invaluable edits and enthusiastic support; Olivia Yu and Simon Young for their encouragement and trusted feedback; Tim Beever for his support and for sharing his vast resource library that greatly aided my research; and Steve Currier, who provided many newspaper clippings from Oakland newspapers as well as helpful source contact information. I want to give a special thanks to Bob Grove, who not only took the time to speak with me but also did a thorough review of the manuscript and provided many edits that have strengthened the final product. Most important, thanks to my wife, Tracy, and our two children, Lucas and Melia, for accepting my obsession with old newspaper articles and letting me take the time I needed to put this together.

Table of Contents

Acknowledgments   vi

Foreword by Jean Pronovost   1

Preface   3

Part One—Waddling Out of the Gate
(1966–67 Through 1968–69)

1. The Penguins Are Hatched: 1966–67   8

2. Dropping the Puck: 1967–68   15

3. Flightless: 1968–69   23

Part Two—Kelly's Men
(1969–70 Through 1972–73)

4. Breakthrough: 1969–70   30

5. On Thin Ice, Again: 1970–71   40

6. Picking Up the Pieces: 1971–72   45

7. So Long, Red: 1972–73   52

Part Three—A Matter of Survival
(1973–74 Through 1978–79)

8. Punchless Penguins: 1973–74   58

9. Finally, a Winner: 1974–75   63

10. The Great Penguin Crash of '75: Summer 1975   74

11. Penguin Power: 1975–76   77

12. Country Club: 1976–77   84

13. Trader Al: 1977–78   93

14. Trader Baz: 1978–79   99

**Part Four—The Pesky Pens
(1979–80 Through 1981–82)**

15. A Step Back: 1979–80   108

16. The Rick and Randy Show: 1980–81   117

17. One Bounce Short: 1981–82   126

**Part Five—Bottoming Out
(1982–83 Through 1983–84)**

18. Paying the Piper: 1982–83   140

19. The Mario Miracle: 1983–84   148

**Part Six—Mario
(1984–85 Through 1987–88)**

20. Getting on Route 66: 1984–85   160

21. March Sadness: 1985–86   166

22. Fast Start, Hard Crash: 1986–87   173

23. Sour Cream: 1987–88   179

**Part Seven—Building a Champion
(1988–89 Through 1991–92)**

24. Enter Espo: 1988–89   188

25. Backaches and Heartaches: 1989–90   198

26. Top of the Mountain: 1990–91   205

27. Repeat Performance: 1991–92   224

Epilogue   240

Chapter Notes   245

Bibliography   253

Index   255

Foreword
by Jean Pronovost

When I joined the Pittsburgh Penguins in the spring of 1968, I was very excited. I'd been traded by the Boston Bruins, who were just entering their heyday with the likes of Bobby Orr and Phil Esposito. They had drafted me, but I hadn't yet played a game for them. They were stacked with talent, which was going to make it hard for a 22-year-old like me to crack their lineup. Coming to Pittsburgh, an expansion team entering only its second year, meant I would have a great shot at making a big-league club and living my boyhood dream of playing in the NHL.

After failing to win with a roster of mainly older, experienced players in their first year, the Penguins were shifting their focus to youth. I came to training camp knowing I had a great opportunity before me, and I seized it. I made the team and never looked back, staying with the Penguins for 10 seasons.

There was no shortage of turmoil with the Penguins during those years—money shortages, ownership changes, and even a bankruptcy. We also suffered the tragic loss of one of the game's brightest young stars, Michel Brière.

But we also had some very good teams in Pittsburgh at that time. We could really put the puck in the net. It was a pleasure playing with such fine talents as Syl Apps, Jr., Lowell MacDonald, Les Binkley and Pierre Larouche, to name just a few. Unfortunately, in Pittsburgh we did not end up fulfilling the ultimate goal of any hockey player—winning the Stanley Cup. Perhaps if we had won one more game against the Islanders in 1975 and moved on in the playoffs, things would have turned out differently. But it was not to be. I eventually asked for a trade and was dealt to the Atlanta Flames in 1978, and I later played for the Washington Capitals before retiring.

I left the Penguins as the team's all-time leader in goals and games played. Those records didn't last long, though, thanks to a guy with the number 66 on his back! Mario Lemieux, of course, would arrive in 1984 and lead the

Penguins to the Stanley Cup seven years later. It was great watching the team I spent so many years with finally reach the top.

Today, the Penguins organization is virtually unrecognizable from the one I knew back in the 60s and 70s. The modern rink with all its amenities, the training facilities, player lounges, chartered flights, catered meals—it is quite the operation!

But the Penguins of today still share much with the teams of my era. They have the skating penguin with the Golden Triangle on their jerseys, and they wear it with pride. They have the same determination to win as we did. And they have the passion of the city's fans driving them forward. I like to think that the Penguin teams of my era were the foundation of the triumphs that came later. We got NHL hockey truly established in the Steel City, and of that I am proud.

In this book, Greg Enright has captured the history of the Penguins before they were champions as well as the franchise's first taste of being on top of the hockey world. It's a story full of ups and downs, heartbreaks and highlights, tragedies and triumphs. Reading through these pages, those fans who were there can relive it, and those who weren't can get a sense of what Penguin hockey was like all those years ago.

Jean Pronovost played right wing for the Penguins from 1968 to 1978. He still ranks among franchise leaders in goals (316), points (603) and games played (753). A former team captain and NHL All-Star, Pronovost is a member of the Penguins' All-Time Team.

Preface

There weren't many kids in Montreal in the late 1970s who became Pittsburgh Penguins fans. In fact, I knew of only one.

Me.

Why, you ask, would a kid just discovering the great game of hockey choose to cheer for Pittsburgh, a team that hadn't won anything, over the mighty hometown Canadiens, who at the time were making an annual ritual of carting the Stanley Cup around the ice?

For me, a life-long passion for the Penguins started when I first laid eyes on their logo. It was 1977 and I was eight. That hockey-playing penguin was included in a picture I'd come across that featured all (at the time) 17 NHL team emblems. I was fascinated with each one, but the penguin stood out. I liked everything about him—his gloves, his stick, his skates, his fierce expression. It was, as they say, love at first sight. Everything was determined at that moment: I was a hockey fan, the Pittsburgh logo was my favorite, the Pens were my favorite team, and I wanted whoever was wearing that logo to win!

Hockey and the Penguins soon became the biggest things on my mind. I learned more about the team as that 1977–78 season progressed. Like the logo, I was enamored with their double-blue uniforms. I learned who their players were: guys like Jean Pronovost, Rick Kehoe and Ron Stackhouse became instant heroes. And Denis Herron's chevron mask was waaay better than Ken Dryden's or Gerry Cheevers'... don't even get me started.

Word got around that I had made this curious choice of a favorite team, and it really paid off for me on November 29, 1977. My Uncle Bill, a huge hockey fan, remembered I was a Pens supporter and, when he couldn't use his tickets to their game that night at the Montreal Forum, he had them couriered to me. You could have packed 10 Christmas mornings together and I wouldn't have been more excited. Watching them live that night was like a dream. There were my idols, skating right before me, with their uniforms looking sharper than I could ever have imagined. The Pens lost, but I don't remember being too upset. I left the Forum elated, my affinity for the team cemented even further.

I drew that logo all the time. When I played road hockey in front of my house, I was Pete Mahovlich, scoring the winning goal for the Pens in the Stanley Cup final. I even became obsessed with the city of Pittsburgh. To me, it was a far-away dreamland where my hockey-card heroes played in a place called "The Igloo." I even petitioned my mother to move the family there so I could see all of their games and was always dismayed when she'd react like I was suggesting we fly to the moon.

As each season came and went, I lived and died with every game. The unguarded optimism of late childhood, which had me believing the Penguins could win any game, eventually gave way to the sobering realizations of early adolescence. When the Penguins hit their nadir in the years 1982–1984, I was then old enough to realize they were then a very bad hockey team. Quite frankly, they'd become an embarrassment, and as a self-conscious teenager, I started to keep my fandom under my hat.

When Mario Lemiuex came on the scene in 1984, however, he brought a renewed hope. Here was a player who could maybe, just maybe, one day lead us to the top of the mountain. Seven years later, of course, he did just that. Finally, unbelievably, my Penguins were the best. That was, to be sure, another 10-Christmas-mornings moment.

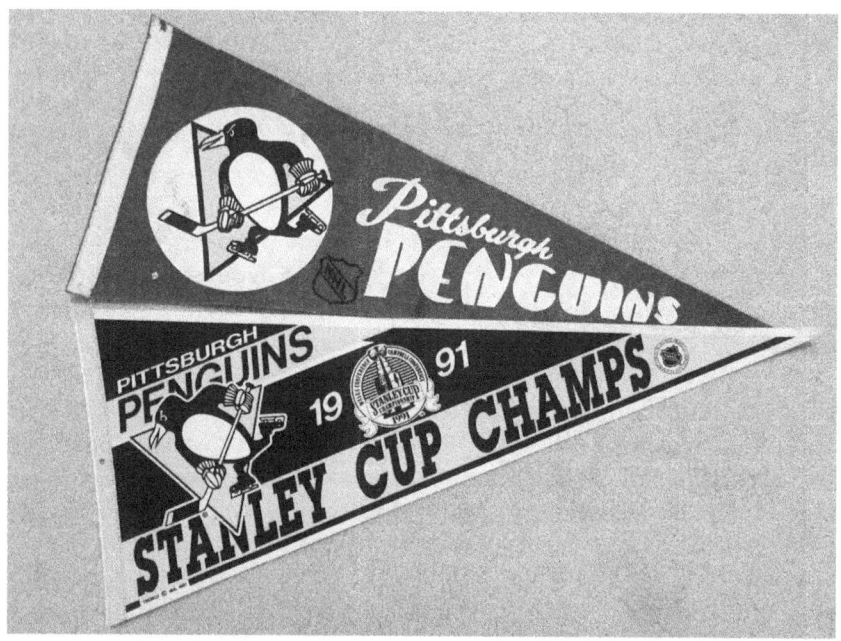

Penguins pennants, 1977 and 1991 (author's collection).

Throughout all these years, one of the most challenging aspects of being a Pens fan where I lived was simply finding enough information about them. In Montreal and, later, Toronto, where my family moved in the early 1980s, Penguin news was in agonizingly short supply.

I gleaned the basic facts of the 10 years of franchise history that was "before my time"—the yearly records, the lists of coaches and captains, the scores of their few playoff games. But the record books and encyclopedias in which I'd found them didn't provide the full story. In those pre-internet days, there was no Wikipedia to go to, no social media platforms or chat groups to throw questions out on. There were certainly no books that I could find that delved into such depths of Penguin history. I had no access to Pittsburgh newspapers. I couldn't get their games on the radio, and I mostly only saw them on TV when they were playing the Leafs or Canadiens.

It wasn't until 2008, when Google started posting the archives of countless newspapers, that I experienced my Howard-Carter-discovering-King-Tut's-tomb moment. Fortunately for me, Google included both the *Pittsburgh Post-Gazette* and the defunct *Pittsburgh Press* in its back-issue treasure trove. Instantly, available right in the comfort of my home office, were reports of almost every game the Penguins had played between 1967 and 2007; all the player profiles those papers had published; hundreds of pictures; day-by-day reports of every major event in team history, from the founding to the 1975 bankruptcy to the drafting of Mario Lemieux to the first two Stanley Cups.

I giddily spent hour after hour combing the archives, feeling a palpable sense of excitement with each issue, anticipating what great article or old picture was going to pop up with my next click. I soon set up a blog to share my top finds with others and later a Twitter feed. My research jumped all over the historical Penguin map.

I realized, however, that with this tsunami of information now at my fingertips, I'd be able to write a comprehensive history of the Penguins' first 25 years. There was a narrative there, from the fragile beginnings in 1966, through all the struggles for survival, up to the triumphs of 1991 and 1992. I'd read some fine books about the team's past, but was dismayed that a comprehensive work that told the entire story of their first quarter-century chronologically wasn't available.

So, in the summer of 2016, I started to write one. Day by day, season by season, I pieced together the bulk of the story that forms this book. Some of the greatest thrills of my reportorial life came next, when I interviewed many of the players I'd cheered for over the years and spoke with many of the reporters who covered the team at different points in its history.

I wrote this book to satisfy my curiosity and because I felt it was important to capture the Penguins' colorful early history. The years continue to roll by and memories continue to fade—even the period of Lemieux's initial ascent is now starting to seem like a long time ago. I wanted to make sure the story was there for anyone who, like me, wanted to know it. I hope you enjoy reading it as much as I did writing it.

Part One

Waddling Out of the Gate
(1966–67 Through 1968–69)

1

The Penguins
Are Hatched:
1966–67

The Pittsburgh Penguins began life as an idea in the mind of Peter Block, a successful young Pittsburgh lawyer and an avid hockey fan. In the 1960s, Block could regularly be found at the brand-new Civic Arena, cheering on the city's minor-league team, the Hornets. When the National Hockey League announced in 1965 that it would be expanding to six new markets for the 1967–68 season, Block felt a responsibility to do what he could to make sure his city got one of the big-league franchises. He set out to gather a group of local investors to cover the $2-million franchise fee.

Much to his chagrin, Block's attempts to sell the idea on the deep-pocketed money men he approached were met with indifference. Discouraged and unsure how to proceed, Block unloaded his feelings one morning to his old law school buddy Jack E. McGregor as the two drove to the state capital in Harrisburg, Pennsylvania, where McGregor was serving as a state senator. He'd heard about the NHL's expansion plan and was quick to agree with Block that Pittsburgh deserved a top-tier hockey team. They stopped for breakfast along the way to ponder the idea. As McGregor recalled a year later, "We talked about it a little, and I said, 'Let me make a few calls. Let me see if I can develop some interest.'"[1]

With the ambitious and influential young senator now on board, Block's vision began to take shape. Selling the idea in part as a way to contribute to an ongoing urban renewal of Pittsburgh—which was once dubbed the "Smoky City" due to the air pollution its steel mills unceasingly pumped out—McGregor worked tirelessly to secure the commitments of numerous local high-rollers. There was H.J. Heinz III from the renowned ketchup maker, W.D. George III, a prominent Pittsburgh stockbroker, as well as Ira Gordon, president of Swift Industries, a maker of prefabricated homes. Perhaps most importantly, there was Art Rooney, owner of Pittsburgh's National Football League Steelers. By early 1966, McGregor and Block had built an investment group of 20 individuals that would collectively foot the $2-million bill.

On February 8, 1966, McGregor, Block and Rooney presented their case to the NHL Board of Governors in New York. Through his involvement in the world of horse racing and boxing, Rooney had links to both Detroit Red Wings owner Bruce Norris and his brother Jim, who owned the Chicago Black Hawks. Exploiting those associations to full advantage, Rooney lobbied both men hard to choose Pittsburgh's application over one from Buffalo.

The Pittsburgh bid nevertheless faced an uphill climb.

"We were a long-shot to get one of the franchises," remembered Joe Gordon, a public relations official for the Hornets who was working with the McGregor-Block group. "A big reason was that the Civic Arena only had a seating capacity of 9,800 and the NHL required at least 12,500. So it was far below their standards."[2]

In the end, Rooney's boardroom machinations paid off. When the NHL announced the successful expansion bids the next day, Pittsburgh was on the list. NHL hockey would be returning to the Steel City after a 37-year absence.

The Civic Arena, home to the Pittsburgh Penguins from 1967 to 2010. Built in 1961, it was affectionately nicknamed "The Igloo" after its dome-shaped design (courtesy City Planning Department Records, City Archives, Office of the City Clerk, City of Pittsburgh).

Pittsburgh's first NHL team, the Pirates, had lasted five years before moving to Philadelphia in 1930 due to an inadequate arena and ownership's inability to weather the financial hardships inflicted by the Great Depression.

But now, big-league hockey was back. Pittsburgh would join Philadelphia, St. Louis, Minneapolis-St. Paul, Oakland and Los Angeles in what came to be known as the NHL's "Great Expansion."

"We plan to do everything possible to ensure a top-flight team for Pittsburgh," Block said the day the franchise was granted.[3]

Gordon, who became the new team's first public relations director, remembered the happiness of that day. "Back in Pittsburgh, we had a tremendous party at the William Penn Hotel with all the investors and all the partners, and it was a very joyous occasion."[4]

Aside from opening a downtown office and electing a board of governors from the group of investors, Block and McGregor's first task would be to find a general manager to build and run the entire hockey organization. "We'll be looking for the best in the business," Block said.[5]

They found their man three months later when they hired Jack Riley, then the president of the American Hockey League. The 46-year-old Toronto native had enjoyed a solid minor league career as a right winger before moving into coaching and management. Riley served as general manager of the AHL's Rochester Americans for five years before taking the league's top post in 1964. He was a hot management commodity when the Great Expansion hit, with other new clubs expressing interest in hiring him, including the Philadelphia Flyers and St. Louis Blues. But the calm and personable Riley chose Pittsburgh and was given complete control over the hockey operation.

"Jack had a laid-back personality," Lou Prato, a reporter who covered the Penguins for the *Hockey News* during their first two seasons, remembered. "He had a soft tone and he wasn't rigid when you were around him."[6]

Dick Mattiussi, a defenseman on the first two Penguin teams, remembered that Riley was "one of the nicest people I played for. He was one of the fairest management people in hockey. He was one of the good ones. He could relate to you. You could go to see him with any problem you had. He'd always treat you with respect, whether you were the best player on the team or the worst. I don't think anybody disliked Jack."[7]

Riley's first move was to hire George "Red" Sullivan as coach, which was announced on the same day as his own hiring. Sullivan had previously served as bench boss of the New York Rangers for two-plus seasons before being let go during the 1965–66 campaign. Earlier, he had enjoyed a career as a steady centerman for the Rangers and Black Hawks. Sullivan had been the youngest-ever NHL head coach when he signed on with New York at age 33. At the time of his hiring by the Pens, he owned the AHL's single-season scoring record, having notched 119 points for the Hershey Bears in 1953–54. That performance earned him that year's AHL MVP award.

Riley knew he'd be getting a strong motivator in Sullivan. "He'll blister the plaster off the walls if [the players] aren't moving," he said.[8]

"He was a fiery guy. Kicked the wastebasket a few times," attested Mattiussi.[9]

In Prato's view, Sullivan "wasn't gruff. He was up front with everything. He didn't try to evade. He probably did criticize players but I don't think he criticized them openly. He and Jack were both very likeable people."[10]

Sullivan was confident he'd have an entertaining squad. "I can promise you this: nobody will fall asleep in the building watching us play."[11]

The next major step for the young team was to choose a nickname. Both Riley and Sullivan, harkening back to their Irish roots, liked "Shamrocks," but to no avail. A name-the-team contest that had garnered over 26,000 entries received 716 votes for "Penguins," and on February 9, 1967, a contest committee officially chose it as the winner. Other popular submissions included Pioneers, Pipers and Golden Triangles. Hornets, the nickname of the American Hockey League franchise then in Pittsburgh, also received a good number of votes. According to Gordon, the main reason for forgoing Hornets was that it was associated with a minor league team and ownership wanted a fresh start for the major league club.[12]

Gordon was disappointed with idea of a flightless fowl representing the new club. "I didn't think that was synonymous with a hockey team and a very physical sport," he said. "From the outset, I thought it was going to be difficult to market the team."[13]

He wasn't the only team official displeased with "Penguins."

"It's a bird, and one of the dirtiest birds in the world," Riley said.[14] Sullivan agreed. "The day after we play a bad game," he growled, "the sportswriters will say, 'They skated like a bunch of nuns.'"[15]

It was later revealed that McGregor's wife, Carol, had a strong preference for Penguins because the team would be playing in the Civic Arena, which was nicknamed the "Big Igloo" due to its distinctive dome-shape construction. Having a bunch of penguins skating inside it seemed right to Mrs. McGregor.

"It was definitely different," remembered Earl Ingarfield, a veteran center who played on the first two Penguin teams, when asked about the nickname. "You say 'Penguins' and it kind of gives you a little chuckle. But I think that nickname started it where teams named themselves differently than in the past."[16]

Riley did, however, get to choose the team colors. He went with a double-blue scheme like that used by his old junior team in Toronto, St. Michael's

College. When it came time to order uniforms, Riley made sure there was no mention of "Penguins" on them, lest the owners come to their senses and go with a different nickname before the season began. They simply displayed the word "PITTSBURGH" diagonally across the front.

Also nowhere to be seen was the club's logo, which featured a portly, scarf-wearing penguin developed by local artist Bob Gessner. Gordon suggested the addition of an inverted golden triangle, emblematic of Pittsburgh's downtown area that was formed by the convergence of the Allegheny, Monongahela and Ohio rivers. "So we put the golden triangle behind the penguin and it's still there," he remembered proudly.[17]

By September 1967—less than a month before the team's first game—the nickname was still Penguins. A resigned Riley had finally come to accept it and was even prepared to alter the uniforms for the team's second season to include the logo.

"And if we're in first place, Penguins will sound just great," he rationalized.[18]

• • •

The 1966–67 season came and went. As Riley continued to build his new hockey operation, the Pittsburgh Hornets won the Calder Cup as champions of the AHL during their final season in the Steel City. With that kind of success, Pittsburgh hockey fans had been used to seeing a champion on the ice, Penguins ownership reasoned. They concluded that their team needed to be as successful as possible right out of the gate. Building slowly with youth simply would not do.

At the NHL's expansion draft in June 1967, therefore, Riley and his management team went looking for veteran players who could use their experience to get an edge on the other new expansion teams, and maybe even surprise some of the six older clubs. To that end, the Pens used many of their 20 picks from the unprotected lists of the established teams to select seasoned players. They didn't take their centerpiece until the second-to-last round: 35-year-old right winger Andy Bathgate, who had starred for years with the Rangers and was a shoo-in for the Hockey Hall of Fame whenever he decided to hang up his skates.

"I remember Jack Riley joking that Bathgate was the best seventeenth-round draft choice in the history of sports," said Bill Heufelder, the *Pittsburgh Press*'s first Penguins beat reporter.[19]

Long on leadership and experience, Bathgate was, however, clearly in the twilight of his career. Playing the previous year for Detroit, Bathgate had managed only eight goals in 60 games and had even been sent down to the Wings' farm team—the Hornets, ironically—for six games.

Other veteran names who became Pittsburgh property on that momentous day in Montreal's Queen Elizabeth Hotel included defensemen Leo Boivin and Al McNeil and forwards Earl Ingarfield and Ken Schinkel, all of whom coach Sullivan knew from his days with the Rangers. The Pens also chose former Hornets Ab McDonald, Bob Dillabough and Art Stratton.

"The Hornets were pretty successful, so the fans expected instant success, particularly when they added some of those Hornet players," said Prato.[20]

"I think a lot of people missed the Hornets, the way they just dominated the American League," remembered Mike Hanczar, a long-time Penguins season ticket holder who developed a love for hockey watching the Hornets play while in his teens. "The Hornets were doing so well that last year they played, it felt like it was going to be a step down when the Penguins got here because you knew they weren't going to be as good."[21]

Heufelder also remembers a rather ho-hum reception in Pittsburgh to the news of a new NHL team coming to town, even within his own sports department. Originally from Detroit, Heufelder had caught the hockey bug as a kid watching Gordie Howe and the Red Wings. Arriving in Pittsburgh in 1963 to take a sports-writing job at the *Press*, he soon found himself covering the Hornets. When it was announced Pittsburgh was getting an NHL team, Heufelder knew the beat reporter job for the new club was his—simply because no other writers wanted it.

"It wasn't like there were three guys vying to cover the Penguins," he recalled. "The feeling was, 'Oh that's nice, the Penguins are in the NHL.' Those guys, they grew up in Pittsburgh, so for them it was Pitt football and basketball, the Steelers and the Pirates. I can remember when they were going to announce the six expansion teams, I was right at the teletype machine, the wire service. And when they announced the six teams, as soon as I saw Pittsburgh was on the list, I knew I was in. It was au-

Les Binkley emerged as the Penguins' starting goalie during the team's first season, 1967–68. His six shutouts that year stood as a team record for 30 years (courtesy Doug McLatchy).

tomatic that I was going to cover the Penguins. Nobody else in the sports department gave a crap about it. And that's reflective of the attitude [in Pittsburgh] about having NHL hockey."[22]

Many of the future Penguins, by contrast, were more than a little excited about the new team, including veteran Earl Ingarfield. "I wasn't really surprised to be drafted in the expansion draft, considering my age. I was happy to go to Pittsburgh for a couple of big reasons. Andy Bathgate was also going there and some other players that I had played with previously on the Rangers and other teams. Also, the coach was Red Sullivan, whom I played with on the Rangers and played for when he coached there. He was a good coach. He was demanding but fair. If you did your job, you got your ice time and if not, you got less. But, all in all, I enjoyed playing for Red. He was a good friend and a fine man."[23]

Aside from its veteran flavor, that first Penguin roster was largely defined by the type of player Sullivan admired: tough, hard-checking, old-school. It was this group of oldtimers and castoffs, punctuated by a few hopeful youngsters looking to break into the big leagues, that in the early fall of 1967 would begin the Pittsburgh Penguins' NHL journey and ultimate quest for the Stanley Cup.

"There was a good mood on the club," Ingarfield said. "There were players who had been in the minors and were getting an opportunity to play in the NHL, and there were players who were drafted from other NHL teams. It was certainly a change, but something to look forward to—to see what everyone could do."[24]

2

Dropping the Puck:
1967–68

The newly expanded NHL now consisted of two divisions, with the Penguins grouped into the West bracket with their five expansion cousins, while the six established clubs remained together in the East Division. To make the playoffs, the Pens would have to finish among the top four teams in the West. Those clubs would battle each other for two rounds until a winner emerged to face the East survivor in the Stanley Cup Final. The league's aim was to give the newcomers a chance to play for the Stanley Cup right away—and drive fan interest in the new markets.

On Wednesday, October 11, 1967, the Penguins played their first-ever game, taking on the mighty Montreal Canadiens at the Civic Arena. GM Jack Riley had requested that the Flying Frenchmen be his team's first opponent, hoping they might catch Montreal in less-than-peak form at such an early stage of the season.[1] The schedule during the early part of that first season was built in such a way that the Penguins' home games would be played on either a Wednesday or a Saturday. PR man Joe Gordon convinced Riley to play the first game on a weeknight—traditionally a tougher draw than a weekend game—figuring that having the high-powered Habs in the building would surely mean a sellout, thus saving a Saturday for a less-appealing opponent.

"I told Jack, 'Why waste a Saturday when we can have the home opener on a Wednesday against the Canadiens,' who obviously were the royalty of NHL hockey. He agreed, and I thought we'd have a helluva crowd."

Things didn't quite work out that way. When the puck dropped, only 9,307 fans were in the stands, leaving about one-quarter of the seats empty. "I was really disappointed," lamented Gordon.[2]

On the ice that night, the Pens came out strong, only to be repelled on every rush by a young Rogie Vachon in the Montreal net. Gilles Tremblay beat Hank Bassen on a breakaway late in the first period and Habs legend Jean Beliveau scored his 400th career goal early in the second to put Montreal up 2–0. Andy Bathgate answered back at 7:06 of the third, scoring the Penguins' first-ever goal when he blistered a 35-foot slap shot past Vachon. Montreal, though, limited Pittsburgh to six third-period shots and escaped with a tight 2–1 win. Canadiens coach Toe Blake came away impressed with these pesky Penguins. "Vachon saved the game for us," he told the *Montreal Gazette*. "On any given night, with everyone playing well, Pittsburgh is going to win some games against the old clubs."[3]

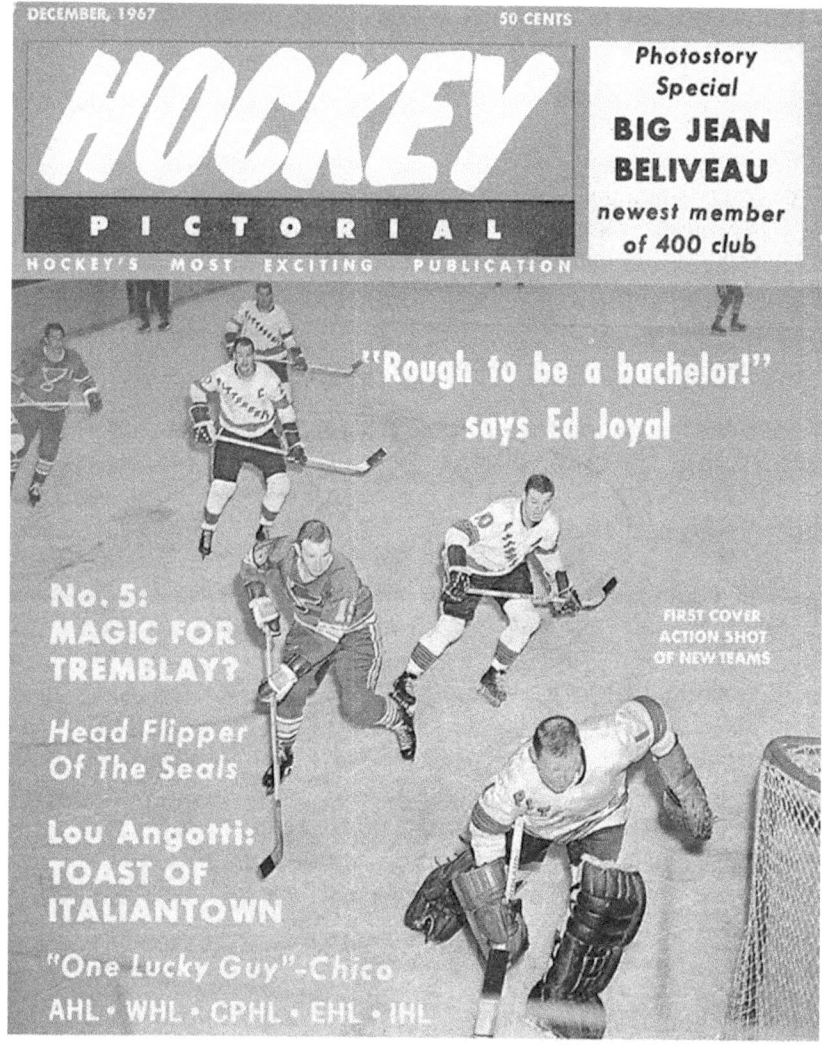

A 1967 hockey magazine cover featuring a picture from the Penguins' second-ever game, and first-ever win, 3–1 over the Blues in St. Louis, October 13, 1967 (author's collection).

Mike Hanczar had a close-up view of Vachon's play that night from his seat at one end of the rink. "The Canadiens didn't go with their veteran goalie, Gump Worsley, that night. Little did we know how good Vachon was going to be."[4]

The Penguins earned their first win two nights later in St. Louis when they beat the Blues 3–1. Art Stratton scored the winning goal on a power play late in the second period and Earl Ingarfield added the insurance marker 5:59 into the third.

The biggest highlight of Pittsburgh's young season came on October 21, when Bobby Hull and his Chicago Black Hawks came to town. Ken Schinkel scored the first hat trick in team history to lead the Pens to a 4–2 win and earn the distinction of being the first expansion club to knock off an established East Division team. Ironically, Schinkel had entered the game with the assignment of making sure Hull didn't score, but it was the 34-year-old right winger who emerged as the offensive hero.

Despite some strong showings against a few members of the NHL's established elite, the Penguins' first month was a rocky one, ending with a 3–6–1 mark. Coach Sullivan attributed the start partly to tight nerves. "Some of these guys still can't believe they're in the NHL," he said after a 4–2 loss in Boston on October 29.[5]

"Playing in the NHL was a little different than the American League. Some of the players were a lot bigger at that time in the NHL," remembered Mattiussi, who was getting his first shot in the big league after eight years in the AHL. "It was certainly a step up. When you line up on the ice and you look and see the Montreal Canadiens on the other side, you're like, 'Whoops!' In the minors, we'd read about the NHL in the *Hockey News*, and then you look at all the names in front of you, like Claude Tremblay on defense. At first, it's a little overwhelming, but you get used to it after a while."[6]

As the season wore on, the West Division race devolved into a battle of six clubs comprised mainly of castoffs who couldn't crack the NHL during the six-team era and faded veterans winding down their careers. Like the other expansion clubs, the Penguins approached each game against the older clubs with the goal of keeping things close by relying on tight checking and, hopefully, standout goaltending.

"We knew the established teams' arenas were going to be tough, but [all the expansion teams] were sort of equal. All the games were tough. They were all hard games," said Mattiussi.[7]

The Pens' offense took a hit when center Earl Ingarfield tore knee ligaments in a collision with the Seals' Bobby Baun in late October.

"I was carrying the puck through center ice and Baun was coming charging at me," Ingarfield said. "I saw him coming so I thought, 'Well, I'd better be ready for this.' So just before we got together, I kind of turned a little bit, and the impact really hit my knee the hardest. It was something that I could have avoided if I'd have used my head."[8]

With Art Stratton the only natural center left on the shallow roster, wingers Paul Andrea and Val Fonteyne were forced to fill the gaps in the middle. As a result, many games ended with no more than two goals on the board for the Pens. It wasn't until a 5–0 win against the Flyers on November 15 that they scored more than four goals in a game.

With the team winning only two of their first seven home games, not many Pittsburgh sports fans were falling in love with the Penguins, and the players admitted they were having their troubles in their home rink. "We just don't seem to be as loose in this building," said winger Ken Schinkel after a 1–1 tie versus the Flyers on November 8 before only 4,719 spectators.[9] Added former Hornet Bob Dillabough, "I think the biggest thing is that we're afraid to make a mistake in front of the home fans."[10]

Said Sullivan, "We've got to tighten up [defensively]. It seems as soon as we get behind in this building we go to pieces."[11]

Noel Price was an early target of the rafters' boo birds. "It's got to hurt anybody," he admitted before putting the situation in perspective. "A lot better guys than me have been booed so I don't lose any sleep over it. It bothers my wife more than it does me."[12]

Mattiussi remembered the fans being excited about their new team, but demanding, too. "They wanted you to win, for sure. They were almost like any team's fans: when something good happens they like you and if something bad happens you're going to hear about it. But they were really enthusiastic. Pittsburgh was a great hockey town. The people were really good hockey fans there. They could never do enough for you."[13]

Gordon attributed the sometimes-harsh treatment to the type of fan the team attracted early on. "We still hadn't really expanded the base of hockey fans. So the ones who were probably the most critical were holdovers from the Hornets. So it was not a major factor."[14]

The season did offer a few pleasant surprises. Another defeat at the hands of an East Division team seemed in the offing when the Pens paid their first visit to Maple Leaf Gardens in Toronto on December 13. The defending Stanley Cup Champion Leafs had yet to lose to an expansion team or lose a home game. But Les Binkley stopped 30 shots, the defense stood up for 60 minutes, and the offense never stopped checking the surprised Leafs. The Pens left with a 2–1 win, much to the satisfaction of forward Art Stratton, who scored the first Pittsburgh goal. "When we go up and down our wings, we're all right. That way our defense can stand up and hit. It showed [tonight], didn't it?"[15]

Binkley's impressive play was becoming commonplace. His consistently steady and often spectacular efforts had helped him win the starting position in the Pittsburgh nets, forcing Sullivan to abandon his original plan of dividing the duties between Binkley and Bassen.

"Bink kind of took over the reins and that was it," remembered Ingarfield.[16]

A 32-year-old rookie, Binkley was the classic example of a capable player who hadn't been able to land a job in the pre-expansion NHL because there were only six employers at the time. He was the rare goalie who wore contact lenses, which he felt general managers held against him. "They figure that if a goalie wears contact lenses he can't see."[17]

The Penguins didn't seemed bothered by Binkley's use of contacts. In fact, he was the first player the franchise signed, inking him to a deal in the summer of 1966, more than a full year before they were scheduled to play their first game. Binkley bided his time by playing with San Diego of the Western Hockey League in the 1966–67 season and now, given his big chance with the Penguins, he was proving how little vision those who questioned his own had displayed. On January 28, Binkley earned his fourth shutout of the season by stopping 33 Bruin shots and making George Konik's second-period wraparound goal stand up for a 1–0 Pittsburgh win. Binkley's performance was so good that it earned him some applause from the traditionally hostile Boston Garden crowd. "You've got to be doing something right to get an ovation like that from these fans," remarked Sullivan after the game.[18]

The victory came at a costly price, though, with Schinkel and Price, two of the Penguins' better performers, suffering injuries. And in the true inconsistent spirit of the season, the Penguins followed up one of their finest performances with one of their biggest duds when they were crushed in St. Louis three nights later to the tune of 9–4.

"This is the most unpredictable club I've ever been connected with," lamented Sullivan.[19]

The disappointments weren't limited to those on the ice. The average attendance as of early January was only 6,800. For instance, a game against Montreal—the most storied franchise in hockey history, featuring the great Jean Beliveau—attracted only 5,580 fans. By Jack McGregor's estimation, the average would have to climb to 9,000 for the team to break even. He was hopeful the Pens could reach that figure, given that the football season would soon be ending and more weekend games were scheduled for the latter half of the season.

"We hardly hoped to break even this year and may not do so next season," McGregor rationalized to the *Montreal Gazette*. "The third year should turn the corner."[20]

Despite McGregor's optimism, there were causes for concern about the franchise's stability. The less-than-impressive attendance figures—midway through the season, the Penguins had still not attracted a crowd of 10,000 or more—prompted NHL president Clarence Campbell to include Pittsburgh as one of his two "points of concern," with the other being the Oakland Seals, whose attendance was even worse than Pittsburgh's.[21]

Some members of the Penguins' ownership group were clearly itching to sell their interest in the team after having taken a bath to the tune of $700,000 on a failed pro soccer team known as the Pittsburgh Phantoms. This raised concerns that the Penguins would be sold to an out-of-town owner who would move them to another locale. Adding fuel to that fire was the revelation in early January that the owners had approached Pittsburgh Steelers president Art Rooney with an offer to buy the team for $4 million, but were rebuffed due to the high asking price.[22]

Campbell also made it clear that the league would not offer any help to a struggling franchise. "When we gave the franchises to these people, they took on their own destiny."[23]

As January wound down, the Penguins were making little progress in the standings, unable to put together any kind of winning streak. "I thought we'd be better than we are at this time, and that's why I'm teed off," said an edgy Sullivan as he waited for his veteran-heavy team to start showing its worth. "It's just a matter of some guys not pulling their weight. I'm sick and tired of it."[24]

A 5–3 loss to the Big, Bad Bruins February 27 at home had Sullivan fuming over his team's soft play. "You got to have a mean streak in you and I don't have enough of these guys. I can't understand it for the life of me how they can get pushed around and don't retaliate."[25]

Things went from bad to worse on March 2 when Oakland came to town. Not only did the Penguins fall asleep and allow the Seals to score five goals in the second period, leading to a wild 6–6 final score, but more importantly Les Binkley broke the middle finger of his right catching hand. Hank Bassen filled in during a crucial two-game road trip against St. Louis and Minnesota and performed admirably, but the Pens' offense was punchless, resulting in a loss to the Blues and a 2–2 tie with the North Stars. The dismal results left them three points back of St. Louis for the final playoff spot in the West with only 11 games to go.

They came up for air in their next game with a crucial 3–1 win over the Kings at home, but once again ran into an "Original Six" wall right after, losing three in a row on the road to Chicago, Montreal and New York.

Just as the season's last 10 crucial days were set to play out, the Penguins' ownership conglomerate announced that they were collectively selling 80 percent of the club to a group of nine investors from the Detroit area, led by Donald H. Parsons. The 37-year-old lawyer had amassed a fortune in the banking world and held the position of chairman of the board for the $1-billion Bank of the Commonwealth in the Motor City. Parsons and team president Jack McGregor were quick to reassure Penguins fans that the team would be staying in town.

"If there is anything overriding in this agreement, it's [the new group's] total commitment to stay in Pittsburgh," said McGregor.[26]

The sale did not come as a big surprise, as McGregor had earlier indicated that some in the original ownership group never intended to be hockey team owners for long.

"Maybe 12 to 14 of the stockholders fit into the category of hardcore hockey fans, but living with the daily operation of a franchise was never a motivation [for the others] in this," he said.[27]

Joe Gordon remembered that lack of commitment amongst the original investors. "None of them really had a substantial investment in it because there were so many of them. These were all very prominent and wealthy Pittsburghers to whom that investment was not a very significant part of their portfolio."[28]

Indeed, an ultimately unsuccessful attempt to sell 40 percent of the club to the Atlanta Braves baseball team had fallen through in November. Part of the owners' motivation to sell was their Phantoms-related losses and higher-than-expected costs associated with running the Penguins, including ballooning player salaries.

Under the Parsons agreement, the original ownership would control the other 20 percent of the club, with McGregor remaining as the top representative. Parsons would accompany him to NHL meetings, with the two jointly serving as governor. The well-heeled new ownership would bring a badly needed infusion of working capital to the Penguin operation. The top priority would be building a farm system through which the team could develop talent. Parsons and his group also had their eye on the ultimate prize.

"It is our joint aim to bring an NHL championship to Pittsburgh," he told the *Pittsburgh Post-Gazette*.[29]

If the 1967–68 edition of the Penguins was to have any hope of fulfilling that goal, they'd have to first make the playoffs. With only seven games left, their fate would essentially be decided by their next three contests, the first against the Blues at home and the other two against the North Stars in a huge home-and-home series. The Pens trailed each by six points, meaning anything short of three wins would doom them to an early trip to the golf course. They took care of St. Louis 4–2, giving them a boost of confidence heading into Minnesota. "You played well out there," Jack Riley told his team in the dressing room afterward. "Now keep believing it."[30]

The Pens came out flying in the first leg of the Minnesota mini-series, blistering the North Stars with 14 shots in the first period. The only problem was that Stars goalie Cesare Maniago stopped all of them—and all other Penguins shots the rest of the way, too. Ray Cullen's goal 31 seconds into the second period gave Minnesota all the scoring they'd need en route to a 3–0 blanking. The next night in Pittsburgh, Bill Speer hit the puck into his own net and the Penguins blew a two-goal lead in the third to settle for a 4–4 draw.

One point out of a possible four against Minnesota was not going to cut it. Even though the Penguins would win each of their remaining four games, they had dug themselves too deep a hole. They were officially eliminated the day before their last game when St. Louis beat the Stars and clinched the final West Division berth. All that was left to do in the season finale at home versus the Flyers was to hand out the MVP award to Binkley. His six shutouts established a club record that would stand for 30 years. Despite the disappointing season, the hometown fans gave the players a standing ovation as they left the ice.

Riley and Sullivan knew, however, that the owners' edict to build a veteran-heavy lineup in the hopes of creating an instant winner had been a major miscalculation.

"McGregor's thinking was that the Penguins had to win right away and build on the momentum of the Hornets winning the Calder Cup," remembered Pens beat reporter Bill Heufelder. "Well, as it turned out it wasn't really a wise decision. Jack never bought into that personally because he knew you needed young players [to build a franchise], not older ones. And that team was old—guys like Ingarfield and Boivin, Noel Price and Bathgate."[31]

Joe Gordon saw the logic in management's decision to go with experience at the time they made it. "The strategy of it made sense. It was an established hockey town and the Hornets had just won. Going into a new endeavor, it made sense to do it that way, but I think down the road it may have cost us a little bit."[32]

The Penguins would now have to enter a rebuilding mode after only one year of existence. Their expansion competitors were already that far ahead of them.

3

Flightless:
1968–69

The Penguins opened training camp on September 13, 1968, once again in Brantford, Ontario. Helping Sullivan evaluate the 61 invited players and run them through drills was Rudy Miguay, a former Pittsburgh Hornet who had scouted western Canada for the Pens the previous season. This year, Miguay would be serving as head coach of the Pens' new Central Hockey League farm team in Amarillo, Texas, nicknamed the Wranglers.

Establishing the minor league team filled a gaping hole in the Penguins organization. In their inaugural season, an injury to a starting player could not be offset by a simple call to the farm team, because there wasn't one. Trades or signings of available pros were the only options available, and neither route was ever a speedy one. Some of the Pens' expansion cousins, however, were already far ahead on this front, having outright purchased American Hockey League clubs to serve as farm teams.

"The Flyers bought the Quebec Aces and the Kings bought Springfield," said Heufelder. "Those were huge acquisitions because the Penguins didn't have anybody. They had a working agreement with Hershey, but buying those AHL teams gave those two clubs a real edge because players were at a premium, especially good ones, when you double the size of the league."[1]

One of the most welcome additions to the Penguins' second-year roster was center Lou Angotti, whom they had acquired in the off-season from Philadelphia. He brought speed and scoring ability to a position that had been lacking in both the year before.

On the downside, Andy Bathgate, last year's leading scorer and the top point-getter not only for the Penguins but in the entire Western Division, came to camp overweight and was having a hard time getting in shape. Riley and Sullivan, displeased with Bathgate's slow progress on the conditioning front and lack of production through four exhibition games, decided to cut the 36-year-old former star. Riley went to work trying to arrange a deal for the right wing but could find no takers. Bathgate eventually caught on with the Vancouver entry in the Western Hockey League. He would, however, remain property of the Penguins and, as time would prove, this would not be the last chapter in his Pittsburgh Penguin story.

The Pens would be sporting a new look for their second campaign. Gone was the nondescript design featuring a dizzying number of horizontal stripes and the diagonal "P-I-T-T-S-B-U-R-G-H" lettering on the front of the jerseys. It was replaced with uniforms that would later become known as the "classic baby blues," which featured a more conventional design based on a light blue theme and an actual logo. The pudgy, scarf-wearing penguin of the original symbol was replaced with a more determined and muscular-looking bird that required no flowing neckwear. He was still encircled by the club's name, which was rendered in slightly bolder lettering.

As they had in their first season, the Penguins opened at home against the Montreal Canadiens, who this time were Stanley Cup Champions. They once again put up a spirited fight, as they had in 1967 when they narrowly lost 2–1. This time, however, they were rewarded with a point when they held the Habs to a 1–1 draw. Les Binkley was in fine form right from the get-go, making 36 saves.

The tie was a rare bright spot in an otherwise disastrous October, which the Pens finished with a 1–4–2 mark. They managed only 16 goals and gave up 28, a figure that would have been much worse had it not been for the consistently brilliant performance of Binkley. But even he couldn't stop the spiral from getting worse in November, when the Pens fell into a seven-game losing streak. To their credit, Pittsburgh stayed close in each of the losses, including their 5–4 loss in Montreal and 6–5 defeat in Chicago. The Pens simply didn't have the talent to overcome the one or two errors that nearly every team makes during the course of a game.

"It seems that every time we make a mistake it costs us. Other teams make mistakes and seem to get away with them," lamented Sullivan after the seventh loss, a 5–2 decision at Maple Leaf Gardens.[2]

Added veteran Val Fonteyne, "One miscue and we fall apart. It seems like that's all it takes for us to go to pieces."[3]

Symbolic of their sad state was the situation of their mascot, Pete the Penguin, a live Humboldt penguin from Ecuador who lived at the Pittsburgh Zoo. Pete had made a few appearances at Pens games early in the season and was even fitted with a pair of tiny skates in hopes that he would learn the art of skating. But the little critter came down with pneumonia and after a short battle died on November 24.

"It was a penguin that didn't like ice," remembered Pens original PR man Joe Gordon. "It got a lot of media attention initially, which it was designed to do. The crowd would get a kick out of it. But it didn't sell any tickets."[4]

One key asset the Penguins were promoting was rookie right wing Jean Pronovost, whom the Pens had acquired in an off-season trade with Boston. Pronovost, the younger brother of Red Wings legend Marcel, was displaying some fine defensive play and an ability to manufacture goals. His talents, which were putting him into early Rookie of the Year discussions, were on full display in Oakland on December 1. With his team trailing 4–3 midway through the third, Pronovost took a Gene Ubriaco pass just outside the Seals' blue line and whistled a 30-foot bullet past goalie Gary Smith. That marker, and his earlier first-period goal, enabled the Penguins to emerge with a point.

Pronovost remembered his move to the Penguins fondly.

"I was very happy because they gave me a chance to play in the NHL. I knew that Boston would've been a tough [lineup to crack]. I was given an opportunity to make it and I basically seized the day. They were putting the emphasis on youth and I played on the power play and penalty killing, so it really helped me. I had a lot of learning to do, but I was willing to learn."[5]

Pronovost was somewhat less impressed by the city in which he was being given his chance. "When I got there, Pittsburgh was in transition because the steel mills were closing. I can't say I was very impressed with the city, but now you go back and it's a beautiful city and everything has been rejuvenated. It was a different feeling [at that time]. But I didn't care, because my goal was the NHL. I didn't care if I played in Timbuktu, as long as it was in the NHL."

Despite Pronovost's strong showing, points were scarce for the talent-thin Penguins. By January, they found themselves in the West basement. Desperate for a win, Sullivan increased the number and intensity of practices. One 75-minute session on December 18 was particularly grueling. "They never saw the puck. It was strictly skating. When your club isn't skating you may as well forget it," he growled.[6]

Sullivan wasn't the only one growing angry. Crowds at the Civic Arena were becoming impatient with their new team that had done nothing but miss the playoffs in their first season and sink to the bottom of the standings through three months of their second.

"The fans seem to be waiting for you to make a mistake," said center Lou Angotti. "I've played in a lot of cities. The fans in Chicago are very demanding and at times can be very nasty, but they don't come close to the Pittsburgh crowds."[7]

The fans were particularly venomous to Sullivan, Jack Riley and defenseman Noel Price. Even visiting players were surprised at how hard the fans were on their own team. North Stars center Andre Boudrias believed Pittsburgh fans just needed to be patient with their new club. "The team finished fifth last year and the fans don't think it is in the same league as the other clubs, but they should realize it is in the NHL."[8]

The Pens suffered from a porous, mistake-prone defense that had by that point surrendered the most goals in the league, as well as a lack of overall depth. As soon as injuries hit, as they did in January, the cupboard was simply too bare to replace any top-line talent. Injuries were particularly frequent up front during the dismal January–February run of ineptitude, with Keith McCreary, Earl Ingarfield and Lou Angotti, all in the top six on the Penguin scoring list, each being forced to the sidelines at various times.

Sullivan tried everything to improve on their dismal record at the Civic Arena, even switching the home bench with the visitors for home games. When such tactics didn't get the desired results, GM Jack Riley looked to the trade market to get them. After the North Stars had handed the Penguins a 3–1 setback at the Big Igloo, the teams announced a swap. Aging defenseman Leo Boivin was shipped to Minnesota for the slightly younger Duane Rupp, a 31-year-old blueliner who had had a few pre-expansion cups of coffee with the Rangers and Maple Leafs before securing a full-time spot in the bigs in 1967. Sullivan wasn't sad to see Boivin move on. "I thought he could have given a little more," he told the *Pittsburgh Press*. "He's supposed to be a body-checker but he wasn't hitting anyone to speak of."[9]

A few days later Riley engineered another, even bigger, trade. Captain Earl Ingarfield, Gene Ubriaco and Dick Mattiussi were sent to Oakland for forwards Bryan Watson and George Swarbrick and 6'2", 195-pound defenseman Tracy Pratt. Watson had made a name for himself as a hard and effective checker, having neutralized the great Bobby Hull in a 1966 playoff series while with the Red Wings. That performance had earned him the nickname "Superpest."

"We have been after Watson for a long time," explained Riley. "We feel he will provide the spark that has been lacking on our club."[10]

Perhaps most importantly, the Penguins had gotten younger. All three additions were under 26, while the players going to the Seals were all in their 30s. Riley was slowly turning the ship that had been founded on veteran players in the direction of youth, as had been new owner Donald Parsons' directive.

The toughness the three newcomers injected into the lineup was also more than welcome, as the Penguins had already developed a reputation for being soft. In their first season, for instance, Pittsburgh finished with the least number of total penalty minutes among all clubs (548), far behind such rough and tumble teams like Boston (1,032) and Philadelphia (976). Watson's feistiness helped put an end to an ugly nine-game winless streak on February 5 when an altercation with New York's Jim Neilson resulted in the Ranger defenseman rapping his stick over Watson's head, drawing blood and sending him to the sin bin for a five-minute major. The Pens capitalized twice on the ensuing power play, with the two goals proving to be the difference in a 3–2 win, their first ever over Sullivan's former team.

For the current season, however, the moves came too late. By March 20 the Penguins were officially eliminated from the playoff race. The reality hit the franchise hard.

"The expectations were great because we'd come so close [to qualifying for the playoffs] the previous year," remembered Joe Gordon. "Not making it that second year was definitely a greater level of disappointment than in year one."[11]

The Penguins had suffered the ignominy of being the only 1967 expansion team to have missed the playoffs in each of their first two seasons, and it cost Sullivan his job. The board of directors ordered his firing after the season's final game on March 30. Sullivan's hard-nosed style had not endeared him to his players. Said Earl Ingarfield a few weeks after being traded to the Seals, "Going to Oakland is like getting out of jail. Sully couldn't fire up a furnace."[12]

Speaking a few months after the firing, Pens goalie Les Binkley opined that Sullivan's tactics were too old-school for the modern NHL.

"Time changes and so have hockey players. Guys today just don't like to be pushed too hard…. I felt [Sullivan] just worked [his] guys too hard. Instead of helping matters, it hurts."[13]

Even Riley admitted that a rocky relationship between Sullivan and one of his key players hindered the team.

"One of the things that hurt us was Earl Ingarfield's inability to get along with Red. If Earl had been happy and if he had played well, it might have made a big difference."[14]

Sullivan would remain with the Penguins for two more years as Director of Professional Scouting. "I would have liked to have been more successful in Pittsburgh," Sullivan told the *Pittsburgh Press* nearly 20 years later. "I liked Pittsburgh, liked the organization at that time, and it was a great city. I always thought it could be a great hockey town."[15]

The original ownership's directive to ice a veteran-based winner right out of the gate in hopes of attracting a large fan base had produced the exact opposite result. The Penguins' losing ways and inability to bring the excitement of Stanley Cup playoff competition to the city left an already cynical fan base disenchanted and—most importantly—disinterested in the team. Single-game attendances barely above 4,500 diehard souls were not uncommon. The season total for 38 home games was 228,296 for an average of only 6,008.

McGregor and Parsons seemed to understand that a losing hockey team would not be successful at the gate in Pittsburgh. Around the midway point of the season, however, McGregor stated that if and when the Penguins did start to win, larger crowds would have to be seen in order for the team to stay. "If we go through a season playing as well as Oakland is now, yet drawing as poorly, our situation would have to be re-evaluated."[16]

Speaking a week later, Parsons called the 1968–69 season a "learning year" and reiterated that ownership's plan was a "minimum three-year building program with the club and the fans," and that this was only year one.[17]

Parsons told the *Pittsburgh Press* that his pat response to anyone inquiring about taking the Penguins off his hands was to tell them to "go jump in a lake." He added: "There is no intention, either at present or in the future, to sell the club or apply, in any way, shape or form, to move to another city."[18]

For Penguins fans, the reassurances were welcome, and there were also some rays of hope with the product on the ice. Riley had, by season's end, begun to inject some sorely needed youth and toughness into the lineup. Many players present from the start of the year showed good results. Jean Pronovost had enjoyed a fine rookie campaign, playing in all 76 games and scoring 41 points while displaying a maturity beyond his 22 years. Veteran Ken Schinkel had rebounded after a slow start that was partly caused by lingering knee troubles to lead the team in scoring with 52 points. Keith McCreary proved to everyone that he was a threat to score every shift, leading the Pens in goal-scoring with 25. Forward Charlie Burns quietly put together a strong year, finishing only a point behind Schinkel with 51 points.

In the stands, seeds of a resilient loyalty amongst some supporters had been planted. A curious fan club devoted to defenseman Bob Woytowich—Woytowich's Polish Army—had sprung up in the nosebleeds, cheering on their favorite son and hanging banners in his name. On some nights, the chant of "Let's Go Pens" could even be heard echoing through the near-empty Igloo in hopes that the Penguins would finally put something together.

In the end, though, there loomed a monumental challenge for General Manager Jack Riley, whom Parsons had spared Sullivan's fate. Standing amidst the rubble of two lost seasons, it would be his job to find the right coach to guide the floundering team out of the darkness to the promised land of the playoffs. The very existence of the franchise in Pittsburgh seemed to depend on it.

PART TWO

Kelly's Men
(1969–70 Through 1972–73)

4

Breakthrough:
1969–70

On July 2, 1969, at the Civic Arena's Igloo Club, the Penguins introduced Hockey Hall of Famer Red Kelly as their new head coach. A winner of eight Stanley Cups over a 20-year career with Detroit and Toronto, the former Norris Trophy winner had spent the last two seasons coaching the Los Angeles Kings. Not having got along with micro-managing owner Jack Kent Cooke, Kelly left La-La Land after having guided the Kings to two successive playoff appearances.

"I'm aiming for first place [in the West Division], because there's no use to shoot for anything less," the new coach told the gathered reporters.[1]

Jack Riley was confident Kelly's extensive history of winning would have an effect on his charges. "Only once in his 22-year career as a player and coach has he finished out of the playoffs," Riley said. "Perhaps some of that spirit will rub off on our players."[2]

Curiously, even through the Penguins wanted to ink Kelly to a multi-year contract, he insisted on signing only a one-year deal. It was an approach he had always followed as a player. "It gives you something to work for. It makes you strive to go ahead."[3] Kelly added with a sly grin, "Of course, if you have a good first season you can always go back and ask for more money the next season."

Meanwhile, Riley was making some key additions to the roster Kelly would be coaching. Evidently pleased with the toughness he'd seen from mid-season additions Bryan Watson and Tracy Pratt, he added brawny Glen Sather from Boston at the intra-league draft in June. He also picked up veteran left wing Dean Prentice from the Red Wings and traded Lou Angotti, who had not proven to be the answer at center the year previous, to St. Louis in a deal that netted 27-year-old center Ron Schock.

That same month, in the third round of the NHL amateur draft, the Penguins selected Michel Brière, a scoring sensation out of the Quebec junior league who had piled up 320 points in his previous two seasons with Shawinigan. His 165-pound frame had made other clubs reluctant to take him, out of fear that he would not be able to stand up to the rigors of the NHL. Quiet but confident, Brière came to camp in Brantford, Ont. in September on a mission to make the big club. On October 2, Kelly announced that he'd succeeded.

"If he comes down the ice with one man to beat, you have a feeling he might get around the defenseman or make a big play," said the coach. "You don't always have that feeling with everyone."[4]

Despite all the retooling, the beginning of the season saw the 1969–70 Penguins looking exactly like the two previous versions that had missed the playoffs. They suffered through a six-game winless streak to start Kelly's tenure and had won but two of their first 12 by mid–November. There simply wasn't enough scoring. In one nine-game stretch, they could muster only 15 goals and were shut out four times. "They can't put the puck in the ocean," Kelly complained. "I'm going to take them down to a pier and see if they can hit the water."[5]

Compounding the problem was the quality of Penguin goaltending, which Kelly called "fair, but not great." Rookie Al Smith was forced to fill in for ailing starter Les Binkley and often displayed the jitters. "He's fighting the puck now," observed Kelly.[6]

Rookie Michel Brière scored 44 points in 76 games during the 1969–70 season. His life was tragically cut short as a result of a car accident that occurred shortly after the season ended (courtesy Doug McLatchy).

As the Penguins tried to hit their stride, team president Jack McGregor decided to hit the road. Since launching his campaign with Peter Block to bring an NHL franchise to Pittsburgh in 1966, he'd divided his time between Harrisburg, where he served as a state senator, and Pittsburgh, where his Penguin and business interests resided. Knowing that sooner or later he would have to choose one endeavor over the other, he announced in early January that politics had won the day. He would be throwing his hat in the ring for the Republican nomination in the 1970 election for Pennsylvania governor. Two weeks later, Jack Riley was handed McGregor's Penguin presidential duties on an interim basis.

Gradually, Riley's injections of additional muscle started to pay off. On a cold Pittsburgh night on the last day of January and the St. Louis Blues in town, the Penguins let the rest of the league know that they were not going to take the punches and cheap shots anymore without giving their own in return. Led by young coaching genius Scotty Bowman, the Blues had combined the right mix of veteran goaltending, provided by Glenn Hall and Jacques Plante, with no-holds-barred toughness in the likes of the Plager brothers, Barclay and Bob, and a decent amount of scoring, to emerge as the class of the expansion West Division. They'd gone to the Stanley Cup Final each of the first two seasons since expansion. On this particular night, they sat a full 14 points clear of second-place Philadelphia.

In the second period of a tight, scoreless game, Bryan Watson and Barclay Plager were sent to the box for spearing each other. When their sentence was served, Plager went right back toward Watson but was intercepted by new Penguin policeman Glen Sather. Their haymaker-fest sparked another bout, and when goalie Al Smith jumped into the fray, both benches emptied. As the punches flew, Bowman was yelling from the bench and even GM Jack Riley came down to the penalty box area to get a ringside seat. In the end, 49 penalty minutes were doled out and the game was delayed 20 minutes. The Pens would go on to win the game 2–1 on third-period goals from Keith McCreary and Wally Boyer, but more importantly, they'd won a different kind of victory with their fists.

The win propelled the Pens to six wins in their next nine games, vaulting them into sole possession of second place in the West, a full 11 points clear of fifth-place Minnesota. After crowning the Kings 6–1 in L.A., Bryan Hextall—who scored two of the Pens' goals in that game—gave voice to the team's confidence: "We go out there now and know we're going to win."[7]

Much of the Penguins' turnaround was being attributed to Kelly, who some in the press were mentioning as a Coach of the Year candidate. "We have a different attitude this season," defenseman Bob Woytowich told the *Hockey News.* "He just instills something in you."[8]

Young Jean Pronovost appreciated the leadership Kelly provided. "He was very respected because of who he was and the type of hockey player he was," Pronovost reflected years later. "He was not a flamboyant coach that gave great talks or anything, but he knew the game and he knew how to coach. He helped us in many different aspects of the game and we just followed his lead."[9]

Pronovost also remembered that Kelly took a different approach to dealing with players than did most coaches at the time.

"He didn't come at you all guns-a-blazing. He tried to talk to you and make you understand [what you were doing wrong]. He was almost like a father talking to a son, which was a different approach because coaches were kind of whipping the players back then. He never got mad, never swore. I never saw him get mad on the bench or get upset at a referee's call. That's a rarity because usually this game can be frustrating, and you can easily lose it."[10]

Kelly's approach helped the Pens clinch the franchise's first post-season berth by the end of March, and a 4–1 win over Philadelphia on April 1 guaranteed them second place in the West. Getting the expansion division's silver medal earned each Penguin $1,250 and the prospect of more bonuses in the playoffs.

"This is just the start. We've still got a lot of money to make," grinned defenseman Bob Woytowich.[11]

The road to riches for Woytowich and his mates would begin with a best-of-seven series against the Oakland Seals, who had finished the season on a strong note, going 5–3–5 in the stretch run and managing to tie Philadelphia for fourth place in the West. The Seals got in by virtue of having 22 wins to Philly's 17.

Like the Pens, the Seals' lineup featured no bona fide stars. Centers Ted Hampson and ex-Penguin captain Earl Ingarfield were the top scorers with 52 and 45 points, respectively, while a young Carol Vadnais anchored the defense and proved to be a contributor in the offensive zone, finishing third with 44 points, including a team-leading 24 goals. Starting goalie Gary Smith, a gangly 6'4", 215-pound giant, provided respectable goaltending with a 3.11 goals against average. Oakland had won the season series with a 3–2–3 mark, but had not managed to win in Pittsburgh, going 0–2–2.

"I think we'll be all right," said a confident Red Kelly as the series was set to get underway. "The guys were flying yesterday in practice."[12]

The Penguins played their first-ever playoff game on April 8, 1970, which was proclaimed "Pittsburgh Penguins Day" in the city by Mayor Peter F. Flaherty. Before a disappointing crowd of just over 8,000, Nick Harbaruk fired a shot from 10 feet out with less than eight minutes to play that beat Smith and proved to be the difference in a tight 2–1 Penguin win. Oakland protested that Glen Sather had interfered with Smith in the crease as the puck flew into the net, but referee Bruce Hood pointed out that "Slats" had been pushed into the goalie, meaning the goal would stand. Smith was livid, throwing his mask to the ice and chasing after Hood. The Seals complained about the call after the game, but Kelly would have none of it. "I saw nothing wrong with [the goal] at all. If the Seals squawked, it was only because they were the losing team. They had to say something, didn't they?"[13]

In game two, Harbaruk came through in the clutch again. With Oakland leading 1–0 midway through the second period, the right-winger slammed a shot past Smith after the goalie had made two big saves on Ron Schock. Wally Boyer followed that up 34 seconds later with a 20-footer and suddenly the Pens had a 2–1 lead.

The Seals had made it easy on the Penguins, with their defense looking slow and uninterested in any rough stuff. It was up to Smith to get physical against the Pens, taking two penalties when he tripped Keith McCreary and later punched Jean Pronovost.

"You're in trouble when your goaltender has to do some of the heavy work," said Seals coach Fred Glover.[14]

Dunc McCallum made it 3–1 in the third, which would hold up as the final score. The win gave the Pens a commanding 2–0 series lead heading to the west coast, but unfortunately not many Pittsburghers were on hand to see it—only 7,253. It appeared that building a solid base of support for the Penguins was proving to be an even tougher climb than anyone had imagined.

Out in Oakland for game three, Earl Ingarfield gave the Seals a 1–0 lead after one period, but unlikely scoring hero Harbaruk did it again, beating Smith at 5:20 of the second to tie the game. The Seals defense once again wilted after the goal, allowing Ken Schinkel to tally his first of the playoffs two minutes later and Jean Pronovost to give the Pens a 3–1 lead at 11:38. After Ted Hampson got one back for Oakland, Schinkel struck again midway through the third in the waning seconds of a power play, giving the Pens a 4–2 lead and some much-needed breathing room. The assists went to Schock and Dean Prentice, and a few minutes later the exact same combination connected again to put the game—and for all intents and purposes, the series—out of reach. Schinkel's hat trick was the first of the season for the Penguins.

Carol Vadnais came to life for the Seals in game four, scoring in each of the first two periods. Each time, however, the Pens answered back, with Prentice tying things up in the opening frame with his first of the playoffs and Bob Woytowich netting his first in the middle period. Les Binkley kicked out all 11 third-period Seal shots and Gary Smith stopped all nine Penguins drives, sending the game to overtime.

Just past the eight-minute mark, Jean Pronovost took the puck off an Oakland defenseman near the Seals net and got it to Val Fonteyne, who whizzed a drive at Smith, forcing him to make a sensational save. Michel Brière, however, was standing at the left side of the net and gathered in the rebound. Despite a sharp angle, the rookie made no mistake, firing home the first overtime goal in Penguins history and sending his club on to the second round.

"They never gave up," said a proud Riley after the game. "They came in here where they didn't win one game during the season and beat Oakland twice."[15]

Brière was already looking ahead to greater things for himself and his team. "I hope I have the opportunity to score an even more important goal in the playoffs."[16]

The next evening the victorious Penguins were welcomed back to Pittsburgh by a few hundred fans at the Pittsburgh airport. Finally, the flightless fowl were winners. Their first two floundering years now seemed like a distant nightmare. They were on to the Stanley Cup semi-finals where they would meet their new rival, the St. Louis Blues, who had knocked off Minnesota in six games in the other West Division semi-final.

"We will give them a battle," predicted Riley. "They won't push us around. They'll try, but I don't think they'll be successful."[17]

Before a madhouse of nearly 17,000 Blues fans, the teams got reacquainted with each other in game one mainly with their fists, slugging it out to the tune of 149 penalty minutes. The Pens kept pace with the Blues for most of the game, but a breakdown in the second period allowed the home team to explode for all three of their goals and assume a 3–0 lead. The Blues' defense stifled the Pittsburgh attack and probably would have shut it down completely had veteran goalie Glenn Hall not lost a race for the puck with Bryan Hextall early in the third, allowing Ken Schinkel to fire the Pens' lone marker into a wide-open net.

In game two, a Jean-Guy Talbot goal only 31 seconds in put the Pens on their heels and before the first period was done they found themselves down 3–0 again. Brière got one back five minutes into the third but the Blues cruised the rest of the way and won 4–1. A mere five shots in each of the first and third periods irked Kelly. "In practice our guys really shoot the puck, but in a game they never do," he said. "I've never known the puck to go into the net if you don't shoot it."[18]

In the upbeat Blues' post-game locker room, however, wily vet Jacques Plante sounded a note of caution as the series headed back to Pittsburgh: "This series is not over yet," he said. "Pittsburgh doesn't quit. They didn't win four games from Oakland for no reason."[19]

The biggest hockey crowd ever to witness a game in Pittsburgh—12,923—turned out for game three and was treated to the brilliance of their new young scoring star Brière. After Dean Prentice had given the Pens a 1–0 lead in the first period, Brière dominated the second. Seven minutes in, he weaved past Blues defensemen Al Arbour and Barclay Plager with the poise of a veteran, getting to the back of the net and feeding linemate Jean Pronovost, whom the Blues' pair had forgotten while trying to catch Brière. Pronovost made no mistake and connected from 20 feet out.

Less than four minutes later, with Bob Plager in the sin bin for hooking, Brière blasted a long, hard shot toward Plante, who could only get a piece of it with his catching glove. Make it 3–0 Penguins and cue the roar of the crowd.

Larry Keenan did his best to spoil the party with two goals early in the third period, but Les Binkley and his mates held on for a 3–2 victory. Kelly attributed the win to solid penalty killing, which shut down two two-man advantages, and the raucous Pittsburgh fans.

"Do you think that doesn't help a team?" he asked a reporter. "We've had good fans, but we haven't had them in vast quantities and boy, that has to help. It picks you up and makes your hair stand on end."[20]

Remembered Pronovost: "There was definitely a different sense around the arena. That's when the team really gelled together. The fans were behind us and we wanted to go and be in the final."[21]

Long-time Pens fan Mike Hanczar remembered that Penguin Fever "just kept building" as the playoffs went on. "The games against St. Louis were selling out, people were waiting in line to get into the games, and there were actually lines to buy tickets. They'd win a game and right after it was over, there would be a long line of people to buy tickets to the next one."[22]

Kelly had also fired up his charges with a secret operation he'd engineered earlier in the day. With the help of two team officials sworn to secrecy, the coach borrowed $7,250 in cash from the Penguin coffers. That just happened to be equal to the share each player would receive from the league should they win the Stanley Cup. Just before game time, Kelly entered the buzzing dressing room and turned the bag holding the bills upside down, letting the money flutter to the blue carpet. The room instantly went silent. "That's your money," the coach told them. "Don't let anyone take it." On the ice, they exploded after seeing what their financial reward could be.[23]

"They were so excited," said Dean Prentice of his teammates. "They hit everything that moved."[24]

For game four, St. Louis coach Scotty Bowman decided to use the size of his two most intimidating defensemen—6'3", 215-pound Noel Picard and 6'0", 200-pound Bob Plager—to try to slow the 5'9", 150-pound Brière every time the speedy scorer touched the ice. Kelly, anticipating the move, had some words of wisdom for Brière.

"Red told us that if Bowman wants to play his big defensemen, that's all right because they're slow," Brière said later.[25]

With the score tied 1–1 nearly seven minutes into the second period, Brière went about proving his coach correct. Taking a Jean Pronovost pass at the Blues' blueline in stride, Brière headed toward Plager. He drifted to the outside and deftly whizzed by the startled defenseman before cutting back to the net and slipping the puck between the pads of surprise St. Louis starter Ernie Wakely. The Igloo exploded and the Birds, as they were sometimes called in the press at the time, maintained their slender 2–1 lead all the way to the final buzzer to tie the series at two games apiece. The once-timid Penguins were staring down the toughest team in the West and giving them a run for their playoff lives. It was now a best-of-three fight for the finals.

"[The Blues] play a dirty, rough game," said defenseman Nick Harbaruk, "but we keep dishing it out, too. Now they respect us."[26]

Somehow, Pittsburgh was going to have to manufacture a win in St. Louis, something they had not done all season. Kelly decided a change in hotel accommodations might help alter his players' mindset, but the move backfired when the Holiday Inn they checked into had its air conditioning system break down. Temperatures in the city had reached 92 degrees, leaving the Penguins to literally sweat it out until game time.

The St. Louis Arena certainly offered no relief, even throwing up some fog patches throughout game five. One caused goalie Al Smith to lose sight of a Frank St. Marseille shot on its way into the back of his net. That goal made it 3–0 Blues. Earlier, Smith had allowed the second St. Louis goal by mistiming a poke check on Andre Boudrias. At the other end, Jacques Plante was playing it cool and stopping everything the Pens sent toward him. St. Marseille ended up with a hat trick and the Blues rolled to a 5–0 win.

Back in Pittsburgh for a do-or-die Game Six, the Civic Arena was once again sold out. The raucous crowd threatened to blow the building's dome-shaped roof off when their hometown heroes jumped out to a 2–0 lead on goals by Duane Rupp in the first and former Blue Ron Schock early in the second. Red Berenson countered for St. Louis before the middle frame ended, and Bill McCreary tied things up in the third. Brière gave the Pens the lead again at 6:17, but it would turn out to be the last Penguin goal of the season. Tim Ecclestone tied things up 40 second later and a Bill McCreary shot at 14:25 that goalie Al Smith juggled and let fall to the side of the crease was banged home by Larry Keenan. The plucky Pens seemed to have run out of gas in that final frame, suddenly making poor passes and having a next-to-impossible time clearing their zone.

"You can't make those mistakes and survive," said Kelly afterward. "And I think we were tired."[27]

With two seconds left on the clock and the game and series decided, the Pittsburgh fans gave the team a standing ovation and later cheered Kelly with another "standing O" as he left the ice after the handshakes.

"I'm proud of these guys, every one of them," said the coach. "We got here by being a team and we went down as a team."[28]

The club that most pundits had picked to finish last in the West had come within two victories of reaching the Stanley Cup final. Jack Riley had hired the right man to coach his team and had finally seemed to have found the right mix of talented youth and solid veterans to form a respectable NHL entry, if not yet a legitimate Stanley Cup contender. With their inspiring play-off run, the club had turned the city on to the excitement of big-league pro hockey.

At long last, these Penguins looked like they were ready to fly.

• • •

With the season done, most of the Penguins scattered to their homes and families across Canada. For Michel Brière, home was Malartic, Quebec, a small gold-mining town about a four-hour drive northwest of Montreal, where his parents and three siblings lived. The summer of 1970 was going to be an exciting one for the young NHL star. Not only would he be able to reflect on a successful rookie campaign in the company of close friends and an admiring townsfolk, Michel would be getting married to his sweetheart, Michelle Beaudoin, in June. The couple had welcomed a son, Michel Jr., into their lives the previous year.

The future could not possibly have looked any brighter for Mike Brière.

At about 9 p.m. on May 15, Brière and two of his closest friends were driving in Michel's pride and joy, a 1970 Mercury Cougar that he'd purchased with the bonus money of his first contract with the Penguins. They were heading south on Highway 117, the spine that connects the various towns, mines and logging operations scattered throughout the region. Snaking its way through deep brush and forest, the two-lane road is full of twists and turns. About halfway between Malartic and the town of Heva River to the north, the car—it has never been determined who was driving—failed to negotiate one of those turns and flew off the road. A police officer said the car "flipped one or two times, probably went on to the shoulder for a short distance and then came back onto the road."[29]

It landed upright, completely demolished. One of Michel's companions suffered cuts to his face and arms, while the other emerged with four broken ribs.

Brière was not so lucky.

He was thrown from the car upon impact and suffered a fractured skull. Unconscious, he and his two friends were rushed by ambulance back down Highway 117 toward the hospital in the town of Val-d'Or. In a cruel twist, the ambulance struck and killed an 18-year-old friend of Brière's, Reauld Perreault, along the way.

Brière was in a coma. He was soon flown to a hospital in Montreal to undergo brain surgery to remove a blood clot. He survived the surgery but was eventually listed by doctors as merely "clinically awake." His eyes were open but he was mostly unresponsive to visitors, simply staring out at a world of which he now had virtually no comprehension. His easy smile, quiet confidence and inspiring determination were, at least for the foreseeable future, no longer to be a part of his family members' lives, the world of his young wife and child, nor the locker room of the Pittsburgh Penguins.

"All you can do is pray, I guess," said a despondent Red Kelly back in Pittsburgh. "Maybe Mike will be all right."[30]

5

On Thin Ice, Again:
1970–71

A week after Michel Brière's accident, owner Donald Parsons announced some positive hockey-related Penguins news: the team's management had been solidified for the upcoming campaign. General Manager Jack Riley was being promoted to executive director, while holding on to his position of acting team president, which he had held since Jack McGregor stepped down midway through the 1969–70 season. His role would focus on player development and liaising with NHL officials and other team management personnel on behalf of the Penguins.

Parsons also put to rest the persistent rumors that coach Red Kelly would be moving on to Detroit or Toronto by not only bringing him back as the Pens' bench boss, but also handing him Riley's GM role. Kelly had high hopes for 1970–71. "We only missed [winning] the Stanley Cup by six games this season. Maybe we can do a little better next year."[1]

However, as Brière lay in his Montreal hospital bed, another cloud developed over the Penguins franchise as the season-opener neared. On October 3, Mellon Bank filed a lawsuit against majority owner Parsons and eight others with a stake in the team. The owners were behind on their payments of a $3.5-million loan and also owed $63,500 in unpaid interest. Parsons' finances had taken a downturn and it appeared that the only way out of his predicament was to sell the Penguins. Once again, the proverbial For Sale sign went up outside the Civic Arena, with the NHL instructing Parsons to find a buyer by December 1. Although they seemed to be finding their feet on the ice, the Penguins, it was clear to all, were still on shaky financial ground.

Parsons' high-risk method of wealth accumulation was akin to a house of cards, according to Bill Heufelder. "Parsons was a big banker, but he was one of those guys who would invest in banking—invest, invest, invest. And as soon as someone called him for the money he owed them, it all just collapsed. That was typical of what was going on in the Penguins' front office. Not that everyone was a crook or anything, but it was always one financial mess after another."[2]

Said Joe Gordon bluntly, "Parsons was a smooth, suave guy—except he didn't know diddly about hockey."[3]

Despite everything happening off the ice, there was still hockey to be played. Apart from Brière's absence, the Penguin roster remained largely the same as the successful 1969–70 campaign. The Pens picked up former Pittsburgh Hornet Lowell MacDonald from the Los Angeles Kings in the intra-league draft in June. Andy Bathgate, after spending the past two seasons playing for Vancouver of the minor Western Hockey League, came to camp. The 38-year-old Hall of Fame shoo-in had remained Penguin property after being cut at the team's 1968 training camp, and after hemming and hawing over an offer from Kelly to come back to the Steel City, he eventually accepted a few games into the season. Bathgate's hesitancy stemmed from his concern about getting enough ice time with the Pens. As he told the *Hockey News*, "I have to play a lot. I have to break a sweat and keep sweating to be loose and effective. If I sit around, I tighten up, and when I go out there I'm no good."[4]

Bathgate chose to remain with Pittsburgh, but neither he nor any other forwards were doing much twine-bulging. Five games in, the Pens had mustered only six goals. "Sometimes it looks like they are trying to set up the perfect play," said an already frustrated Kelly. "Other times they seem to be shooting too soon before setting up anything. Anyway, they've made every goalkeeper they've faced look good."[5]

Brière's absence, both as a person and as a player, was being felt. After a 4–2 loss in Minnesota October 15, Kelly lamented, "I had one guy last year who I don't have this year and as of yet, I don't have a guy who can fill that spot."[6]

Brière's former linemate Jean Pronovost, with whom he had teamed up on many a pretty goal, echoed similar sentiments and tried to rationalize his feelings. "I miss the little kid," he told a reporter. "It makes a difference but it shouldn't. He's not here, that's all. Playing with someone else shouldn't be any problem if I go up and down my wing."[7]

Pittsburgh Press beat reporter Bill Heufelder, however, recalls that the 1970–71 Penguins did their best to keep playing hard in spite of Brière's absence.

"Nobody really talked about it that much," he said. "I think everybody felt terrible, but the game goes on, life goes on, and he'd only been there one year, so it wasn't enough to really have a brutal impact on them."[8]

One Penguin rookie was helping make Brière's missing production somewhat easier to take. Left winger Greg Polis, Pittsburgh's first choice in the 1970 draft, was enjoying a solid start playing on a line with Ron Schock and Nick Harbaruk, lighting the lamp 10 times by the end of December. The problem was that that total was leading the team. This fact illustrated just how talent-poor a team they were, one that had to hustle and scrape for every point they earned. When they failed to play that kind of game, they fell in the standings, as they did during one eight-game stretch in December when they could muster only one win.

"I found out last year that if I didn't stay on top of the team, keep working them in practice, they lapsed into bad habits," Kelly said. "It looks like it's the same with this team. We haven't been checking well and we haven't been playing our positions properly."[9]

Things weren't going well for any part of the Penguin operation. As Kelly looked to solve the issues on the ice, Donald Parsons was having no luck in his efforts to offload the team to a new buyer by the December 1 deadline the NHL had imposed on him. If he didn't meet that deadline, Parsons would be forced to relinquish all control of the Pens to the NHL. According to one source, he had been close to a deal with a Minnesota group that intended to move the Penguins to Denver. The NHL, however, had been encouraged by a few home dates that had each attracted impressive crowds, including 12,909 to see Bobby Orr and the Boston Bruins on November 7; 11,075 versus the lowly California Golden Seals November 14; 11,298 to catch Detroit November 21; and 13,050 for a return matchup against the Bruins on December 26—the biggest Penguin crowd to that date. Based on these showings, NHL president Clarence Campbell seemed to have become convinced of Pittsburgh's viability as an NHL market, and henceforth insisted that any sale be to a group committed to keeping the team in Pittsburgh.

The December 1 deadline came and went, with the NHL assuming control of the franchise. The wheeler-dealer Parsons was out of the Penguin picture.

The league was rumored to be close to a purchase agreement with Metromedia, Inc., New York–based owner of the popular Ice Capades skating show. After the initial reports and excitement, though, talk of the sale dried up. In late January, Campbell assured everyone that the club would be sold by June. In the meantime, the league would continue to operate it. Most importantly, the Penguins would be staying in Pittsburgh. "We have given no consideration at all to moving the franchise," he said.[10]

The franchise apparently wasn't making a move, but Riley knew he had to make some on his roster. Looking to offload some of the grit he'd accumulated in exchange for more scoring, he traded popular pest Glen Sather to the Rangers for center Syl Apps, Jr., son of the long-time Toronto Maple Leafs star. Before Apps's first game in a Penguin uniform, played at home against the Leafs, some of the 9,000 fans who were unhappy with Sather's departure proceeded to boo the new arrival's name when the lineups were announced. Unperturbed, Apps put on a performance that made them quickly forget all about Slats. At 13:16 of the first period, he set up Polis to give the Pens a 1–0 lead. Apps himself made it 2–0 late in the second when he picked up a loose puck at the Toronto blueline, sped to the net, calmly deked legendary goalie Jacques Plante and put it into the cage.

"If tonight is a sample of what he can do, he can put us over the hump," said an elated Kelly after the game. "He could be the difference between being in the playoffs and not making it."[11]

As the Pens entered the season's home stretch, the playoffs seemed like a distinct possibility—until starting goalie Les Binkley injured his right knee, the same one that had required surgery in the off-season, during a 4–0 win over Montreal on March 3. Neither Al Smith or Paul Hoganson could prove an adequate replacement for Bink, whose injury was but one in a long line of ailments that decimated the team's top talent. Ken Schinkel had been out since late December with a broken collarbone. He came back in late February but was soon sidelined again when he hurt another bone in the same area. Keith McCreary went down with a back injury at about the same time. Defenseman Bob Blackburn was forced out for a few games with a shoulder injury. Veteran Lowell MacDonald played only 10 games due to a badly injured knee. The not-so-sweet icing on the cake was a case of mononucleosis hitting Polis in early March. It meant the end of the 18-goal-scorer's fine rookie season.

The Pens would win only two of their final 21 games to finish second-last in the West Division and 10 points out of the playoffs. It was a monumental letdown of a season that bore no resemblance to the hope and excitement that characterized the one that came before it.

"We haven't been right all season," said Kelly. "We started off blowing games early and we never did get off the mark. You can't wait until the last month to make a move."[12]

It was a season of numerous losses, but the biggest one came shortly after the final game had been played. At 4:20 p.m. on April 13, following a valiant, 11-month fight that involved four brain operations, Michel Brière died at Montreal's Marie-Clarac Rehabilitation Hospital. After Brière had lived most of that time in a coma, his death did not come as a surprise to his loved ones or those in his Penguins family.

"It is hard to say it this way, but we have been expecting it, so that when it came, it was with a feeling of relief," said Kelly. "Mike is better off and so is his family."[13]

Kelly and acting president Jack Riley were the Penguins' official representatives at Brière's funeral four days later in Malartic. The team sent a floral wreath with Michel's number 21 in the center. Riley said the club might possibly retire the number that fans remembered seeing flashing across the Civic Arena ice, eluding defenders and making magic happen around the opponent's net.

"It's so sad," Kelly said. "Mike was so young, with a full life ahead of him."[14]

Nearly 50 years after Brière's passing, Pronovost reflected on the effect the tragedy had on he and his teammates.

"It was tough because he was going to be the big superstar for the team. So you lose a guy like that and it affects your outlook. We really needed a grief psychologist to help the players deal with it, but there was no such thing at the time."[15]

Pronovost lost not only a teammate but a good friend whom he was just starting to get to know. "When we learned he had died, it was discouraging because he was a kid who had a lot to offer," Pronovost reflected. "We were very close. But when he got to Pittsburgh he was 20 years old and there was a family that kind of took him aside and he lived with them, which was the best thing for him. They took care of him, and I helped him get acclimated to Pittsburgh, this U.S. city that was so new to him. He was a good kid. I was a kid, too, but I was a bit older than him. He came to play. He loved the game. Loved to play in the big game. He was a big-game player. Unfortunately, we lost him."[16]

The loss of such a promising player hit Pens fans hard, too. "I remember watching Brière," said Mike Hanczar, who delighted in seeing Number 21 buzz around the Igloo ice from his vantage point in the stands. "He would have been a superstar, there's no doubt about it. He just had a flair for his play. A little guy. He was just so good. Fast, crafty. Everybody was looking forward to a bright future for him and the team. But that was it. It was pretty sad."[17]

Beat reporter Bill Heufelder remembered Brière's quiet determination to win while covering the Penguins during the 1969–70 campaign.

"I remember one time when he really showed himself. We were waiting for a bus after a game in Philly. The Penguins had lost and I guess they hadn't played that well. Brière was standing there by himself so I walked over and he just said something like, 'You have to work hard.' What he said was reflective of the way he was. He had that inner [drive]. You gave 100 percent every night—that's the way you play the game. What he was basically saying, ever so quietly, was that he didn't get much help around him that night. Not everyone was pulling their weight. That's what I remember about him because that's all there was. I mean, this kid was really quiet."[18]

Brière's play reminded his friend Pronovost of one of the era's greatest players.

"I always compared him to Davy Keon: very good passer, good vision, and very intelligent. He wasn't big but he was pretty tough. Only God knows what his potential was. We didn't see him long enough, but we saw him one year to say this guy could be a Mario Lemieux. But we will never know."[19]

6

Picking Up the Pieces:
1971–72

Through all the dark clouds of the 1970–71 season, one ray of sunshine pierced the gloom: the fans came out to the Civic Arena.

The year before, sparked by Brière's lightning-quick rushes up the ice and the Penguins' exciting playoff run, Pittsburgh had caught enough of hockey fever to leave them wanting more. This feeling carried over into the 1970–71 campaign, even though their young scoring hero wasn't there. Finally, the Penguins were attracting respectable-sized crowds. Despite the lackluster results on the ice, the Pens' attendance rose by an impressive 42 percent over the previous year.

After having lived through the difficult early years, Jack Riley was impressed not only by the size of the crowds but also their enthusiasm. "Even on Saturdays I can remember coming to the office and saying, 'I hope we get 7,000 tonight.' Now I ask, 'Are we sold out?' The way the fans have been hollering, you wouldn't think the Arena was the same place anymore."[1] Whomever the NHL decided to sell the club to would be inheriting a team that was on its most solid financial footing ever.

By mid–April, NHL president Clarence Campbell had five offers for the Penguins on his desk. One, from singer Andy Williams and former Philadelphia Flyers president Bill Putnam, looked promising. In the end, though, the NHL opted for a group of Pittsburghers led by Thayer R. (Tad) Potter, a marketing executive with a local natural gas company. The cherubic-faced 38-year-old was the grandson of William F. Rockwell Jr., long-time head of aerospace giant Rockwell International Corp. One of the other partners was a familiar face to Penguins fans: original partner Peter Block, who, along with Senator Jack McGregor, was a driving force in obtaining the franchise for Pittsburgh.

Potter said the impetus to put together the new ownership group was a newspaper story he read indicating that the team might be sold to out-of-town owners. It didn't matter that the day he saw it he was set to leave for a skiing vacation in Colorado with his wife.

"I apologized to her, told her we'd have to cancel the trip, and then went to work with my associates here to get the franchise for Pittsburgh," he said.[2]

The Penguins hockey bug had bitten Potter much earlier. He and another member of the new ownership group, Elmore Keener, Jr., had been part of the "Hockey Hounds," a group of passionate fans who helped sell season tickets for the team.

The price tag on the franchise was $7 million, which covered the losses incurred by previous owner Donald Parsons, payments to members of the Penguins' original ownership group, and about $1 million to the NHL to cover operating capital used during the previous season.

Potter promptly signed coach Red Kelly to a five-year contract, and Riley and Director of Player Personnel Jack Button to three-year deals.

The 1971–72 Penguins press guide summed up the situation as the team prepared to embark on its fifth season: "With the worries of financial difficulties now history, Potter can work on selling out the arena and Kelly, Riley and Button can work on building a Stanley Cup Champion."

Both tasks would prove to be much easier said than done.

• • •

The new ownership stressed a need to build the Penguins with youth, which meant there were a few more fresh, young faces at training camp replacing some of the older ones from the previous year. Gone were Jim Morrison and Andy Bathgate. In were winger Rene Robert, obtained from Buffalo in June's intra-league draft; promising young defenseman Dave Burrows from the Chicago system; and 22-year-old goalie Jim Rutherford from Detroit.

Kelly did bring in one old-time defenseman to help show the kids how things were done: 41-year-old legend Tim Horton, who had been Kelly's teammate during the Toronto glory years of the 60s. The Rangers had left him unprotected, figuring he'd retire to tend full-time to his growing chain of doughnut shops. Universally recognized as the strongest man in hockey for years, Horton dished out checks the way Gordie Howe scored goals—consistently, spectacularly and, for many a season, better than anyone else. Aside from helping the kids find their way, Horton, Kelly felt, still had enough gas left in his tank to be a key contributor.

"He can mean so much to a team. He can play with my young guys. He can take a guy out with authority. He makes the big play at the blue line when you need it. He helps put heart in your team."[3]

Legendary Pittsburgh sports writer Bob Smizik, who covered the Penguins during the 1971–72 season, remembers Horton being regarded as "kind of a god" by the many young players on the Pens roster that year. "He was such a legend by that time," Smizik reflected in 2019. "Even Red Kelly didn't like to tell him what to do. I remember the training camp up in Kitchener, where Horton came and went as he chose, rather than adhering to the rules. It was such a big deal when they acquired him."[4]

The Penguins sprinted into first place in the West Division thanks to a 5–1 record to start the season. That included winning all legs of a three-game west coast road trip, a total that equaled the team's entire win total on the road during the previous season. Horton, who had scored only 112 goals in just over 1,000 games throughout his long NHL career, surprised everyone by netting both goals in the Pens' 2–1 victory in Vancouver. When they got back to Pittsburgh and trounced the Kings 8–1 on October 20, which tied the team record for consecutive wins at four, Kelly was feeling confident about his latest flock of Penguins. "With this team, I'm not afraid of any other club in the league," he told reporters.[5]

He had reason to be afraid, however. The Pens were dealt a huge blow during the victory over L.A. when, during the second period, Horton broke his right ankle. At first, it didn't seem like much. He even took another shift before heading to the dressing room. The next day, however, the full extent of the injury became known. Horton would be lost for at least six weeks. It was a disheartening turn of events for a club that had allowed only nine goals in its first six games.

Horton's injury seemed to break the Pens' positive spirit. They went winless over their next nine games and, thanks in large part to a lack of scoring, went into a prolonged slump. Horton's long-awaited return came December 18 in Boston and helped spark the team to a tie against the mighty Bruins. The hard-earned point, however, turned out to be only a short waystop along a long, cold and dark winter road. The Pens would garner a mere two wins over 24 games from the beginning of December through to the end of January. A low point came on January 19, when the second-year Vancouver Canucks came to town. In what *Pittsburgh Press* writer Bill Heufelder deemed "their darkest hour since the franchise came to life nearly five years ago,"[6] the Pens flopped and floundered their way to a humiliating 6–1 loss. When it was done, a livid Kelly made sure no one other than the he and the team entered the dressing room, even denying entrance to one of the team's partners, Elmore Keener. Inside, he unleashed a bellowing tirade on his troops. "It's embarrassing to be associated with you," he said, saying they had "no effort, desire or will to win." The coach was set to march them back onto the Civic Arena ice for a practice in front of what remained of the crowd of 7,189 who had witnessed the embarrassment. In the end, however, he relented. "I'm not taking you out there in front of those people, but I should," he snarled.[7]

Kelly had tried everything to wring more goals from his players. He yelled at them. He shuffled his lines and even moved defenseman Darryl

Edestrand up to the wing. He traded D-man Bob Woytowich to the Kings for promising young winger Al McDonough, who proceeded to take nine games just to register an assist, let alone a goal.

Eventually, Kelly made a move that involved himself. On January 29, he relinquished his general manager position to focus solely on coaching. Jack Riley would return to the post he had held for the first three years of the franchise before the Donald Parsons ownership group stripped him of the job in favor of Kelly. Red admitted to being burnt out while wearing both the coach and GM hats. "There's so much paperwork, a lot of details with being general manager. It's a time-consuming job. You're working like hang and you get fatigued."[8]

The scoring gradually returned in February and as the Penguins climbed in the standings and a playoff spot became a possibility, the team's braintrust decided to deviate from their youth movement, at least in one instance. On March 4 they traded underperforming winger Rene Robert to Buffalo for veteran Eddie Shack. A former linemate of Kelly's during many of Toronto's championship years in the 1960s, Shack was an effective winger with a larger-than-life personality and enough energy to fill an entire roster. Shack loved playing to the crowd and had earned the nickname "the Entertainer" for good reason.

Both his scoring and entertaining skills were on display as soon as he donned a Penguin uniform. After scoring two goals in a win over Boston at the Civic Arena, Shack was named the first star. When his name was called, he burst out from the tunnel, sprinted toward center ice and did a few hard-charging circles around the faceoff circle. The fans loved it, and they kept coming out for more Shack-style entertainment.

The fourth and final West playoff spot came down to the Penguins and Flyers and a crucial head-to-head matchup on the second-last day of the season for both clubs. Trailing Philadelphia by two points, the Pens entered the Spectrum needing a win or a tie to stay alive. Things were looking bleak in the second intermission after Bobby Clarke had his second goal of the game to give the Flyers a 3–1 lead. Greg Polis sliced the deficit to one with a goal only 12 seconds into the third with a pretty backhand shot, but Ross Lonsberry restored the two-goal margin six minutes later. Bob Leiter fired a shot from the right faceoff circle that went between goalie Doug Favell's legs to make it 3–2 as the period approached the midway point.

Tasting the final playoff berth, Philadelphia went into a defensive shell to protect their lead. The clock ticked steadily down until, with just under one minute to play, a Shack shot from the left point was deflected by Polis past Favell, tying the game and keeping the Penguins' playoff dream alive.

The race would be decided on the final night of the season. Pittsburgh still trailed the Flyers by two points, but if they managed to beat St. Louis at home and the Flyers lost at Buffalo, Pittsburgh would get the nod in the tie-breaker thanks to winning the season series with Philly, 3–2–1. By the midway point of the third period, the Penguins were rolling to an easy win, holding a commanding 6–2 lead over the Blues. Throughout that final period, everyone in the Civic Arena kept a watchful eye on the score in Buffalo, which showed the Flyers leading 2–1 in the third. Rene Robert, however, helped out his old mates by bringing the Sabres even with a power play tally at 8:47.

As they had the night before, the Flyers stuck to a tight defensive scheme to protect the tie. This night it was working to perfection as the clock ticked down, minute by minute. That was, until Sabres centerman Gerry Meehan crossed the Philadelphia blue line in the dying seconds and fired a hard slap shot toward the goal. The low blast beat goalie Favell and clanged into the net with only four seconds left. Miraculously, the Flyers had lost.

Back at the Civic Arena, public address announcer Beckley Smith told the crowd what had happened in Buffalo, sending the fans and the Pens bench into a delirious celebration. In one of the craziest endings to a playoff race in NHL history, the Penguins had come out on top and claimed the second post-season berth in their five-year history.

Their reward was a first-round matchup against the powerful Chicago Black Hawks, led by 50-goal-scorer Bobby Hull and goalie Tony Esposito, who led the league with a 1.76 goals against average. The Pens had failed to beat the Hawks all year, going 0–5–1.

The Penguins rode the momentum of their regular season finale into Chicago Stadium for game one of the best-of-seven series and managed to grab a 1–0 lead only 1:25 in when Bob Leiter took a nice feed from Eddie Shack and put it behind Esposito. Playing a solid defensive game, the Penguins saw the Hawks answer back but stayed with Chicago until the third period, when Pit Martin set up Jim Pappin for the go-ahead goal, and then scored his own goal to make the final 3–1.

In game two, Martin picked up where he left off by scoring only 35 seconds in. With Chicago leading 2–0 in the second, Jean Pronovost, the Penguins' leading goal-getter in the regular season with 30, drove a 10-footer past Esposito for a shorthanded goal. Pittsburgh would get no closer, however, trading third-period goals and coming out on the short end of a 3–2 decision.

"You can't spot [Chicago] two goals and expect to catch them very often," observed winger Nick Harbaruk.[9]

The players came back to Pittsburgh knowing they'd played two good games, with relentless forechecking and rock-solid defense. The mood ahead of game three at the Civic Arena was anything but negative. "We've been playing these tough games for the last few weeks, and we can survive a few more. This series is going the full seven games," said defenseman Bryan Watson.[10]

Eddie Shack was doing his best to get the Hawks off their game, hitting and pestering their stars every time he was on the ice. In game one he high-sticked Keith Magnusson, opening a gash that required 13 stitches. The Hawks tried to get him all night, and the next night, too. The Entertainer's antics resulted in eight Chicago penalty minutes in game two. At one point, Magnusson dropped his gloves to fight Shack but Eddie just turned away. "Has he ever won a fight?" Shack wondered to the press after the game. "I've never seen him win one. He's a little scared of me."[11]

Keith McCreary, out since January 23 with a knee injury, returned to the lineup for game three, but neither he nor any other Penguin managed to get a puck behind Chicago backup Gary Smith all night. The lanky Smith stopped all 31 Penguin shots, including 14 in a third period that saw Pittsburgh, trailing 2–0, open things up. But the scoreboard didn't change and when the final horn sounded, the Pens found themselves in a 3–0 series hole.

They trailed despite having held Bobby Hull off the scoresheet in the

first three games. The "Golden Jet," however, was not to be denied. He exploded for three goals to help the Hawks establish a 5–4 lead late in the third. Bob Leiter, however, scored his third of the series from the side of the Chicago net with only 2:08 left to keep the Pens' season alive and send things to overtime.

After Chicago grabbed possession on the opening faceoff and put the puck deep into the Penguin zone, Jim Pappin got possession and fired a shot at goalie Jim Rutherford, who saved it with his chest. The puck bounced to his left and he fell toward it. Before he could smother it, however, the disk bounded further away from him, into the slot. Chicago's Pit Martin swiped at it, knocking it off Tim Horton's skate and into the open net.

Game over. Season over.

"The puck went off my skate. I just wish it hadn't happened this

Defenseman Dave Burrows was a mainstay on the Penguin blueline for much of the 1970s. His strong, shut-down style earned him three All-Star Game appearances throughout his 11-year career (courtesy Doug McLatchy).

way," said a sombre Horton after the game. "This team's got a lot of moxy. We could have given up a lot of times this season."[12]

Surprisingly, the Penguins could feel positive despite having been swept in a playoff series.

"[Chicago] should have won the Stanley Cup last year, and this year they're even stronger," said Kelly. "We played 'em tough. We lost four straight but I don't think we disgraced ourselves."[13]

7

So Long, Red:
1972–73

If the Penguins were to have any success in 1972–73, it would be on the backs of go-to forwards Syl Apps, Jean Pronovost and Greg Polis. The fruits of the team's youth movement that began after their disappointing first season were now on full display on defense and in goal. Promising sophomore Dave Burrows, 24, was the centerpiece of a blueline corps that included five members who were 27 years old or younger, while 23-year-old Jim Rutherford would be given the bulk of the goalkeeping duties. Gone were Les Binkley, who signed with the Ottawa Nationals of the upstart World Hockey Association, and Tim Horton, who signed with Buffalo Sabres.

The team once again got off to a good start, winning four of its first five games and scoring 23 goals in the process. Up front, the "SH" line of center Ron Schock and wings Eddie Shack and Ken Schinkel was clicking. A pleasant early surprise was the play of a goaltender even younger than Rutherford. Chosen in the third round of the 1972 amateur draft, 20-year-old Denis Herron won his first game and followed it up with two shutouts in his next three starts, beating the Islanders 5–0 on Long Island and then blanking the Canucks 4–0 in Vancouver.

"I didn't expect a shutout so early, but my teammates, they help me so much,"[1] said a happy Herron after the New York game.

The good times were also rolling on November 22 when the Penguins, playing at home against the St. Louis Blues, set an NHL record that still stands to this day. The game was a typically close battle between the bitter expansion rivals for the first two periods, with the Pens holding a 5–4 lead with a little over eight minutes to go. Bryan Hextall widened the lead by tipping in a Jack Lynch slap shot at 12:00. Jean Pronovost then took a feed from Greg Polis 12 seconds later and buried it past Blues goalie Wayne Stephenson. Al McDonough completed a hat trick at 13:40 off a pass from Syl Apps to make it a rout at 8–4. The crowd of 12,405 had barely even started celebrating that marker when Ken Schinkel lit the lamp only nine seconds later. The shell-shocked Blues could not pull themselves together enough to stop Schock from adding a 10th goal only 18 seconds later.

The traditionally goal-starved Penguins had scored five goals in only two minutes and seven seconds, easily obliterating the previous mark for fastest five goals by one team of three minutes, 46 seconds set by the Rangers in 1942. The fourth and fifth of those Penguin goals, only nine seconds apart, set a new team record for fastest two goals, and the overall tally of 10 marked the first time the Pens had gone into double figures.

"Our guys were driving," observed GM Jack Riley. "They seemed to have an obsession like Rocket Richard used to have to get down toward the goal and to get a shot. Everything seemed to be going our way."[2]

Indeed, everything was going the Pens' way throughout November.

Eddie Shack was doing a fine job of living up to his "Entertainer" nickname, delighting the fans with reckless dashes up the ice and frequently putting the puck in the opponent's net. After scoring a hat trick during a 7–4 Penguin win against his old Toronto team on November 29, Shack said he "just gave our fans a sample of my figure skating prowess. I'm saving my big effort for Toronto on December 27 when we'll bomb the Leafs in their own rink."[3]

The real engine for the Penguins during their most successful month in team history was the line of Syl Apps centering Al McDonough and Lowell MacDonald. Apps had 22 points during November, McDonough had 18 and MacDonald, progressing nicely in his comeback from knee surgery, scored seven goals.

The good times, however, didn't last and the Penguins soon tumbled below the .500 mark. On January 12, a day before the 17–19–6 Pens were to take on the Kings at the Civic Arena, Red Kelly spoke to the press about what changes might be made to the lineup. Adjustments were necessary both because defenseman Bryan Watson had suffered a knee injury during their last game against Detroit, and because the team was in a goal drought.

"I'm still uncertain just which players will work together against Los Angeles," he said. "We have to start scoring some goals if we hope to remain in this race."[4]

It turned out that within 24 hours of making that observation, Kelly would no longer have to worry about the Penguins lineup for the Kings game, or any other game, for that matter. The morning of the 13th, the coach was informed that he had been relieved of his duties.

"We believe this year's team has more ability than last year's team and is not living up to its potential," explained Penguin owner Tad Potter. "We feel that the worst thing we could do is nothing."[5]

Although many fans voiced their displeasure at the move, Kelly was not completely shocked. "I had heard the rumours," he said. "They were like vultures waiting for an excuse for a long time."[6]

Kelly had been the favorite son of previous Penguin owner Donald Parsons, who had given him the GM reigns after the successful 1969–70 campaign. Potter did not seem to hold the Irishman in quite as high regard, and perhaps didn't feel his observations and suggestions were being welcomed by the coach. It was also no secret that Kelly and GM Jack Riley had often been at odds over coaching and managing strategies.

Stepping behind the bench on an interim basis was right wing Ken Schinkel, who would relinquish his playing duties. The only remaining Penguin from the team's inaugural season and its all-time leading scorer, "Schink" would bring to the job an in-depth knowledge of the roster and the organization. "I have been personally involved with the guys and I hope to use this as an advantage," he said. "They have been able to talk to me in the past and should still be able to in the future."[7]

Schinkel immediately tried to instill a more relaxed atmosphere in the dressing room, making days off more common, relaxing the rules of wearing ties on road trips, and doing away with Kelly's doghouse, in which many players took up residence after a single bad performance.

Greg Polis, who had been a frequent tenant in that doghouse, had more than just a new boss to adjust to at the time. He and his wife welcomed their first child, a baby boy, on January 29, the day before he was set to fly to New York for the 26th NHL All-Star Game. Although his season had not been as productive as he or the Penguin brass would have liked—he sat sixth in team scoring with 29 points in 48 games—Polis was nevertheless chosen. Hoping to score a goal and present the puck to his new son, Polis did far better. Playing on a line with Philadelphia's Bobby Clarke and teammate Lowell MacDonald, Polis scored two goals and was named MVP, for which he won a new Dodge Charger.

A late-season surge, combined with the stumbling of the Kings and Blues down the stretch, gave the Penguins some hope of pulling off another miracle to squeak into the playoffs. A pair of wins against the expansion Atlanta Flames set up a showdown in St. Louis in the second-last game of the season for both teams. The Penguins trailed the Blues by three points for the final playoff spot. Only a win would do, but Pittsburgh came out nervous and found themselves down 3–0 after the first period. The Blues cruised to an easy 7–2 win, keeping the Penguins out of the playoffs for the fourth time in their six-year history.

There were some positives. Lowell MacDonald captured the first major award by a Penguin when he was named the winner of the Bill Masterton trophy, awarded for perseverance, sportsmanship and dedication to hockey. Putting three knee operations behind him, MacDonald netted a whopping

34 goals. Had he not missed an empty net in the Pens' last game of the season he would have tied team leader McDonough. Syl Apps had another fine year, leading the team in points with his new club-record total of 85. Perhaps most importantly, however, the Penguins easily set a new attendance record with 436,601 for an average of 11,195, eclipsing the old mark with an entire month left in the season. It appeared that, finally, the Penguin hockey club had gained a toehold on the Pittsburgh sports scene, silencing much of the relocation discussion that had hung around the Civic Arena like a bad smell since the team first hit the ice. The installation of 3,500 new Civic Arena seats was tangible proof of the Pens' off-ice success.

"Hockey has caught on in this town and now it's up to us to repay the fans for their support by giving them something to cheer about," said GM Jack Riley.[8]

It would now be up to Schinkel, who it was announced would be returning as head coach, to get his Penguins to start generating those cheers.

PART THREE

A Matter of Survival
(1973–74 Through 1978–79)

8

Punchless Penguins: 1973–74

When Ken Schinkel looked at the roster of his 1973–74 Pittsburgh Penguins, he had no concerns with the forwards. The group would remain largely the same as the one that had set a team record with 257 goals the previous year. "We have talent," he said. "You can't score that many goals and not have any talent."[1]

He also knew that he'd never be in a panic as long as little Jimmy Rutherford, who had emerged as a bona fide NHL starter in 1972–73, stayed healthy. Andy Brown and a young Denis Herron would probably also provide adequate backup help when needed.

It was the defense that Schinkel knew was his big worry. Beyond Dave Burrows, who had been named team MVP for his steady defensive play and an upsurge in offense to the tune of a career-high 27 points, the cupboard was at best circumspect, if not outright bare. Bryan Watson provided grit but not many points. The rest of the blueline would be patrolled by a largely unproven group including Jean-Guy Legace and youngsters Larry Bignell and Yvon Labre.

Knowing he'd need help in this area, the career right-winger Schinkel enlisted the help of an assistant coach who would concentrate on the defensive end. Forty-one-year-old Fred Hucul had patrolled the bluelines of the minor Western Hockey League for 13 seasons and also got into 164 NHL games, mostly with the pre-expansion-era Chicago Black Hawks.

"I'm limited in what I can teach defensemen," Schinkel admitted. "Freddy, on the other hand, was always a first-rate defenseman."[2]

The NHL was entering an era where toughness was the name of the game. Led primarily by the roughhouse Philadelphia Flyers, whose intimidating style of play had already garnered them their soon-to-be-famous "Broad Street Bullies" nickname, hard checking, cheap shots and fighting—lots of fighting—became the model that many teams tried to adopt. It became clear early on, however, that the Penguin roster was filled with many players who seemed to want no part of that kind of game.

And they soon started to pay the price—on the ice, at the turnstiles and in the standings. The Flyers manhandled the Penguins twice in nine days, pummeling them 6–0 at the Civic Arena on October 27 and hitting them hard the next time they met to the tune of 7–0.

The Pens were quickly gaining the reputation of being patsies.

"We're always able to get up for Pittsburgh, and they weren't too aggressive," said Flyers coach Fred Shero after the 7–0 beatdown.[3]

After a respectable 4–4 start, the Pens soon entered into a freefall and found themselves in the familiar position of the lower rungs of the West Division standings. A slow start by the top line of Syl Apps, Al McDonough and Lowell MacDonald didn't help Schinkel sleep at night. The trio that had accounted for 98 of the Penguins' goals the previous season was hit by the same goalless dry spell that seemed to afflict the entire team in early November.

The fans soon became angry watching their team get pushed around night after night. Many decided they'd seen enough and stayed away altogether. Attendance figures began to drop back to those seen in the first few years of the franchise. Two months in, the Penguins were 15,000 behind their pace at the same time the year before, and owner Tad Potter was not pleased. The ownership team had invested $1 million to expand the Igloo's seating capacity to 13,300 and install 24 plush luxury boxes, only to see more and more unfilled seats as the season wore on. Potter put the blame on the players.

"The discipline is gone out of hockey," he ranted to the *Pittsburgh Press*'s Bill Heufelder. "I get the feeling that the players think the energy crisis means them, so they only give 85 per cent now."[4]

The fans that were showing up often reacted to their team's poor play with boos and jeers. "They've been down on us so much this season that we look forward to going on the road," lamented Lowell MacDonald.

During an 18-game stretch from late November to early January, the Penguins won only twice—a 9–1 bombing of the bumbling Golden Seals and a tight 2–1 decision over the sophomore Flames. The offense was largely coming only from the top line of MacDonald, Apps and McDonough, which accounted for 40 of the team's 82 goals as of Christmas. That made it easy for opposing coaches to concentrate their defensive efforts on them.

The goaltending was proving unreliable, with Rutherford having a subpar year and Brown going hot and cold from one night to the next. Herron was occasionally brought up from the minors and performed admirably when given the chance, but the inability of any keeper to solidly grab the starter's spot was preventing any upward movement in the standings.

Schinkel tried his best to shake his skaters out of the slump, even having them stay at a local motel for two days before a home game against Chicago.

"I thought it might be a chance for them to get some rest," he said.[5] Unfortunately, the Pens did most of their resting on the ice and fell to the Black Hawks, 3–1.

By January 11, with his team sitting in seventh place in the West Division and 16 points out of the final playoff spot, owner Tad Potter decided enough was enough. The Jack Riley era in Pittsburgh abruptly came to an end. The only general manager the franchise had known was let go, to be replaced by his assistant, Jack Button. The 34-year-old Button came to the job with no experience as a player but a thorough knowledge of the Penguins organization and a reputation for being a master organizer. He'd served as GM of the club's now-defunct farm club in Amarillo before assuming the Pens' assistant GM role under Riley in 1968. He vowed not to meddle with Schinkel's efforts behind the bench.

"I think the general manager should be more of an organizer and planner," he told the press on the day he was hired. "I don't think I can tell a coach who to play."[6]

Button also had opinions on an owner's role, which in large part involved staying quiet about the day-to-day operations of their club. He said as much to Potter, who had never been shy about popping off to the media about his team's play. The head Penguin got the message. "Beginning today," Potter vowed to a group of reporters on the day of Button's hiring, "you will no longer find easy access to my thoughts."[7]

Joe Gordon remembers Potter being "more of a fan" to whom the Penguins were a bit of a toy that, thanks to his family's wealth, he was able to play with. "Tad was a great guy. You'd love to have a drink with him every night of the week," said the Pens' former PR manager. However, "if you were buying [the Penguins] for investment purposes, it was not the deal you'd want to make."[8]

Despite his pledge, it was Potter who was the lead man on the first trade that took place under the Button regime, only six days after the GM shuffle. St. Louis Blues president Sid Solomon III called Potter directly, looking to acquire left winger Greg Polis. Potter negotiated the deal that saw Polis, longtime Pen defenseman Bryan Watson and a second-round choice in the 1975 draft go to St. Louis in return for promising forward Ab DeMarco and two bruisers, 22-year-old Steve Durbano, known for having a short temper that resulted in ill-timed penalties, and Bob "Battleship" Kelly, a huge, hard-nosed left wing who was more inclined to putting up his fists than big point totals.

The very same day, Button sent starting goalie Jim Rutherford and blueliner Jack Lynch to Detroit for rangy defenseman Ron Stackhouse. An early-season slump and a contract that was expiring at the end of the season contributed to Button's decision to move the team's go-to goalie. The 24-year-old Stackhouse would bring size and some point production to the Pens' blueline.

The wheeling and dealing paid some early dividends. In Vancouver, Durbano scored a goal and demolished the Canucks' Dave Dunn in a fight, landing a right hook that broke Dunn's nose and sent him to the dressing room. Stackhouse also scored in the 6–2 win. The victory kicked off a three-game winning streak, including an increasingly rare victory in Philadelphia and a vanquishing of the hated Blues in Pittsburgh, in which the new musclemen's toughness was on fine display.

"The Blues won't be bothering us too much anymore," said a grinning "Battleship" Kelly after the 4–1 win in front of a packed Civic Arena. "I don't think anyone will bother us too much."[9]

The turnaround, however, would be short-lived. The Pens would lose their next five, causing Button to end Schinkel's short reign behind the bench and replace him with Marc Boileau, coach of the Penguins' International Hockey League affiliate in Fort Wayne. The choice of Boileau was seen to be a bit of an odd one, given that the 41-year-old Montreal native, whose playing career was spent mostly in the minors along with a 54-game stint with the 1961–62 Detroit Red Wings, had zero NHL coaching experience. He had, however, led Fort Wayne to the IHL championship the previous year, and Button was impressed with his confidence and energetic attitude.

"I want to get the players believing in themselves," Boileau said after spending some time with his new charges and realizing that the attitude in the locker room needed some adjusting.[10] To that end, the new coach adopted an "everybody plays" approach that saw each player get a fair share of ice time. It was a big boost to players like right winger Chuck Arnason, who had been struggling to find the net prior to Boileau's hiring. Arnason promptly popped in six goals in five games under the new coach.

"Marc gave me a lot of ice time and that has to help my confidence. Now the goals are coming," Arnason told the *Pittsburgh Press*.[11]

Boileau's methods of loosening up a tightly wound bunch included some unorthodox methods, such as inviting his nine-year-old son Luke to tell some jokes in the locker room before a game. And such moves began to pay off. While the Pens could not seem to string more than two wins together, the losses did become less frequent. A four-game unbeaten streak, capped by a wild 7–5 win in St. Louis, had Boileau thinking the unthinkable: a playoff spot. His Penguins sat second-last in the West, 10 points behind fourth-place Los Angeles, with only 14 games to play.

"The teams ahead of us can lose seven, eight in a row. If we win five or six, we're right in the thick of it," said the coach.[12] Boileau knew something about late-season streaks. The year prior in Fort Wayne, he'd led his Komets to 20 wins in their final 25 games to get into the playoffs and eventually win the IHL championship.

The Penguins' 1973–74 hole, however, proved to be too deep. They stayed alive as late as March 30, when a 4–3 loss to the Blues—thanks to a Garry Unger goal with five seconds to play—officially eliminated them.

The surprising hire of Boileau, however, had provided some hope in the midst of a lost season. The Penguins won as many games under the fiery Frenchman (14) as they had all year before his arrival. His 14–10–4 record earned him a chance to return behind the bench for the 1974–75 campaign. Little did anyone know, amidst the rubble of the season just ended, that it would be the Penguins' finest hour yet.

9

Finally, a Winner:
1974–75

Jack Button knew that the offensive attack of his Pittsburgh Penguins was a one-trick pony. To be sure, the team's top line of center Syl Apps, right wing Jean Pronovost and left winger Lowell MacDonald was a potent weapon. Together, they formed the second-highest-producing line in the NHL during the 1973–74 season. After that, however, the Penguins offense ran quite dry. The top line had accounted for 44 percent of Pittsburgh's scoring, which made opponents' game plans simple: stop the top guns and you have a great chance of winning. During the summer of '74, Button set out to build a quality second line to give those opponents something else to worry about.

His first move was to acquire aging left wing Vic Hadfield from the Rangers, who had once formed part of New York's famous GAG (Goal a Game) line with Jean Ratelle and Rod Gilbert. A 50-goal-scorer three years earlier, Hadfield had notched 27 goals in 1973–74. Button hoped he still had enough left in his 33-year-old tank to put up a similar number.

On the right side, Button swooped in and plucked a disgruntled Rick Kehoe out of Toronto, sending their first-round pick in the 1973 draft, right winger Blain Stoughton, and their number one pick in the 1977 draft to the Leafs in return. Button felt the seemingly high price was worth it: Kehoe was a sharpshooter who had notched 131 points in 184 games over his first three seasons in Toronto. A falling out with Leafs coach Red Kelly had led him to demand a trade if the ex–Penguin coach remained behind the Toronto bench. The 23-year-old had named "about three teams" he'd agree to go to, with Pittsburgh being one of them. Kehoe took a liking to the less-pressurized atmosphere of Pittsburgh.

"In Toronto, you're always in the public eye, whereas in Pittsburgh, [the Penguins] were a few rungs down because the Steelers were winning and the Pirates won in the early 70s," he reflected years later. "You could go places and nobody really knew who you were. In Toronto, it was a different time back then. You didn't wear helmets and you were on TV twice a week, so people recognized you."[1]

Veteran Ron Schock was a shoo-in for the spot between Hadfield and Kehoe, but Pierre Larouche, the club's first-round pick in the 1974 draft, quickly put himself into the mix at center as training camp opened in Brantford. The 19-year-old Quebec scoring sensation came to the Pens brimming with a brash confidence and a skill set that had veterans turning their heads. Larouche had scored an incredible 94 goals and 251 points in his final year of junior for Sorel of the Quebec junior league. The talent that got him those numbers was often on full display in camp drills, scrimmages and preseason games, but Penguin management was on the fence as to whether to keep him with the big club or send him to Hershey of the American Hockey League for some seasoning at the pro level. To Pierre, however, there was no doubt he was going to be playing in the Steel City—and playing well.

"I will settle for 20 goals and 50 points this year," he told reporters.[2]

When McManama contracted a nasty intestinal flu that affected his preseason play, it made Button and Boileau's decision on Larouche an easy one: he would indeed be wearing a skating penguin on his jersey when the season opened.

Throughout their less-than-impressive history, the Penguins had at least usually been able to rely on strong goaltending to make many a final score look respectable. Les Binkley had been the man to rely on in the crease until his departure to the WHA in 1972, and Jim Rutherford had performed admirably afterward. But even he at last faltered behind an often-leaky defense before being shipped to the

Pierre Larouche scored 53 goals in 1975–76, only his second year in the NHL. His often-stormy stay in the Steel City ended when he was traded to the Montreal Canadiens in November 1977 (courtesy Doug McLatchy).

Red Wings. The Penguin cage this year would be guarded by Gary Inness and Bob Johnson, a pair of untested youngsters with only 32 games of NHL experience between them heading into the 1974–75 campaign. Their inexperience was evident early in the season, with Johnson in particular showing his nerves repeatedly. He was blasted for four goals in the opening period of a game in Vancouver on November 1 and had to be relieved by Inness. Both netminders weren't given much help by the defense, which too often shied away from battles in the corners and frequently looked in disarray in their own zone.

Fortunately, their teammates up front were scoring goals at a clip never seen before from a Penguin team. The days of playing dull, close-checking hockey in the hopes of eking out a one-goal victory appeared to be over. Thanks in large part to the abundance of talent up front, a new identity was taking hold, one full of confidence and looseness.

No better example of this new spirit was seen than on November 20, when the Pens headed into Maple Leaf Gardens to take on Toronto, their fourth game in five nights. Down 3–1 after the first period, it would have been easy to throw in the towel and take solace in the fact that they'd won three of the first four of this demanding stretch. Instead, the Pens stormed back with four second-period goals and three more in the third to run away with an 8–5 win.

"We have an identity now," said Syl Apps after tallying two of the Penguin goals. "We are the Pittsburgh Penguins. We have a good team and we know we can beat the other team. We used to think about how we would defend against the opponent, but now we play our game and let the other team worry about us."[3]

It appeared not everything had changed about the Penguins, however. With every success seemed to come a setback. This time the dark cloud took the form of Larouche, who was apparently steamed over having to watch most of the third period of a game at home November 30 against Buffalo from the bench. The game was tied 5–5 and Boileau was none too pleased with the rookie's lack of defensive coverage.

Larouche decided to show his displeasure by not showing up at the airport for the Pens' charter flight to Buffalo, where they were to meet the Sabres the next night to complete the home-and-home series. The no-show left management and players bewildered as to where their young hotshot centerman was.

"I didn't know he wasn't coming," said veteran Jean Pronovost, who had taken his fellow Frenchman somewhat under his wing. "I even brought some sandwiches to the plane for him."[4]

Larouche was eventually located, and it was up to Pens marketing director Marv Parliament to drive him to Buffalo. It would be just the first in a long line of petulance displays by "Lucky Pierre" that would test the patience of Penguin coaches and managers.

Button's efforts to build a deeper offensive attack began to pay dividends as the season rolled along. Schock was enjoying a career year playing with Kehoe and Hadfield and was leading the team in scoring at the Christmas break with 39 points. The third line of Larouche, Chuck Arnason and Bob Kelly offered coach Boileau a viable option to throw at opposing defenses. Larouche had 17 goals by mid–January and was being mentioned in NHL Rookie of the Year discussions.

When the Pens topped the visiting California Golden Seals 7–5 on January 22, it pushed them to a record of 18–17–10, marking the first time a Penguin team had been above the .500 mark later than Christmas. The win also extended the team's home unbeaten streak to 14 games (8–0–6). Despite the impressive record on Igloo ice, however, the fans still weren't warming to their big-league hockey team. For the California game, for instance, only 7,730 Civic Arena seats were filled—an obvious disappointment to owner Tad Potter but also to the players.

"What do we have to do to get the fans?" wondered winger Bob Kelly after the win. "We haven't lost at home since November and we're still not drawing. The ones who come are great, but they are the same people every game."[5]

The low attendances were doing nothing to alleviate the financial strain Tad Potter and his ownership group was continuing to feel. In December it was revealed that the NHL had advanced the Penguins $250,000 over the summer of 1974 to help pay the bills. A report in February pegged the amount owed to the league at $500,000.[6] To dig out of that hole, Potter was looking to sell about 25 percent of the club to any investors who could supply the necessary cash to keep the Penguin ship afloat. Even Potter admitted, however, that the low attendances were scaring off potential partners. They were also discouraged by the team's radio broadcast deal, which, unlike most teams, netted the team no money.

NHL president Clarence Campbell and the board of governors seemed to be running out of patience with the Penguins. In January, Campbell indicated to the press that two cities that had been granted conditional expansion franchises for 1976–77, Seattle and Denver, might enter the league a year earlier with relocated existing teams. Talk soon arose in Seattle about the strong possibility of the Penguins moving west to become the Seattle Totems. Potter steadfastly maintained that the Pens would be staying in Pittsburgh, but until new investors could be found, the rumors persisted. Meanwhile, Pittsburgh's top politician was doing his part to save the city's hockey team. Mayor Peter Flaherty summoned many of the city's top business investors to his office on February 3 and asked them to purchase all 84,842 remaining unsold seats for the last 14 Penguin home games.

If the Penguin players were at all distracted by their team's financial uncertainty, they showed no indication of it on the ice.

"I don't think it really bothered guys," remembered defenseman Ron Stackhouse. "I wasn't aware of it at all. People knew that the team was struggling and you could see we weren't drawing big crowds and stuff. But I don't think that affected our play. If it did, I was oblivious to that sort of being a cloud hanging over us or anything."[7]

Similarly, Rick Kehoe wasn't losing any sleep over his team's financial situation. "We knew what was going on maybe two months before the season ended, that we were in financial trouble," Kehoe remembered. "It didn't bother the guys because everybody was still getting paid. It's when you're not getting paid that it bothers you."[8]

As the season wound down, the Pens continued to win more than they lost, securing impressive wins in March against such elite teams as Montreal, Boston, and defending Stanley Cup champion Philadelphia—the latter an 8–2 home-ice drubbing that had the Igloo faithful gleefully chanting, "Go home, Flyers!" The only cause for concern was the location most of the club's victories were being attained. Despite rolling to their best-ever record, the Pens were garnering a reputation as a great team in their own rink but woeful away from it. At season's end, their home record stood at a spectacular 25 wins, five losses and 10 ties, while on the road they were a limp 12–23–5. After the Canadiens had answered their loss on Pittsburgh ice with a 6–0 demolition of the Pens at the Forum in Montreal, even Habs goalie Ken Dryden was left wondering about the Penguins' Jekyll and Hyde act.

"I can't see why that team is so inconsistent. I can understand some difference between a home and a road record, but certainly not as dramatic as this one."[9]

The extreme difference made it that much more important to secure home-ice advantage for the first round of the playoffs. For once, the Pens enjoyed the luxury of a guaranteed playoff spot long before the season ended. In the recently expanded and realigned NHL, the winners of the league's four divisions received a bye to the second round. Pittsburgh, being in the same division as Montreal, had no hope of capturing their section's title. They would have to instead jockey for one of eight first-round spots that were awarded to the league's best non-division-winning teams.

When the season's dust had settled, the Pens' team-record 89 points were good enough to secure the coveted home-ice advantage in the short best-of-three preliminary round series against their old rivals, the St. Louis Blues.

The Pens could look at the season statistics and see a lot to be proud of. Jack Button's moves to add depth to the offense had paid off in spades, with a whopping nine players notching 23 or more goals. Schock maintained his lead in team scoring right to the end, finishing with 86 points. Larouche ended his first season with an impressive 31 goals. Only a handful of players sported negative plus-minus ratings, with defensemen Barry Wilkins and Colin Campbell leading the way with plus-29 and plus-28, respectively.

In Game One against the Blues before a sold-out Civic Arena, the Pens rebounded from a mostly nervous performance through most of the first two periods to pound three third-period goals past St. Louis goalie John Davidson—two by winger Chuck Arnason—en route to a come-from-behind 4–3 victory. Pierre Larouche sent the crowd into a frenzy when he scored the go-ahead goal at 17:29 of the third, speeding into the slot and converting a Vic Hadfield pass from behind the net.

"We proved a lot by coming back like that," said Hadfield afterward. "We can stand up to the playoff pressure."[10]

They continued to prove that in the second game, two nights later in St. Louis. Jean Pronovost snapped a nine-game scoring drought with an early goal in the first period, Gary Inness stopped 39 shots and Colin Campbell netted the winner with a shorthanded goal 4:33 into the third to give the Penguins a 5–3 win and only their second playoff series victory in team history.

"This was the best game we've had in at least a month," said Syl Apps. "We didn't want to play them a third time. [The Blues] are a rough team."[11]

Dave Burrows had the same impression of the Blues when reflecting on the series years later.

"We had quite a rivalry with St. Louis at that time. And it was always a very physical series, but it was a short series, too. It was very intense and we played well. To get one round under our belts was a wonderful feeling and a good confidence-builder."[12]

Up next would be a best-of-seven quarterfinal series against the New York Islanders, who had knocked off their cross-town rivals the Rangers, thanks to a Jean-Paul Parise goal 11 seconds into overtime of the deciding third game. In only their third year of existence, the Isles had emerged as a strong, young club built around emerging stars like defenseman Denis Potvin, forward Bob Nystrom and goalie Billy Smith. Led by coach Al Arbour, the Islanders promised to be a significant test for the high-flying Penguins. Pittsburgh, now the fourth-highest seed remaining in the playoffs, would again enjoy home-ice advantage.

Thanks to the strong goaltending of Gary Inness, the Pens held on for a 5–4 victory in game one, after nearly blowing a 5–2 third-period lead. It was Parise again who provided the firepower for the Islanders, scoring two goals to make it 5–4 with 2:13 left to play. A tripping penalty to Ron Schock and a pulled Billy Smith gave New York a two-man advantage in the last minute, but Inness made two more big saves to secure the win.

The Penguins fired 47 shots at Smith in game two and came away with a 3–1 victory to take a commanding 2–0 lead. More great play from Inness had the Igloo crowd chanting, "Gary! Gary!" Said Inness after the game, "I've been booed here before and I was cheered here tonight. Who knows what will happen next week?"[13]

With Pens backup goalie Michel Plasse on the sidelines with an injured ankle and the often-shaky Bob Johnson filling the second-string role, it was clear that it would be up to Inness to carry the Pens load in goal. The 25-year-old Toronto native seemed unphased by any apparent pressure, instead looking loose and confident.

"These guys have worked hard," he told the *Pittsburgh Press* after game two. "I'm not about to let them down now. Ten more wins and we get the Cup."[14]

The team brought that total down to nine with a 6–4 win in game three, which saw them come out of the dressing room flying, grabbing a 2–0 lead just over seven minutes in. Bob Kelly notched his second of the game early in the middle period to extend the lead to 3–0. The tenacious Islanders, however, refused to give up and the Pens only secured the victory when Lowell MacDonald scored into an empty net with 12 seconds left. In all three games, New York had come back from 3–0 deficits to make the games interesting. The Penguins knew that getting the fourth and final win of the series would not be easy.

"They're like a disease," Kelly observed. "Most teams, you get ahead of them 3–0, they're making reservations to get out of town. The Islanders don't seem to do that."[15]

Inness was again phenomenal in the game three win, but a hit to the back of his head by New York's Gary Howatt during a collision behind his net with just over four minutes to play left him feeling blacked-out. After being down on the ice for a minute, Inness shook it off and finished the game, but not before giving up two late goals that allowed the Islanders to turn things into a nail-biter. The first was a slapshot from the blue line that Inness, according to *Pittsburgh Post-Gazette* beat writer Bob Whitely, "had been routinely stopping and clearing to the wings in the same motion."[16]

After the game, Inness was quickly deemed by the Penguins training staff to be well enough to play in game four three days later. Meanwhile, the Islanders, despite their predicament, sounded a note of optimism in their post-game dressing room.

"The Penguins won three in a row, why can't we?" asked Potvin. "We've got to get our heads on right in the next couple of days and come back with our kind of hockey. If we do that, I don't see how we can lose to the Penguins."[17]

The series ran into a scheduling blip for game four. If the regular pattern of playing one game and taking the next night off had continued, the teams would have played on Saturday, April 19. However, the Nassau County Coliseum schedulers had booked the building months earlier for a concert by popular singing star John Denver. The NHL proposed game four be played the night after game three, on the Friday, but both teams rejected the idea.

A second option was to play the fourth game three days after game three, on the Sunday. Problem was, Denver was booked to play the arena that day as well. The NHL was becoming desperate to stage the game on the Sunday to fulfill its national TV commitment to NBC. With the other three teams that were hosting games that day unable to support such a broadcast, the desperate NHL even began preparing to transfer the game to Pittsburgh. Denver himself came to the league's rescue by agreeing to cancel his Sunday night gig, thus clearing the path for the Islanders and Pens to drop the puck at 3:30 p.m.

With the schedule squared away, Penguin management decided it would be easier—and cheaper—to keep the team in New York over the extended weekend break rather than fly back to Pittsburgh and then back to Long Island. Up 3-0 in the entertainment capital of the world had the Penguins in a good mood—perhaps a little too good. The layoff was a recipe for distraction, and disaster. A team party held right after the game three victory didn't help the players' concentration.

"After that third game, there was a John Denver concert and they didn't want to take us back to Pittsburgh because it would've cost too much," said Rick Kehoe. "So they kept us there and we kind of lost a little bit of our focus. And [the Islanders] got theirs."[18]

In game four, the Penguins let the Islanders beat them to almost every puck and send things back to Pittsburgh with a hard-checking 3-1 win.

"They had control of the game all day," said Ron Stackhouse. "We did nothing to take it away from them."[19]

The Islanders' confidence continued to grow.

"The pressure is all on the Penguins," said rookie Clark Gillies. "We got our game together again. They are expected to win. No one expects anything from us."[20]

Nevertheless, things still looked good for the Pens. They were coming back to the Civic Arena, where they were riding a 12-game winning streak, not having lost since February. The only problem was the goaltending of Islanders rookie Glenn Resch, who had replaced Billy Smith after the Pens had built their 3-0 series lead. He stopped all 16 Penguin first-period shots and watched as his teammates put two behind Inness at the other end before the buzzer sounded to end the frame. Pittsburgh got to within a goal twice but a 200-foot fluke empty-netter from Jude Drouin sealed the deal and sent things back to New York for a sixth game.

The Islanders were also doing a better job of standing up to the dangerous Penguin attackers as they hit the New York blueline. Suddenly, the fancy moves that had resulted in so many goals throughout the season were not having an effect on the suddenly ferocious defensive wall the Islanders were putting up.

"We were fooling around with the puck in the middle of the rink instead of just firing it into their end," said Jean Pronovost.[21]

Some Penguins admitted to looking ahead to a date in the semi-finals with the Philadelphia Flyers, who awaited the winner of the Pittsburgh-New York series. "Some of us were thinking about going to Philadelphia, but we won't be thinking that way [in game six]," said Dave Burrows. "I hope we finally realize how tough it's going to be to beat these guys."[22]

Resch again made a number of spectacular saves in game six, keeping the frustrated Pens at bay with 31 saves and getting five more from his goalposts on the way to a 4–1 Islanders win. It was a tense affair for almost the entire game until Ed Westfall and Garry Howatt hit on empty-netters in the final half-minute.

The series would return to Pittsburgh for a decisive seventh game, putting the Penguins in danger of suffering an ignominy experienced by only one other team in NHL history: losing a seven-game series after building a 3–0 lead. If they lost, the Pens would join the 1942 Detroit Red Wings, who fell in Game Seven of that year's Stanley Cup Final to the Toronto Maple Leafs.

Coach Boileau was nevertheless encouraged by his team's play, and despite the precarious situation, some of his trademark brashness shone through before the decisive contest. "Our team played a lot better [in game six] than it has in the last two games. We had the opportunities but the puck bounced away. There is no way they are going to hold us to one goal again."[23] A day later, his faith in the high-powered offense that had fueled the Penguins throughout the season was on clear display, telling the *Pittsburgh Press*, "I guarantee we will score more than one goal" in game seven.[24]

Those were bold words, given how well Resch was playing and how the Isles' had elevated their checking game to a much higher level since game four.

A capacity Civic Arena crowd sat on the edge of their seats as the puck dropped and the Penguins took their effort to another level against the stingy Islanders defense. They fired 26 shots on goal in the first two periods but couldn't put one by a red-hot Resch. At the other end, the Pens "D" allowed the Islanders nothing, limiting them to a mere 11 shots.

The stalemate continued through the third, each team battling for their lives as the tension rose higher and higher in the stands. Even Pittsburgh mayor Pete Flaherty was doing his best to urge the Penguins on, twice sprinting through the aisles holding up a huge sign that read "Go Pens—I Believe!"[25]

The fans' faith looked like it might just pay off when Pierre Larouche found himself alone on Resch with 7:30 left. He deked the goalie out of position but was caught from behind by Denis Potvin before he could get a decent shot off. Both players went crashing into the boards. Lucky Pierre later claimed he was tripped, but there was no call and the teams soldiered on.

Not long after Larouche's chance, New York captain Ed Westfall found himself unchecked to the right of the Penguin crease. Receiving a pass from Bert Marshall at the blue line, Westfall held the puck long enough to notice Inness leaning a bit to his right. Westfall shifted the puck to his backhand and fired the puck toward Inness's left catching hand ... and bulged the twine, giving the Islanders a 1–0 lead. Only 5:18 remained on the clock. The Penguins did little the rest of the way, and New York held on for the 1–0 win and a trip to the semi-finals that the Penguins only a few days earlier thought for sure was theirs.

"I remember the atmosphere in the building that night. You could cut it with a knife," remembered Dave Burrows years later. "It was just so intense the whole game. And then when Westfall scores, you're just ... you're done. It's just such a sudden mixed emotion that it's hard to believe it's over that quickly. I remember when that goal went in. I was on the bench. I'd just got off the ice and man, you're just heartbroken. It's done. The whole season's done. But it was just the best series—great hockey to watch, great for the game, but we came up short."[26]

In his Civic Arena office adjacent to a shell-shocked Penguin dressing room, Boileau sipped on a can of beer and admitted to reporters that "we got overconfident. [In game four] we were terrible. We were a little better [in game five]."[27]

Captain Ron Schock pointed to Game Four as a turning point. "We let them off the hook."[28]

Islander coach Al Arbour revealed after the series that he had made two key adjustments following game three: concentrating on the speedy Pittsburgh wingers rather than the defensemen when the Penguins were bringing the puck out of their own zone, and keeping the Pens out of their slot and forcing them to the outside.

When the shock of their collapse had dissipated, the Penguins could look back on a number of positives from the season. They had won their first playoff series since 1970, against the hated St. Louis Blues, no less. Pierre Larouche had met and exceeded all expectations in his rookie year and looked like a budding star the team could build around. Perhaps, finally, the club had absorbed the Michel Brière tragedy and was ready to move on. In goal, Gary Inness had emerged as a bona fide Number One NHL puck-stopper. Up front, the offensive engine appeared to be capable of revving loudly for years to come, with stars such as Pronovost and Apps now in their prime.

Nevertheless, blowing a 3–0 series lead and a chance to count themselves among the final four teams in contention for the 1975 Stanley Cup was sure to leave an embarrassing stain on a franchise already soiled with a mostly bumbling history.

"That was a killer," remembered Jean Pronovost. "We took it for granted [after game three]. We forgot that it takes four games to win, not three. When you lose one, you think 'Oh we're going to get them next time.' But then when you drop that one, too, I tell you, the pressure mounts up a bit and you hold your stick a little tighter and you miss opportunities. And then you end up being tied 3–3 in the series and then it's anybody's game. It's too bad because we had a great team."[29]

Defenseman Ron Stackhouse, reflecting on the series in 2019, felt the specter of going into the Philadelphia Spectrum to face the Broad Street Bullies in the next round played a role in the loss to the Islanders. The Flyers had advanced to the semi-finals a day after Pittsburgh went up 3–0 and were lying in wait for the winner of the Pens-Isles series.

"I hated going [to Philadelphia] because I was always going to end up in a scrap, and it wasn't because I was starting it. That's just how it was back then, and I hated that aspect of hockey. We had a lot of guys that were amazing hockey players but it was just that they didn't fare well in that heavy-going." Stackhouse added: "I honestly think if we hadn't known we were going to play Philadelphia next, we would have probably won. We were just lacking a little bit of toughness, and I wasn't the guy to provide that sort of toughness, but I think that was a factor. We were very, very talented, but we weren't really good in the trenches."[30]

Dave Burrows has often wondered what a victory in game seven would have meant for the Penguins. "I believe that [series] was the Islanders' catalyst to winning Stanley Cups. They came together as a team because of that series and they went on to have a dynasty. You wonder: if we could have just won one more game, would that have been us?"[31]

10

The Great Penguin Crash of '75: Summer 1975

As the summer of 1975 beckoned and Penguins players and fans began trying to put the Stanley Cup playoff nightmare behind them, Tad Potter's worst nightmare was just beginning.

On the morning of June 12, Potter arrived at the Penguins' Civic Arena offices, ready for another round in his long fight to solve his financially floundering club's cash woes. For a number of months, the Penguins had owed money to three groups: the bank, the league and the government. Potter had done his best to hold each at bay throughout the 1974–75 season, primarily through his tireless work to find a buyer to take the team off his hands and, hopefully, keep it in Pittsburgh. Each potential deal eventually collapsed, however, and sooner or later one or more of the Penguin debtors was sure to come knocking.

On this fateful morning, it was Uncle Sam.

The Internal Revenue Service was finished with waiting for the Penguins to pay $527,346.55 in employee withholding tax—money deducted from Penguin employees during the season but never forwarded to the IRS. The result was that a padlock was put on the Penguins offices and the team went into voluntary receivership. The legal maneuver gave the Penguins protection against any creditors they owed and allowed them to maintain possession of the business. They would, however, be accountable to the court regarding their day-to-day activities.

The court appointed Jack Button receiver, meaning he would handle all assets and, in general, operate the team. Potter and fellow owner Peter Block were now out of the picture. It would be up to Button to do what his bosses had failed to do for months—find a buyer who was willing to handle the approximate $6.5-million total debt load and run a hockey club that had never come close to turning a profit in eight years of existence. And he'd have to do it by September 30, when the court would need to see a reorganization plan.

The bankers were quick to follow the government's footsteps to the Penguins' doors. Two days after the padlocks were applied, Equibank filed 10 lawsuits against the club, looking to recover the $4,997,450.27 debt the Pens had piled up over the previous two years.

Block, the longtime Pittsburgh hockey fan who first conceived of bringing the NHL back to the city as part of the league's 1967 expansion, articulated the determination felt by many to see the franchise survive what was its most trying hour to date. "If people think this is the end of the Pittsburgh Penguins, they're sadly mistaken."[1]

With the lawsuits set to wind themselves through the courts, Jack Button turned his attention to the Penguins' other main creditor, the NHL itself. At the league's annual summer meetings in Montreal only four days after the padlocking, Button began the process of lobbying the governors to allow the Penguins to remain a member of the club. There was the possibility that, given the Pens' dire financial picture and spotty ledger-sheet history since their inception, the league's power-brokers could simply liquidate the franchise.

Button was grilled hard by the governors, particularly around the Penguins' ticket prices, which were some of the lowest in the league. In the end, however, his performance at the meetings succeeded in helping sway the NHL in the direction of giving the team a chance to find a buyer, preferably before August 15, when a schedule for the upcoming campaign would have to be finalized. NHL president Clarence Campbell, however, did not let the man he saw as the chief culprit of the Penguin catastrophe get off without a scolding. Tad Potter, he said, did a "masterful job" of accumulating debt. "The whole thing was [our] fault. We made a mistake in who we allowed to own the franchise."[2]

The cash-flow situation had become so bad that by the time the playoffs rolled around, there wasn't even enough money to supply the players with the basic tools of their trade.

"People didn't really know what was happening behind the scenes," remembered Rick Kehoe. "[Ownership] wasn't really paying the bills. I remember when we played the Islanders [in the playoffs], I ended up having to borrow some sticks from Jude Drouin, who was playing with the Islanders. Those things went on, but nobody said anything back then and nobody wanted to make an excuse."[3]

The Penguin financial predicament was eased further when the NHL indicated its general willingness to forgive the debt owed to it by the Pittsburgh club. And even Equibank was sending signals that it would be open to negotiating the $5-million sum owed to it with any new owner.

Button went back to Pittsburgh and began putting his sales efforts into overdrive. With the debt burden no longer a source of concern for any prospective buyer, reports of a number of interested parties soon emerged. They included Vince Abbey, a Seattle hockey man still interested in moving the Pens to the Pacific Northwest; Jerry Wolman, former owner of the NFL's Philadelphia Eagles; and Frank Fuhrer, owner of the Pittsburgh Triangles professional tennis team. In all, about 35 offers were reviewed.[4]

The highest bid, however, came from a group headed by the owner of a Columbus, Ohio, mortgage brokerage. Al Savill's offer of $3.8 million was accepted by U.S. District Court Judge Hubert Teitelbaum—who, it became clear during proceedings, was a Pens fan who did not seem keen on his favorite team leaving town—on July 9, and then by the NHL two days later. The price was a bargain compared to the $7 million Potter's team shelled out four years earlier.

Buying a hockey team was not a foreign concept to Savill, who owned the Columbus Owls of the International Hockey League. But now, he'd made it to the big leagues.

"This is the day I have long dreamed about," he said when the deal was done. "I'm thrilled to death. Pittsburgh is a great sports town, steeped in hockey tradition. I see a lot of hard work ahead of us, but Pittsburgh has given the club tremendous support. Just recently, 19,000 people signed a petition asking for the club to remain in Pittsburgh. This, of course, it will do."[5]

Savill's group included Otto Frenzel III, chairman of the board for Indianapolis-based Merchant's National Bank, and Wren Blair, a fellow owner in the IHL (Saginaw Gears) and former general manager of the Penguins' expansion cousins, the Minnesota North Stars. With an ex-GM on the incoming team, it appeared certain that Button—the man who had been most responsible for saving the Penguins during this, their most troubled period of a mostly troubled history, the man who had presented the new ownership's very offer to the NHL for approval—would not be part of the Penguins' future. Before the month was out, Button had left Pittsburgh behind him, headed for the NHL's head office in Montreal and a post as the league's first director of central scouting services.

"I regret leaving Pittsburgh because the people here were great," he told an interviewer. "I think there's great potential for a National Hockey League franchise here."[6]

Thanks to the tireless work of Button, a judge who was on their side, and perhaps a little more luck than they'd ever had on the ice, the Penguins were going to keep skating in Pittsburgh and trying to realize that potential.

11

Penguin Power: 1975–76

The new regime's first major move was to bring back coach Marc Boileau, whom they signed to a one-year deal over the summer. Boileau's emotional, fiery approach to coaching could often work in his favor, motivating players to reach higher levels and sending an energetic charge through the dressing room. It could also, however, rub players the wrong way at the wrong time. For instance, his curious decision to start rookie Gord Laxton in goal for the season opener in Washington, rather than Gary Inness, who had performed so admirably in the playoffs, had Inness steaming.

"Was I surprised? Damn right I was," the goalie howled to reporters after the game.[1]

Boileau also found himself dealing with an upset Steve Durbano, the frequently wild and unpredictable defenseman the Penguins were welcoming back to the lineup after he'd missed most of the previous year with a broken wrist. "Derby" didn't like the practice his boss was leading and decided to walk out of it, punctuating his departure by throwing his stick into the Civic Arena stands. About 10 days later, he walked out of another one. Boileau followed him off the ice, had words with him, and contacted Blair, who suspended Durbano indefinitely, without pay.

"If he's going to act like that," said Boileau, "I don't want him on my team. He gets paid to play hockey, I get paid to coach. I know what I want to do out there."[2]

Durbano tried to downplay the incidents. "I'm not a troublemaker or rebellious. I feel I'm a team man, but I just had to voice my opinion."[3]

The suspension would last for five games and cost Durbano about $2,000.

The Penguins' offense picked up where it had left off the previous year, averaging 4.3 goals over the first 20 games. Any satisfaction Boileau and Blair may have derived from seeing such firepower, however, was overshadowed by the club's mostly abysmal play in its own end. Their average goals against in those first 20 games was 4.5. Often unable to deal with a good forecheck, the defense was prone to turnovers and scrambling. One of the worst displays came November 12 when they blew a 3–0 lead against the lowly Washington Capitals and had to settle for a 6–6 tie.

"We just panicked when we got the puck in our own end," commented Jean Pronovost. "And then we don't work hard enough to make up for it."[4]

Tensions continued to rise right along with the goals-against figure. On November 1 in Minnesota during a 7–3 loss to the North Stars, Durbano got into a shouting match with Boileau on the bench after the coach had criticized him for taking a needless penalty. He also snapped at a teammate who told him to calm down.[5]

The next night in Buffalo, according to Durbano, he was dressed for the game but, just before puck drop, was told by Boileau he would not be playing. Durbano once again exploded on Boileau. After the game, Blair talked with Boileau and left it up to his coach to determine if the defenseman should be reinstated to the lineup or traded. The two parties arrived at a truce a few days later after meeting with Blair. Durbano returned after missing two games.

Just as one attitude problem with a defenseman seemed to have been patched, another one blew up in management's face. During a 7–6 win at home over the Islanders, normally mild-mannered Ron Stackhouse lost it on the Civic Arena fans after being burned on a Bob Bourne goal late in the third. For some time, the fans had taken to booing Stackhouse whenever he made the slightest mistake. They apparently thought the 6'3", 210-pound blueliner should use his size more often and play a more physical game. On this night, he'd had enough abuse and made a rude stick gesture to the crowd, earning him a game misconduct. The boos intensified as he skated off, eliciting another rude stick gesture from Stackhouse to the whole arena.

Blair called Stackhouse's actions "disgraceful" and promised to match whatever fine the NHL levied on him. Cooler heads soon prevailed, though, with Blair suggesting the fans should question if they were being fair in their treatment of "a pretty good hockey player," and Stackhouse himself admitting he was "totally wrong."[6]

The incident was the latest incident in a sour relationship between Stackhouse and Penguins fans.

"They'd kind of had a history in Pittsburgh of apparently having somebody to boo," said Stackhouse during an interview in 2019. "It had been Duane Rupp before me and then a guy named Ronnie Jones and, well, I guess I inherited that sort of role. I have to admit that I was not a fancy player. I had some very good years in Pittsburgh statistically. But the fans didn't particularly like my style."

Stackhouse believes that because he was big, the fans expected him to be more of a bruiser.

"And it's just not in my nature. It wasn't in my nature and it still isn't. When I was young I was a big guy, but my mother told me, 'Don't you hurt those kids you're playing with,' and it kind of sunk in. I guess I couldn't bring myself to go out and physically intimidate somebody. Nobody bothered me very much so I didn't go around bothering anybody else."

Stackhouse remembers the night of inappropriate stick gestures as being like "another *Slap Shot* movie, that's how bad it was. The whole arena was booing me, and this is my home-town arena! Some people were yapping at me and I waved the stick at them and the next thing I know … the ref comes over and tells me I'm out of the game. 'Well, thank you very much,' I thought."[7]

The Pens continued to play loosey-goosey in their own end and, despite the offensive efforts of Jean Pronovost, who was enjoying a career year and sat third in league scoring at Christmas, the team's record gradually sank further below .500. Boileau seemed powerless to get through to his troops. Another flare-up with Durbano, in which the defenseman was benched during a game in Chicago and simply went back to the dressing room and called it a night before the game was over, resulted in Blair finally pulling the plug on Durbano and shipping him off to the Kansas City Scouts.

The atmosphere was bleak. During the first intermission of yet another pounding from the two-time champion Flyers on January 3—this time at home, to the tune of 8–4—Blair made a special appearance in the dressing room to berate the troops. On January 11 in Buffalo, Gordie Laxton let in the first four shots he faced as the Sabres trounced the Pens 6–0. Meanwhile, last season's hero in goal, Gary Inness, was playing in Hershey. The situation made little sense to most observers.

The loss to Buffalo was the latest chapter in an ugly eight-game winless streak. In the eye of the storm stood Boileau, who had clearly "lost the room." As the *Pittsburgh Post-Gazette* described it, "Few of the Penguins contain their contempt for Boileau anymore. When asked about the coach, they either smirk or simply shake their heads and walk away."[8]

The new owners had seen enough. Savill and Frenzel, in particular, insisted that Boileau be fired, despite a caution from Blair that doing so might not make a huge difference. "They countered that at least things couldn't get any worse," recounted Blair.[9]

The day after another loss to Philadelphia, the ax came down on the coach. He was replaced by a familiar face—Ken Schinkel, the man Boileau had replaced two years earlier. Moving down with some reluctance from his front-office position as director of player personnel, Schinkel noted that the team had been failing to carry out one fundamental aspect of the game of hockey: "We weren't skating, and when that happens, nothing else goes right."[10]

Schinkel also set about cleaning up the overall play of the often-porous Penguins defense. This involved keeping the puck to the outside, clearing the puck out of their own zone more effectively, and not getting caught up ice trying to score.

"We don't want the defensemen going to the [opponent's] net. If they do get in, then make one play and get back out."[11]

The players responded immediately. In Schinkel's first game, at home against Buffalo, Jean Pronovost capitalized on a botched Sabre clearing attempt midway through the third period and beat goalie Gerry Desjardins with what proved to be the winning goal in a 3–2 Penguin triumph. They followed that up the next night with an 8–3 drubbing of the Rangers in which newly acquired left wing Stan Gilbertson notched a hat trick and Pierre Larouche tallied four points.

The Penguins were back. In their first 20 games under Schinkel, they lost only twice, going 12–2–6.

One constant throughout the season, even through the darkest last days of the Boileau regime, was the scoring prowess of the Penguins' two French-Canadian stars, the cerebral veteran Jean Pronovost and the spirited sophomore Pierre Larouche. "Prony" led the top line of himself, Apps and MacDonald (dubbed the "Century Line" in 1973–74 by the Penguins' PR staff when the trio scored a combined 107 goals), while Larouche was clicking all season long with right-winger Rick Kehoe. By March 24, when Boston came to town, both players stood on the precipice of major milestones: Pronovost needed only one more goal to become the first Penguin, and only the 14th player ever, to reach the magical 50-goal mark, and Larouche required but one point to become the youngest player ever to score 100 points in a season.

A crowd of 15,699 would witness one of the most magical nights in Penguins history. Late in the first period during a tight 0–0 game, Larouche broke in alone on Bruins goalie Gilles Gilbert on the left side, faked him down, and fired the puck into a yawning cage. The fans erupted and gave him a standing ovation as his teammates mobbed him. The crowd's reaction "made me proud," said Larouche after the game as he puffed on a cigarette. "I don't get too many standing ovations. It was a good feeling for someone so young."[12]

The Bruins answered in the second period with three goals, but the Pens fought back to tie things at three in the third. The stage was set for Pronovost. Getting the puck in front of Gilbert, he fired and was stopped, but the rebound came right back to him. He made no mistake this time, sending the arena into another raucous frenzy.

"I could feel it coming a little," Pronovost said later. "Their goalie was down and I lifted the puck over him. It felt good and it was a relief."[13]

True to his nature, Pronovost later downplayed the accomplishment in the dressing room. As he had frequently mentioned during his long tenure as a Penguin, there was only one objective that mattered. "My biggest goal is winning the Stanley Cup. I want to be on a Cup winner."[14]

Pronovost felt the same way when interviewed in 2019.

"When you accomplish something like this, you figure you're on top of the world. But you don't stay there very long. After you get there, you go, 'Wow I scored 50,' but that's not the end. You feel you have to keep going. You want to win the Cup. That was my perspective, basically."

Pronovost also remembered thinking it would be tough for him to reach the 50-goal mark again. "I was not a 50-goal scorer. It just happened that that year, things were going my way and I had good players going with me and we complemented each other very well."

Pronovost was referring to his Century Line partners, Apps and Mac-Donald. "Lowell was kind of a stabilizer. He was the guy that we could trust. [Syl and I] could take a few more chances up front because we knew he'd be back and he was good defensively, so that allowed us to be more flexible offensively. And Syl was a perfect passer. I mean, he put it on your stick every time."

For a forward line to work well, "you have to gel together," Pronovost added. "You have to have a real unity as a group and an understanding of what the other guy does, and we did that well."[15]

Apps, who came alive after a miserable stretch under Boileau in which he scored only six points in a stretch of 20 games, articu-

Jean Pronovost became the first Penguin to break the 50-goal mark, notching 52 in 1975–76. He scored 316 goals over his 10 years in Pittsburgh (courtesy Doug McLatchy).

lated how a new feeling had spread throughout the dressing room since the coaching change.

"The game's a hell of a lot more fun now," he said. "Now that the team's winning, it makes everything else right.... We have a winning spirit."[16]

Unfortunately for the Pens, they couldn't carry that spirit through to the end of the season. After a 5–3 loss to the Islanders at home on March 7, they welcomed the Sabres to the Civic Arena three nights later—and proved to be too gracious a host. The Pens had exploded for five goals in the second period, three of them by Rick Kehoe, to head into the third with a commanding 6–2 lead. From there on in, the team played "as if they had never seen a puck before," according to Penguin beat reporter Bob Whitley.[17] Goals by Craig Ramsey, Jim Lorentz and Rene Robert suddenly had the Sabres within one with over seven minutes still left. Gilbert Perreault then stuffed a rebound past a shell-shocked Michel Plasse to knot things at six. In the final seconds, Buffalo's famed French Connection line invaded the Penguin zone, passing it amongst each other until Perreault sent the final dagger into the Penguins' hearts. His shot was stopped by the glove of Plasse, but the goaltender fell back into the net and across the goal line with puck in hand. The goal counted and the Penguins could only retreat to their dressing room, dazed and confused.

The missed points would be costly. They finished the season with a mediocre 6–7–1 record, making the playoffs but missing out on home ice advantage in their opening-round series by a single point. Had they won against Buffalo, the Pens would be waiting at home for the Maple Leafs, but instead they'd be travelling to Toronto for Game One of the best-of-three series.

There was still, however, room for optimism. Pittsburgh had won four of five against Toronto during the season, outscoring them by a wide 32–18 margin.

It was the Leafs, though, who took charge of game one, standing up at the blueline and hitting every Penguin in sight. When the forwards did make it deep into Toronto territory, goalie Wayne Thomas was there to stop just about everything. A key pad save on a Pierre Larouche shot heading toward a half-empty cage lifted the Leafs and helped propel them to a dominating 4–1 win.

"Pittsburgh usually makes the pretty play," said Leaf captain Darryl Sittler, "so we had to check them closely. If we don't, they have the passers and shooters to blow us out."[18]

Game two back in Pittsburgh was hardly a blowout, but the Penguins' ability to play it physical on home ice as the Leafs had in game one helped secure a tight 2–0 win, the game not decided until Vic Hadfield scored into an empty net with 39 seconds remaining. It was Hadfield who sent a message to the Leafs, and his own teammates, that the Pens could play it rough, too, when he fought Sittler just 29 seconds into the game.

"We had to show Toronto right off the bat we weren't going to lie down for them," said the wily veteran.[19]

The Penguins were given a golden opportunity to score early in game three when Toronto tough guy Dave "Tiger" Williams wrapped his stick across Barry Wilkins' neck, drawing a five-minute major. However, Pittsburgh's usually potent power play couldn't get on track and the Leafs killed the penalty off, giving them a major boost en route to a dominating 4–0 win and a trip to the quarter-finals.

"The game was decided right there in the first five minutes when we had that five-minute power play and Thomas stopped us cold," said Schinkel afterward. "That just about finished us."[20]

It was once again left to veteran Jean Pronovost to encapsulate the latest Penguin on-ice failure in the most basic terms: "Their team worked harder than ours. We kept saying we had more talent, but we have to put it out."[21]

Remembering the series more than 40 years later, Dave Burrows said an advantage he thought the Penguins might have against Toronto didn't quite materialize.

"Playoff hockey is just so different and so much better than regular-season hockey. I remember the intensity of it all, and not wanting to make a mistake that's going to cost you. And going to play in Toronto, everybody's up for the games in Toronto, so I thought that would be in our favor, because most guys were from Canada. You want to do so well when you're on *Hockey Night in Canada*, and I thought that would help. But we still didn't have enough to get by them."[22]

A team that one year earlier seemed poised to challenge the big boys of the NHL and become a legitimate Stanley Cup contender had fallen back to its more familiar spot in the middle of the pack. However, a pair of familiar faces to the Pittsburgh hockey scene would soon return to help the Penguins start climbing back up the mountain.

12

Country Club:
1976–77

"If I told him once, I told him a thousand times, both here and in Kansas City: He's got to let that puck go and hang tough at the net."[1]

New Penguins assistant general manager Aldege "Baz" Bastien was talking about the team's new starting goalie, Denis Herron. The setting was the Civic Arena, just after the Penguins had played their first game of the 1976–77 season. Despite getting a 9–5 win over the Vancouver Canucks, Bastien was livid that only six minutes in, Herron, re-acquired in the off-season from the Kansas City Scouts, had come far out of his crease to get the puck before hard-charging left wing Gerry Monahan could. The result was a broken arm for Herron and a gaping hole in the Penguins' goaltending situation. With youngster Gordie Laxton suddenly the starter, Bastien would have to find at least a temporary replacement for Herron, and soon.

The injury threw a wrench into what had to that point been a triumphant return to the Steel City hockey scene for Bastien. A star goalie with the old Hornets of the American Hockey League before a horrific training camp injury in 1949 cost him his left eye, Baz later coached the Hornets and, while also serving as general manager, led them to an AHL championship in 1966–67. A strong candidate to become the Penguins' first general manager in 1967, Bastien was passed over for Jack Riley and subsequently went to Detroit to work as an assistant GM for the Red Wings. He held a similar post with the Scouts when Wren Blair offered him the Penguins assistant GM role. Never having lost his fondness for Pittsburgh, the Timmins, Ont. native readily accepted. Bastien's arrival was welcomed by fans and the press. His big smile and outgoing nature would offer a much-needed antidote to Blair's often taciturn demeanor. Laxton's first start ended in a 10–1 humiliation at the hands of the Montreal Canadiens, leading Bastien to trade for New York Rangers backup Dunc Wilson. A free-spirited journeyman who wore a mask painted to resemble the U.S. Confederate flag, Wilson's veteran presence helped stabilize the Penguin net while Herron recovered.

To Schinkel's chagrin, not all his players were giving it 100 percent every night. Even the opposition was noticing. After a 3–0 loss in Philadelphia brought Pittsburgh's record to a miserable 2–6–3, many Flyers ridiculed their opponents in the press. "That wasn't the Canadiens we were playing," said captain Bobby Clarke. "They didn't play too hard."[2]

Added defenseman Tom Bladon, "It would have been nice to have a tough game to tune up for [our next game against] the Islanders. But when you've got nobody going against you, it's not easy to keep going against them. If we were really going tonight, we would have really blown them out."[3]

The comments stung the Penguin players, and it would not be the last time during the season that a verbal assault would wound their pride.

The Pittsburgh roster was getting younger, whether Penguin management wanted it to or not. Knee injuries to veterans Lowell MacDonald and Vic Hadfield opened spots for rookie forwards Greg Malone and 1976 second-overall draft pick Blair Chapman. The centerpiece of the Pens' youth movement continued to be Pierre Larouche, but his immaturity was still a factor in this, his third big-league season. Penguin general managers and coaches had, since his arrival in 1974, generally turned a blind eye to his late arrivals to practices and planes, his glares issued to teammates when a pass wasn't made or a play broke down, and his petulant sulking and arguments with coaches whenever his ice time was not to his liking.

The hope had been that the young star would grow out of it, but early in the year it was apparent such growth hadn't yet occurred. When he arrived half an hour late for a practice in early November, the Penguins' patience had run out. He was told to report to the team's farm club in Hershey, which he refused to do. Larouche was then suspended indefinitely without pay. He would not be on the team plane jetting to Denver for a date with the Colorado Rockies on November 5, even though he showed up at the airport and attempted to talk his way on to the plane.

"Maybe this should have happened a long time ago," Ron Schock told the *Pittsburgh Press* after the news broke. An unidentified former Penguin added, "The Penguins will never be a winner as long as there is a double-standard there. There is one set of rules for Pierre and another for the rest of the team."[4]

Larouche's initial reaction to the incident was one of defiance, telling the *Pittsburgh Post-Gazette*, "Why should I go to Hershey—because I was late for practice? That's not logical. It doesn't make any sense to me." *The Hockey News* reported Larouche had his lawyer working to get him traded.[5]

The issue was quickly resolved three days later when Schinkel, at the request of Larouche, met with the suspended star to talk things out. Satisfied that Pierre's attitude had changed sufficiently, Schinkel reinstated him.

Discord wasn't limited to the Penguin dressing room. Upstairs in the team offices, minority owner and GM Wren Blair's involvement in the team had noticeably diminished in recent weeks. In early December, local papers confirmed the obvious: Blair would no longer be involved in the club's day-to-day management. Blair himself said his "other business interests," including his ownership of the IHL's Saginaw Gears, were demanding too much of his attention to tend to the Penguins as well. Savill denied suggestions that he had pushed Blair out.

"It's absolutely not true," he told the *Pittsburgh Post-Gazette*. "Wren will not be as active as he was, but, when he first got into this, he made it clear he didn't want the responsibility forever."[6] With Blair out of the picture, the task of managing the club would now fall to both Bastien and Savill himself.

Gradually, the Pens righted their ship and climbed back to the .500 mark by mid–December, thanks in large part to Schinkel's incessant harping on the need for better team defense. Even sharpshooter Syl Apps, who never made headlines for his back-checking or play in the corners, was buying into Schinkel's system. "[Early in the season] we were giving away too many goals. We had to switch tactics or we'd get buried in our own division almost before the season was underway."[7]

Rick Kehoe, who had powered the Penguin scoring machine in recent years, was also becoming converted to a defensive mindset. "We've changed," he said. "We used to win a lot of games 7–6, but that's why we didn't do well in the playoffs. Playoff hockey is tight, close-checking hockey, and we couldn't adjust."[8]

The statistics didn't lie; at the mid-season mark, Schinkel's Penguins sat a respectable seventh in the 17-team league in total defense, surrendering an average of 3.3 goals per game.

But things were *still* not feeling right in the Penguin camp. The improved defense hadn't resulted in any significant jump in the standings. After 40 games, the Pens sat in the middle of the pack with a .500 record—16–16–8, good for ninth overall. Before a game against the Maple Leafs in December, Jean Pronovost told a Toronto newspaper reporter—off the record—that he had had enough of the "country club" atmosphere around the Penguins organization and had asked to be traded. The reporter went ahead and published the story anyway. Pronovost did not seem to mind that his cat was out of the bag. "Maybe it will do some good," he said. "I've been trying to get away from this situation for two years."[9]

Pronovost's nine years of playing for a losing club boiled over in a stream of vitriol aimed at just about everyone but the Civic Arena popcorn vendors.

"We don't want to win bad enough.... We're the worst-conditioned team in the league. How many guys do you think stay after practice and work on their skating? Not too many, that's for sure. Are the general manager and the coach blind? Can't they see what's happening?"[10]

Pronovost was also unhappy with Schinkel's revolving door of replacements for the injured left wing Lowell MacDonald on his line with center Syl Apps. Pronovost claimed it was difficult to get any chemistry going. "If they stick with one guy in there for five or six games, Syl and I will adjust."[11]

Larouche wasted no time in joining the "trade-me" chorus, telling a Toronto TV station that Pittsburgh was a "bad hockey town, if the present situation doesn't improve," adding that the city "thinks only of football."[12]

The Pittsburgh fans, who had adored their good-looking, fast-skating superstar since he first pulled on a Penguin jersey, suddenly turned on Larouche. During a 2–2 tie with the Canucks on January 4 at the Igloo, the first home game after his trade demands were made public, the 6,856 patrons rained boos upon their former darling. "I don't blame them," said Larouche after the game. "They figure they've been paying my salary for a couple of years."

Explaining why he wanted out of Pittsburgh, Larouche said "It's hard for me to go on like this. Not when I don't have the confidence of the coach. And it looks like I don't have it."[13]

Schinkel was making every effort to placate his young star. "We like Pierre. So many guys have tried talking to him. I've tried talking to him." He added, "I wish we could make Pierre understand everyone doesn't hate him."[14]

Despite the turmoil that Larouche's act had caused, Pronovost's words had an effect. Shortly after he uttered them, the Penguins went on a six-game unbeaten streak that included a tie against mighty Montreal and a win over the Sabres, both at home. It also, however, included a tie with the lowly Canucks, who sat in last place in the laughable Smythe Division with a record of 11–28–4, and the Washington Capitals, last in the Norris at 11–23–6.

"Two bleep periods and one good one," moaned Schinkel after the Washington tie. "I don't know what it is we do against these [weaker] clubs. We don't seem to get mad at them."[15]

Such inconsistency left Penguins fan wondering what to make of their team. Many, it seemed, decided to stop wondering and find something else to do with their entertainment dollar. With the football Steelers' season uncharacteristically done by the end of December, the Penguins were the only sports game in town, but attendance figures still weren't where ownership needed them to be. Average for each game was about 10,000, but that was down 1,000 from the previous year, when owners Al Savill, Nick Frenzel and Wren Blair finished the season $800,000 in the red. Projected losses for the current campaign were $1.4 million. Since buying the club for the bargain-basement price tag of $3.8 million in 1975, the triumvirate had suffered operating losses of just over $1 million.

How long, observers wondered, would they be willing to take such a financial bashing? Savill, a native of Indianapolis, admitted the thought had crossed his mind to move the Pens to his hometown, where the WHA's Racers were bringing in about 10,000 per game. But, according to the banker, the thought was a fleeting one, and he was resolved to making the Penguin franchise a success in Pittsburgh.

"We're not moving the team," he told the *Pittsburgh Post-Gazette* in January. "Pittsburgh is a good sports town. I think we can make it work there."[16]

In Savill's eyes, the key to making it work was growing the team's season ticket holder base from its current figure of 4,500 to somewhere around 8,000. "If you sell four or five thousand season tickets and the weather's bad or the football teams happen to have center stage, you're hurting…. But if you have a solid [season-ticket] base, you can withstand a few of those off-nights."[17]

But such season ticket growth wouldn't be happening overnight. In the meantime, the owners had to hope the Penguins made the playoffs, ideally with home-ice advantage, so they could reap the extra revenue rewards the additional dates would generate.

The Penguins, still committed to a more defensive style of play than in years past, were doing a decent job of ensuring those extra dates would in fact be played. While there would clearly not be any 50-goal scorers this year, the likes of Pronovost, Larouche, Apps and Kehoe were still scoring at a steady clip. The goaltending situation had stabilized with the solid play of both Dunc Wilson and Denis Herron. The push to drive higher in the standings, however, seemed to be continually impeded by one injury after another to key players, particularly on defense.

Many were long-term situations. Lowell MacDonald banged up his knee on two separate occasions during the preseason and would end up sitting out all but the last three games of the regular season. Ed van Impe suffered an injured shoulder and was gone for the year. Dave Burrows, once again the Pens' best defenseman, tore his knee ligaments in a hit during a game against the Atlanta Flames. Young d-man Dennis Owchar suffered the same injury only a few days later. At one point, the defensive corps was reduced to three starters. After finding themselves still short on blueline bodies after calling up youngsters Mario Faubert and Russ Anderson from the top farm club in Hershey, the desperate Penguins resorted to owner Al Savill's Columbus Owls of the International Hockey League for help, calling up career minor-leaguer Steve Lyon for a few games.

By season's end, the Pens had lost well over 300 man-games to injury. Those who were left standing did a good enough job to help the club finish one game above .500 (34–33–13), good for 81 points and another third-place finish in the Norris division. The result also translated into a playoff spot and another first-round, best-of-three meeting with the Toronto Maple Leafs. The

Leafs also finished with 81 points, but Pittsburgh's extra victory gave them the home-ice advantage this time around.

In game one before a disappointing crowd of 10,033—more than 6,000 short of capacity—the Penguins came out with a spirited first-period effort, forechecking the Leafs every time the puck went into the Toronto end and generating a number of quality scoring chances. Thanks to the strong goaltending of their previous year's nemesis, Wayne Thomas, however, the Pens could only put a Bob Kelly shot into the Leafs' net, which was good enough for a 1–0 lead after one.

The forechecking suddenly disappeared in the second and the Toronto defense was able to come out of its own end virtually unimpeded, giving life to the offense and making Pens goalie Denis Herron much busier than he was in the first. The result was a 2–1 Toronto lead after two, which Dave "Tiger" Williams made 3–1 midway through the third. Mario Faubert brought the Penguins to within one at 18:34, but Darryl Sittler's empty-netter with eight seconds left finished the Pens on this night and gave home-ice advantage to the Leafs.

"We should have run away with the game in the first period," said Pronovost afterward, "but we didn't. We had enough scoring chances but we didn't get the puck into the net."

The Pens did have their chances in the second period, including two Pierre Larouche breakaways, but Thomas stopped him each time. "The best thing to do is to wait on him," said the Toronto goalkeeper.

Frustrated by their team's sudden laissez-fair attitude in the middle period, the crowd began booing. "That stuff shouldn't bother you, but it does," admitted Pronovost after the game.[18]

Winning playoff hockey games was important to everyone in the Penguin organization, but perhaps none more so than owners Al Savill and Nick Frenzel. After all, no one else had roughly $100,000 at stake with each one. That's what each playoff home game was worth to the pair, and with a regular season deficit of $1.2 million staring them square in the face, a nice long Penguin playoff run would go a long way to cutting into that ugly line of red ink. Perhaps that's why Savill chose to watch game two from a seat to the immediate left of the visitors' bench at Maple Leaf Gardens. Earlier in the day at the team's hotel, he had told his employees of the ice to "just give me all you've got. You lose, then you don't have to be ashamed."[19]

Whether it was Savill's pre-game words or his presence, something seemed to be working for the Pens in the first period. They put three goals past Thomas and headed back to the dressing room with a commanding 3–0 lead. By the midway point of the third period, however, the dogged Leafs had tied things up at four. With Savill screaming encouragement at his troops as the tense third period unfolded, Pittsburgh's "kid line" took command in the Toronto zone. Wayne Bianchin corralled the puck along the boards and fed it to Blair Chapman in the right faceoff circle, about 15 feet out. Rather than shoot, Chapman showed the poise of a veteran and instead chose to pass to center Greg Malone, who had snuck into the slot. The rookie took the pass and flung the puck under Thomas for a 5–4 Penguin lead. A few nice saves from Denis Herron and a long empty-netter from Ron Stackhouse sealed a 6–4 victory.

The series would go back to Pittsburgh for a second decisive game three between the two clubs in as many years. The Penguins had their chance at redemption, and this time the fight would take place on their own turf. A win would push the Pens through to the quarterfinals and a best-of-seven series with either Boston or Philadelphia—meaning at least two more precious home dates for Savill.

A crowd of 15,934, the largest playoff attendance in Penguin history, watched the home team get into penalty trouble in the first period—and pay the price. Defenseman Borje Salming opened the scoring at 8:34 with but three seconds left on a 4-on-3 Toronto advantage. A few minutes later, Bob Kelly went to the box on a holding call and the Leafs power play came back out. That unit included one Tiger Williams, league leader in penalty minutes during the regular season with 338. Williams, who famously claimed before game two that "them Penguins is done like dinner," had been a thorn in the side of Pens goalie Denis Herron all series long, camping out in the crease and jabbing, screening and trash-talking the netminder to distraction. When Ian Turnbull's 30-footer sailed past Herron on the power play at 14:14 to make it 2–0 Toronto, Herron could hold in his rage no longer. He punched Williams, whom he claimed had been in his crease when the puck went in. The Tiger punched back, causing a nearby Syl Apps to intervene and save his goaltender.

It was a costly move, however, earning Apps a game misconduct for being the third man in. "It gave us a big lift," said Leafs winger Lanny McDonald of the Apps ejection. "They had to start changing their lines all around, and when you start doing that in a playoff game, it hurts."[20]

Jean Pronovost got one back for the Pens before the period was out, but a pair by McDonald in the middle frame helped the Leafs skate away from the Penguins. Blair Chapman scored before the end of the second to keep it a game at 4–2, but the Leafs played a close-checking third and never let the Pens get too close to goalie Mike Palmateer. McDonald added a late empty-netter to complete his hat trick and send the Penguins to an early tee time for the second straight year.

"We never gave up," said coach Ken Schinkel, but added that "killing off the penalties [in the first period] took the extra zip out of us."[21]

The disappointing loss closed the book on a season of underachievement, marked by internal discord and an often-lackadaisical approach on the part of the players. Too often, nights were taken off and shifts weren't skated with the all-out fervor necessary to turn an average club into an elite one.

Reflecting on the shortcomings of many 1970s Penguins teams years later, Pronovost felt that a big problem was a lack of a winning attitude. "You're content with what you have right now, or you don't want to pay the price. Because the more you advance in the Stanley Cup playoffs, it becomes harder and harder and harder. So sometimes it's just the way the puck rolls and who wants it most and who is willing to put his neck on the line. If you're not all on the same page, if people have selfish goals, that might be a hinderance to go all the way."[22]

Ron Stackhouse was a dependable defenseman who could also contribute his share of points, scoring 71 in 1975–76. He even scored a goal in the 1980 NHL All-Star Game (courtesy Doug McLatchy).

Much of the blame could be left on the doorstep of Schinkel, who it seemed clear to all was just too nice a guy with his players, lacking the motivational mastery of a Scotty Bowman or a Fred Shero.

"The main problem with the team this past season was there were some players who didn't put out," said Savill. "I want a team that is going to put out all the time. We have to get motivation back in our team."[23]

Changes, he promised, would be coming.

13

Trader Al:
1977–78

As the 1976–77 Penguin campaign played out its final weeks, Al Savill and partner Otto Frenzel were working secretly behind the scenes to bring on a new ownership partner. Edward J. DeBartolo, a Youngstown, Ohio-based real estate mogul who owned 39 malls across the country, liked enough of what he saw to assume a one-third stake in the Penguins. DeBartolo had an interest in sports toys to complement his real estate empire, already owning three horse-racing tracks. His family, under the official ownership of son Edward Jr., had recently purchased the NFL's San Francisco 49ers, and there were rumors the clan was looking to buy baseball's Cleveland Indians.

No one seemed to know anything about DeBartolo's very silent partnership until April, when the magnate himself let the cat out of the bag to the press and further stated that he expected to have a controlling interest in the club within a matter of days. The pronouncement caught the entire hockey world off-guard. Even league president Clarence Campbell said he'd never heard of DeBartolo. No one was more surprised, however, than Savill and Frenzel themselves. They were quick to correct their new partner in the papers, even going so far as to hold a press conference to clarify matters.

"If Ed DeBartolo is going to get controlling interest of the Penguins," Savill said, "he'll either have to buy part of mine and part of Nick Frenzel's, or all of mine or all of Nick's. And I don't envision that happening."[1]

Savill clarified matters further. DeBartolo, whom he called "a good friend," had purchased the 20 percent stake of Wren Blair mid-way through the previous season. Savill and Frenzel then increased the stock and diluted their interests, allowing DeBartolo to attain an equal one-third share in the franchise.

A month after DeBartolo made his surprising announcement, Ken Schinkel surprised no one by announcing that he was stepping away from the Pens' bench to take a position as the club's director of player personnel.

The front office seemed to want someone with a more forceful personality directing the often-lackadaisical troops, and they found their man on June 13 in the form of Johnny Wilson. A solid and reliable left winger in his playing days who averaged roughly a point every second game for Detroit, Chicago, the Rangers and Toronto during the 50s and early 60s, Wilson brought an old-school approach that emphasized hard work and strenuous physical conditioning. On that front, Wilson had always practiced what he preached. He'd played 580 consecutive games in the brutal Original Six era and still looked to be in granite-hard shape at the press conference introducing him as the new Penguin pilot.

Wilson's coaching resume included head spots with the Kings, Red Wings, two years in the WHA, and most recently two dreadful campaigns with the Colorado Rockies. His chief task in Pittsburgh would be to somehow take the assembled talent and get it to work together in a way that would finally see it live up to its potential.

"I realize there is rich talent on this hockey club," he said. "I know I can motivate this team. They need some direction in the dressing room and I know they need some leaders on the ice."[2]

At the same press conference, Baz Bastien was officially bestowed the title of Penguin general manager. The 58-year-old had, for all intents and purposes, been performing the GM's duties in the wake of Wren Blair's departure. As the 1977–78 season played out, however, it became clear that Savill was the Penguin GM in practice. In a series of attempts to quickly change the character of his team, Savill would engineer some highly questionable trades throughout the first few months of the season.

The first was to unload aging captain Ron Schock to Buffalo for left wing Brian "Spinner" Spencer, a high-energy character with a mop of blond rock star curls who could throw his weight around, but who was also prone to taking stupid penalties at the wrong time.

This was followed by two deals with the Washington Capitals. The first was a minor swap that saw Bob Paradise reacquired in exchange for underwhelming defenseman Don Awrey. The second was arguably the worst trade in franchise history: a first-round pick in the 1979 draft to the Caps for right wing journeyman Hartland Monahan, who had scored a total of 50 goals in 166 NHL games. Decent numbers, but hardly worth a precious first-round pick that could potentially be used to put a young star on the Penguin roster. A few days after the deal had been completed, even Savill seemed unsure of the move.

"I admit it wouldn't be a deal you would make every day. But I think the jury is still out."[3]

The day before the Monahan trade, the Penguin family received some horrible news from Pittsburgh's Presbyterian Hospital. Winger Stan Gilbertson would have to have the lower half of his left leg amputated follow-ing a single-vehicle car accident near the Penguins' training site in nearby Rostraver Township two weeks earlier. Driving through the hilly country in a teammate's Jeep, Gilbertson rounded a bend and saw another car in his lane, forcing him to swerve to the right and off the road. The Jeep rolled over, pinning Gilbertson's leg. With the nerves damaged beyond repair, the only option was amputation below the knee. Further surgery would remove part of the knee itself.[4]

Gilbertson's grinding ability would be missed on the ice, but his sense of humor in the dressing room would be missed even more. He loved, for in-stance, to pull a prank on reporters by calling them together in the room and, once assembled around him, simply say, "No comment."[5]

Stan took the blow with resilience, grace and determination. He never let his injury stop him from achieving what he wanted off the ice and eventu-ally built a successful career in real estate.

Meanwhile, as the season started, it became clear that it would take some time for Wilson's philosophy to take hold with a team that had rarely been known for playing it tough. Two early games against the Flyers—still very much the Broad Street Bullies two years removed from their last Stanley Cup—brought this fact into painful and embarrassing focus. On October 15, Philly came to town and humiliated the Pens 8–2. Bobby Clarke had a field day with the light-hitting Penguins, racking up a goal and four assists.

Two games later, the Pens travelled to the Spectrum, but apparently no Penguin really wanted to be there. With the pummeling in Pittsburgh still fresh in their minds, the Pens allowed Ross Lonsberry to score a mere nine seconds in, and then let Clarke make it 2–0 at the 1:27 mark.

The rout was on.

Reggie Leach added a pair before the first period was done, a frame that saw the Flyers outshoot the Penguins 21–4. Three more Flyer tallies in the second made it 7–0 after two. In the third, Bill Barber scored a pair, followed by goals from Bob "Hound Dog" Kelly and Barry Dean to make the final 11–0 Philadelphia. The final shot count was 54–20. Perhaps just as disconcerting as the result was the *way* in which the Pens took the lambasting: lying down. No one in double-blue seemed too upset about what was happening, evidenced by not one penalty being called in the final period.

"The Flyers beat us all over the ice," said an ornery Dunc Wilson, who had endured all 60 minutes of the beating in the Penguin net. "There was no pride out there. The biggest disgrace is not to have pride in yourself."[6]

The beatdown in Philadelphia led directly to Savill's next dictated trade. The fuming Penguin owner wanted his birds to get a lot tougher, immediately. To that end, he told Bastien to go get the toughest player in the game: one Dave "The Hammer" Schultz, poster boy for the Flyers' Broad Street Bully

Cup years and now toiling for the Los Angeles Kings. Savill's command was made a reality near midnight on November 2, when long-time fan favorite Syl Apps and the recently acquired Hartland Monahan were shipped to L.A. for Schultz and speedy winger Gene Carr.

Savill was also salivating over the effect he expected Schultz to have at the box office. "Face it: we're struggling for our survival," he said. "I think Schultz is the kind of player who will turn on a lot of Pittsburgh fans…. It's my opinion that Dave will help us put over hockey in Pittsburgh."[7]

Schultz had barely been able to drop his new Penguin gloves a few times before the Pens made an even bigger deal. The Pierre Larouche era in Pittsburgh came to an end on November 29, when he was shipped to his dream destination of Montreal in exchange for former all-star center Pete Mahovlich and young winger Peter Lee. The deal went down mere hours before the Pens were set to face off against the Habs at the Montreal Forum. The three players involved would play against each other wearing the uniforms of their new teams.

Two months into the season, it was clear Larouche's heart was no longer with the Penguins. After 20 games, he sported a woeful minus-13 and was scoring well below his usual clip with only 11 points. Many were quick to criticize the Penguins for trading a budding superstar for Mahovlich, an aging veteran on the downside of his career, and Lee, an unknown quantity. However, Larouche had forced the Penguins into an unwinnable situation. His contract contained a no-trade clause, allowing him to veto any potential deal. He'd previously invoked it, nixing a trade that would have seen him move to the Cleveland Barons for two of their best forwards, Al MacAdam and future 50-goal scorer Dennis Maruk. About the only team Larouche would agree to be traded to was the Canadiens. After the swap was done, Bastien revealed he'd been in talks with Habs' GM Sam Pollock for weeks, trying to get the best deal possible for his team. In the end, that's what they got from their dealings with the notoriously shrewd Pollock.

"I always said Pierre could be one of the best players in the NHL if he applied himself game in and game out," said Pronovost of his teammate years later. "When he wanted to score goals, he did. He loved to play against Montreal. I think he had something to prove there, I don't know. One night we were playing the Canadiens. I was sitting on the bench with him and he said, 'I'm gonna go score a goal against Dryden, just watch.' And he went out there and did just what he said he was going to do, he scored a goal against Dryden."

Pronovost added that Larouche "was a good kid," but was capable of much more as a player. "If he had applied himself and been serious, he would've been a real superstar. He was a free spirit kind a guy, easy-going and liked to have fun. He loved the game but that was not the only thing for him.

He had other ways of looking at life, I guess. But I always looked at him and said, 'Wow, this guy can play hockey, man.'"[8]

A few days after the Montreal trade, Savill summed up his moves with a statement that would make crusty Toronto Maple Leafs owner Harold Ballard proud: "We got rid of losers for winners. The guys we traded were losers, and guys like Pete Mahovlich and Dave Schultz know what it's like to win. Winners are contagious."[9]

The classless utterance was particularly galling in terms of Syl Apps, who had merely scored an even 500 points in 495 games in a Penguin uniform over six and a half seasons, while posting a plus-94 plus/minus rating—astounding when one considers how bad most of the teams he played with were.

Mahovlich's skill and leadership and Schultz's toughness did give the Pens a spark, but all the wheeling and dealing did little to improve their porous blue line. A deal to send Dennis Owchar to Colorado for Tom Edur did not have a significant effect. By early December, Pittsburgh ranked dead last in goals-against. Crucial injuries to Stackhouse and Burrows meant Wilson and Denis Herron were left out to dry most nights. The Penguin organization still didn't have the depth required to withstand the usual number of injuries that are bound to affect any hockey team throughout the course of a season. The Penguin ownership had pared their operation to the bone following the bankruptcy of 1975, and now the product on the ice was paying the price.

Pittsburgh employed but one scout and, unlike most teams, did not have anyone assessing upcoming opponents. Payroll was kept low by maintaining a shallow roster with only a few minor leaguers who could be summoned when a starter went down. The approach cost the club its affiliation with Hershey of the American Hockey League, forcing them to ink a deal with Binghamton of the AHL. The agreement allowed them little or no control over how the few players they had on the roster were used.

"We don't have any depth," bemoaned Wilson in late January. "I was down to three [forward] lines and five defensemen against Boston [on January 29, an 8–2 Penguin loss]. I don't have any maneuverability when we're that short of manpower. Even if I wanted to give somebody a rest, I couldn't."[10]

The Penguins stumbled through the rest of the season, never winning more than two games in a row. A cracked rib to Mahovlich on March 19 during a disappointing loss in Toronto spelled their final doom. With Big Pete out, the rest of the Penguins seemed lifeless, being blown out in their next game by the sad-sack Minnesota North Stars to the tune of 9–1. The season's nadir came in their next game versus the woeful Colorado Rockies at the Igloo. Winners of a grand total of one road game to that point, the Rockies jumped out to a 2–0 first-period lead and cruised to a 5–2 win.

In desperation, Bastien signed perhaps the biggest has-been of the era, former Bruins star Derek Sanderson, who had frittered away his career on booze and drugs. Overweight and out of shape, Sanderson did little to help the Penguins. They were officially eliminated from the playoffs in their third-to-last game when they lost to 3–1 at Detroit on April 6.

In the days after the players had cleaned out their lockers and headed to their favorite golf courses, it emerged just how bleak the Penguins' financial situation had been during the second half of the season. In an article in the April 11, 1978, *Pittsburgh Post-Gazette*, an unnamed source within the Penguin front office revealed that by February, "we weren't paying any of the bills. Just player salaries and people in the office."

If the idea of Penguin ownership skipping out on overdue bills sounded familiar, that's because it was exactly what Tad Potter and Co. were doing prior to the bankruptcy of 1975. In this instance, at least Savill and Frenzel had the sense to place a call for cash to their somewhat-silent third partner, Ed DeBartolo. He dispatched his trusted associate Vincent Bartimo to the Penguin offices with a sac full of cash (roughly half a million dollars) to keep the team solvent.

"He paid the bills," the source told the *Post-Gazette*. "We couldn't even take out a one-inch ad in the newspaper. Things like sticks and pucks weren't coming in."[11]

It took a few months longer than he had predicted the previous April, but DeBartolo was indeed in control of the Penguins. Money, quite simply, talks. The triumvirate of owners soon elected a new front office leadership team consisting of DeBartolo's hand-picked men. Bartimo, manager of one of DeBartolo's race tracks, replaced Savill as president and chairman of the board, while Paul Martha, a local lawyer and former University of Pittsburgh football star, stepped into the dual role of vice-president and general counsel.

At a press conference introducing the new regime, Martha sounded a hopeful note. "This club has always suffered from the lack of a strong financial base," he said. "Although we are not operating with unlimited resources, I would venture to say this is the strongest financial position the Penguins have ever had."[12]

The Penguins were now DeBartolo's. Its long-suffering fans could only hope that his deep pockets to which Martha referred would eventually help transform their team into a respectable franchise.

14

Trader Baz:
1978–79

"I hope nobody thought we were going to sit still with what we had, not after what we went through."[1]

Baz Bastien, speaking to Jim Proudfoot for the sportswriter's annual NHL guidebook, had most certainly not sat still in the summer of 1978. The Penguin general manager's offseason objectives had been twofold: acquire some proven talent to ensure his hockey team was more competitive than the floundering edition of Penguins the year before, and add more depth to the roster by securing players who could work at multiple positions. That way, when injuries or slumps inevitably hit, players could be moved around like chess pieces to fill the holes.

The roster overhaul began the day before the June NHL Entry Draft, when Bastien sent defenseman Dave Burrows and a sixth-round pick to Toronto for promising young defenseman Randy Carlyle and winger/center George Ferguson. The next day he brought in three members of the Flyers' Broad Street Bullies squad that had tormented Pittsburgh teams for years: gritty and driven forwards Orest Kindrachuk and Ross Lonsberry and offensive-oriented defenseman Tom Bladon. The price was yet another first-round pick, this one the number six overall in that day's draft.

Despite the many examples of his fellow GMs using the draft to build Stanley Cup winners and contenders, such as those in Montreal, Philadelphia and Long Island, Bastien repeatedly succumbed to a desire for immediate gains, often in the form of proven talent entering the downslope of their careers or youngsters surrounded by question marks. Before the season was a month old, two more high draft picks would be sent away for these types of players. On October 9, Baz gave the Chicago Black Hawks a second-round pick in 1980 for eight-year veteran Dale Tallon, whose best years of an underachieving career were behind him. Nine days later, Bastien did his best to relive the horrific Hartland Monahan heist of 1977 by sending yet another

Randy Carlyle (left) and Rod Schutt came to the Penguins through trades with the Maple Leafs and Canadiens, respectively (courtesy Ron Kerrigan).

first-round pick, this one in the 1981 draft, to—who else?—Montreal in exchange for 22-year-old Rod Schutt, a left winger who had not yet cracked the Canadiens' starting lineup.[2]

Just before training camp opened, Bastien traded captain Jean Pronovost to the Atlanta Flames in a three-way deal with Boston that saw Pittsburgh attain winger Gregg Sheppard from the Bruins. "Prony" had asked for a trade over the summer and, after putting up some initial resistance to the idea, Bastien acquiesced.

"There were no grudges," Pronovost said later in the season. "I thought it would be good for me and my family to get a new lease on life."[3]

Looking back on the trade years later, Pronovost added that "there was a transition in Pittsburgh at the time, and I was 30 years old. The goal was to win the Stanley Cup and I didn't think we were on that direction so I kind of forced the trade to Atlanta."[4]

Pronovost departed with team records for games played, goals and points—and the immense respect of his teammates.

"Jean was a quiet leader, a tremendous talent. What a great shot he had. He was well respected by everybody, a real good team guy," remembered Dave Burrows.[5]

"Jean was a good family man," said Rick Kehoe. "I think he got tired of what was going on, with players always in and out, and finally he said he wanted out. But he didn't have the success anywhere else that he had in Pittsburgh."[6]

As the 1978–79 season began, the Penguin roster undeniably featured more talent, experience and depth than the previous year's edition. Given the Penguins' continuously perilous situation in Pittsburgh, where the prospect of the team moving out of town always seemed to be part of the picture, Bastien could be commended for doing his best to put what resembled a winning club on the ice, *immediately*. However, the discarding of so many high draft picks created another, more distant dark cloud on the horizon. Only time would tell how big a storm it would bring.

For Dave Burrows, the constant trading of picks for proven yet aging players elicited mixed emotions. "As a player, you want to win this year. So if you can get a good veteran player who can help right now, that's wonderful, but you know you're really trading away your future."

The Penguins' constant financial struggles sometimes forced the hand of their GMs to trade away the future, Burrows added. "We knew that money was always an issue because we didn't always have packed houses. Back then, your money came from the fans. It comes from TV now so it's not the same. I remember when Vic Hadfield came, he was a big name. It was great for attendance, but Vic was kind of at the end of his career. So ownership is hoping that he's got one or two more good years in him, type of thing. It's always a gamble."[7]

However, it wasn't anything the players spent too much time fretting over, he said. "You just kind of have to go with who's there in the dressing room, you know? You don't have any say in the matter, so you just make the best of whoever's there."[8]

Like many a Penguin season past, this one started disastrously, with only one win in their first 11 games. The only difference with this version, however, was that the woeful mark was not the result of porous goaltending, shaky defense or a limp offensive attack. No, these Penguins were playing *well*. It just seemed that on many nights, a strong effort would be negated by a spectacular performance by the opposing goalie or an unlucky bounce at the most inopportune moment.

"I've never seen a team play so well and not come up with anything in the way of points," observed Bastien. "It seems like we're snakebit."[9]

In late November, though, things finally started to click. From November 29 to December 30, they lost only twice, going a torrid 9–2–4, with one of those losses being a hard-fought 2–1 trench battle in one of the places they never seemed to win, Philadelphia's Spectrum. By New Year's Eve, the Pens had crawled all the way back to within one win of the .500 mark. A victory in Detroit that evening would give them their best December in franchise history. The Red Wings, however, had a decidedly different idea of how the night should transpire. A pair of goals in the first period and another two before the second period was half done gave the Motowners a commanding 4–0 lead. Pete Mahovlich's 20-foot shot on a three-on-two at 17:48 of the second got the Penguins on the board, but the score still stood at 4–1 well into the third.

The Pens, however, did not seem interested in spending New Year's Eve drowning their sorrows over a loss. They kept swarming the Detroit cage until Peter Lee trickled a shot between the pads of ex-Pen goalie Jim Rutherford with 8:25 left. With just under three minutes to play, Lee sent a pass into the Red Wing crease, leading to a mad scramble. Greg Malone found the disc and stuffed it behind Rutherford.

Detroit was reeling as the standing-room-only crowd at the Olympia grew more nervous. The Penguins continued to attack, with Tom Bladon taking yet another shot at Rutherford. The little goalie stopped it but left a rebound for winger Gregg Sheppard, who put it in the top corner at the 18:17 mark. The Pens bench emptied to congratulate their heroic goal scorer, as was customary of most teams when a big goal was scored. (This practice was later outlawed.)

The clock ticked down but the Penguins, not content with one point, continued their assault on the Detroit cage. Lee's blast with 10 seconds left was stopped, but defenseman Randy Carlyle was johnny-on-the-spot to tap in the rebound at 19:53. The Penguin bench again emptied, engulfing Carlyle in a wild celebration.

Whooping it up at the other end was goalie Greg Millen, who, with the victory, tied a team mark set by Al Smith in 1970 by winning his sixth straight game. The five-foot-nine, 175-pound Millen, drafted 106th overall in the sixth round of the 1977 draft, had been a pleasant surprise since training camp. He had quickly grabbed solid hold of the backup spot and, with Denis Herron slumping in December, proved he was capable of handling the big-time pressure.

"I like to have fun," said the 21-year-old Toronto native, who often talked to his goalposts and bopped to the arena music during stoppages. "I try to stay as loose as possible when I'm in the net."[10]

The Penguins skated through the second half of the schedule playing solid hockey, not seriously challenging the legitimate Stanley Cup contenders in the standings, but also not falling into the kind of winter funk that had doomed so many past Penguin teams. Following the New Year's Eve win in Detroit, the Pens went 21–16–6 the rest of the way. That included an 8–4–4 mark in March, a month in which they got a pair of embarrassing monkeys off their backs. On March 10 versus Philadelphia before a sold-out Igloo, Greg Malone's tie-breaking third-period goal gave Pittsburgh a 3–2 win, their first win over the Flyers in two and-a-half years. It came at a high price, though, as Pete Mahovolich went down with a separated shoulder and would likely be lost for the season.

An even bigger boil was exorcised two weeks later in Boston, when the Pens beat the Big Bad Bruins, 3–1. It was their first victory in Boston Garden since January 28, 1968, ending an ugly 0–26–2 streak. "A win like this over a team like Boston should help us," said Malone. "It's a real boost to our confidence."[11]

The strong stretch run earned the Penguins a second-place finish in the Norris, five points up on Los Angeles (but a whopping 30 behind first-place Montreal!). They would meet the Buffalo Sabres in a best-of-three, first-round Stanley Cup playoff battle.

The Sabres held home-ice advantage, having garnered 88 points to Pittsburgh's 85. They came out flying in game one at the Memorial Auditorium, outshooting the Pens 12–3 in the first period but only managing a 1–1 tie after 20 minutes, thanks to some spectacular saves from Herron. Ex-Pen Rene Robert put Buffalo up 2–1 in the second, but Pittsburgh's Blair Chapman evened things with just under 15 minutes left in the third period. Later, ex-Sabre Gary McAdam, whom the Pens had acquired in February for Dave Schultz, took a George Ferguson pass, used his speed to blow by a Buffalo defender, and beat netminder Bob Sauve with a hard shot, giving Pittsburgh a 3–2 lead. Orest Kindrachuk got an insurance marker less than two minutes later and the Penguins skated out of the "Aud" with a 4–3 win and a 1–0 series lead.

The Pens' hopes of sweeping their way into the quarter-finals were dashed in game two in Pittsburgh, however, by an all-around solid defensive effort by the Sabres and some hot goaltending from the youngster Sauve, who stopped 30 of 31 shots for a 3–1 Sabre triumph. "He came up with some fantastic saves," said his counterpart Denis Herron. "I guess you could say the first game was my hot game and this one was his. Now it's my turn again."[12]

In the decisive Game Three showdown back in Buffalo, the Sabres built a tight 3–2 lead after two. Both Penguin goals were scored by unlikely sniper Jim Hamilton, a 1977 Pens draft pick who had spent his career going back and forth between Pittsburgh and the minors. Buffalo came out for the third flying like the days of the famed French Connection line, firing shot after shot at Herron, who was stopping everything that came his way.

"I always played well in Buffalo," Herron said 40 years later. "The arena there was a bit smaller than all the others in the league. The blue line was closer to the net."[13]

Just past the four-minute mark, on a rare break into the Sabres zone, George Ferguson put a Jacques Cossette rebound past Sauve to tie the game. The Sabres did not relent, though, sending more rubber at Herron in an all-out attempt to break the deadlock. But when the horn sounded, the Penguin goalie had stopped all 18 Buffalo shots he faced in the period, often in eye-popping fashion. The series headed to a one-goal, winner-take-all overtime.

Before the extra frame was even a minute old, Gregg Sheppard sent an errant pass from his own blue line well in front of his intended target Ferguson, who was skating down the left side. The "Fergy Flyer," however, chased the puck down, corralled it inside the Sabres' zone and bore down on Sauve. "I noticed the left side of the rink was open," he told the *Pittsburgh Press*, "so I just took off, and when I thought I could score, I just let it fly."[14]

Ferguson let a quick, hard shot go that beat Sauve between the legs, ending the series in shocking fashion after only 47 seconds of extra play. The goal gave the Penguins their first playoff series win in four years and only the third in franchise history. Ferguson was mobbed by his teammates in the suddenly silent Aud.

Looking back on the tally years later, the goaltending hero Herron said, "I definitely felt a sense of relief when Ferguson's goal went in, because you knew if we didn't score at the beginning, Buffalo was going to come in pretty strong."[15]

Rick Kehoe added that the short best-of-three format helped the Penguins get by Buffalo. "They had a better team than us, but it was one of those short series where, if you get good goaltending, it's anybody's game."[16]

The Pens were moving on to the quarter-finals and a best-of-seven series against the well-rested Boston Bruins, whose first-place finish in the Adams Division had earned them a first-round bye. Pittsburgh would have little time to savor their dramatic preliminary round win, having to travel to Boston Garden for game one just two nights after the win in Buffalo. Perhaps remembering their loss on home ice to Pittsburgh in March, the Bruins right off the bat made it clear to the Penguins just what they were up against. The Beantowners started strong, racking up a commanding 3–0 lead before the first period was done. They coasted from there to an easy 6–2 win.

"What killed us was how we played in our own end," said Kindrachuk afterward. "You can't give it away against the Bruins because they'll put it in the net."[17]

The Pens played a more tight-checking style in game two and found themselves trailing only by a 3–2 margin midway through the third period. This time, though, it was an unfavorable bounce that did them in. Bruins defenseman Mike Milbury flipped the puck into the Pittsburgh zone from center, which Randy Carlyle, with his back to the play, knocked down with his stick. Unfortunately, it caromed right onto the blade of Boston's Bob Miller, who took one stride and rifled a shot past a surprised Herron. Kindrachuk scored a meaningless marker with six seconds left, making the final 4–3 Bruins.

The Pens received a boost for game three when Pete Mahovlich returned from the shoulder injury he'd suffered in March. Big Pete came ready to play, setting up the game's first goal, a 30-foot howitzer from Gary McAdam only 3:13 in. After Peter McNab tied it up late in the first for the visitors, the Pens played Boston even until Rick Middleton fired home a loose puck in front of the Penguin goal 5:03 into the third. The Bruins clamped the Pens' attack down from then on and left the building with a 2–1 win and a 3–0 series stranglehold.

The Penguins hoped to salvage at least a victory in the series before a sold-out Igloo the following night. An early 45-foot slap shot from Rod Schutt that bulged the twine behind Gerry Cheevers got them off on the right foot, but by the end of the first period, goals by Bobby Schmautz and Jean Ratelle had given Boston a 2–1 lead. After a tight-checking, scoreless second, Ratelle connected again 8:50 of the third, and an empty net goal in the final minute sealed the Penguins' season for good.

In the end, the Pens just couldn't get their sputtering power play revved up, going 0-for-5 in game four and only 2-for-15 throughout the series. Combined with an 0–14 effort in the first round, the Pens' post-season power play worked at a miserable 6.9 percent.

"[Boston] plays a physical game and are willing to take a few penalties for it," said Kindrachuk. "When you're unable to score during those penalty situations, then they've effectively made you play their game."[18]

Looking back on the Penguin teams of the era, Herron believes the absence of one key ingredient continually prevented them from taking things to the next level. "We had a pretty decent team. But we didn't have a super, super, superstar on the team. We had three lines: the first was pretty decent, the second was a little bit less, and the third line was pretty much defensive. But what we were missing was that superstar who can pick up the puck and go out and score a goal once in a while. That makes a big difference, and that, I think, was what was missing."[19]

Despite the disappointing finish, the 1978–79 season was in many ways a big success. The Pens improved by 17 points over the previous year, giving them their second-best season ever. Attendance was up by more than 35,000, an average of 880 per game. Baz Bastien was recognized as the *Hockey News* NHL Executive of the Year. And with Edward DeBartolo, Sr., now pulling the Penguin purse strings, the Pittsburgh papers were mercifully devoid of stories about the team possibly moving. DeBartolo was showing his commitment to the Pittsburgh market by working with local government officials to secure a long-term lease on the Civic Arena.[20] Such a deal would effectively give him control of the facility and help solidify his investment in the team and, by extension, the Penguins' future in Pittsburgh.

For all that good news, however, the club had still lost an approximate

$1.3 million, according to Paul Martha.[21] Its on-ice leader was also not in a particularly celebratory mood at season's end.

"This was a good year, but I hope that doesn't allow for any complacency to set in," said captain Kindrachuk. "This season should be used as a building block. Next season we should improve just that much more."[22]

PART FOUR

The Pesky Pens
(1979–80 Through 1981–82)

15

A Step Back:
1979–80

Baz Bastien was so convinced second-year goalie Greg Millen was ready to assume the Penguins' starting spot that he was willing to trade seasoned starter Denis Herron. On August 30, 1979, he did just that—to the Montreal Canadiens, along with yet another high draft pick, this one the Penguins' second-round choice in 1982. In return, he got young goalie Rob Holland and winger Pat Hughes, whom he had coveted for more than two years. In fact, Baz had wanted to attain Hughes in the 1977 deal with the Canadiens for Pete Mahovlich and Peter Lee.

Why Bastien was so fixated on Hughes remains puzzling. A third-round pick in 1975, Hughes had barely cracked the Habs' lineup since that time, scoring 17 points in 44 games. Most of his pro career had been spent in the minors, where he averaged less than a point a game. Nevertheless, Baz got his man. With Herron gone, the 1979–80 Penguin net would be in the hands of two 22-year-olds and 24-year-old perennial underachiever Gordie Laxton.

The new season brought with it many changes to the National Hockey League. There were four new teams, absorbed in the NHL's long-anticipated merger with the World Hockey Association. With the addition of Edmonton, Winnipeg, Quebec and Hartford, the league was now a 21-team circuit.

The makeup of the four-time Stanley Cup champion Canadiens would also look different, with the departures of key cogs like goalie Ken Dryden, center Jacques Lemaire and coach Scotty Bowman, who was now the GM in Buffalo. The mighty Bruins had fired coach Don Cherry, raising questions about whether they could continue their inspired, lunchpail-style brand of hockey without their emotional bench boss. And in Philadelphia, the Flyers' championship Broad Street Bully days were long behind them.

For the Penguins, coming off an 85-point season and sporting an experienced and relatively deep roster outside of the goalie position, there appeared

Denis Herron takes on his ex–Penguin teammates at the Civic Arena as a member of the Montreal Canadiens in 1980. Herron had three stints with the Pens in the 1970s and 1980s (courtesy Ron Kerrigan).

to be a chance to finally join the league's upper echelon and make a deep run in the playoffs.

The Penguin ship was headed in that very direction throughout the first half of the season. After a win and a tie in their first two games, they went into Boston Garden and served notice that these Penguins were not going to be pushed around as had previous versions. Playing the Bruins tight for the first two periods but trailing 1–0 in the third, Peter Lee fired a long, low slap shot that found the back of the Bruin net at 2:18. The goal ignited the Penguin attack. Four minutes later, rookie Paul Marshall collected his own rebound and put it behind Gilles Gilbert to give the Pens a 2–1 lead, silencing the Boston crowd. Only 11 seconds later, George Ferguson connected with a 55-foot blast over Gilbert's glove. Netminder Rob Holland, replacing an injured Greg Millen, held the B's at bay the rest of the way and the Penguins marched out of the Garden with a 4–1 win—only their third at the Garden in franchise history.

"I've said all along we had the kind of people who would make it possible for us to compete in anybody's building. Maybe tonight we proved it," said a proud coach Johnny Wilson.[1]

Bastien could never have predicted just how important Holland would be to the Penguins in the first three months of the season. Millen had suffered a torn hamstring, keeping him out of action for a number of weeks. When he reinjured it in practice, Holland remained solidly entrenched in the Pittsburgh crease. It was only in early December, after he had set a new Penguin record for consecutive minutes played by a goalie (1,114, breaking Herron's record of 1,060 in 1978) that Holland was relieved by a recovered Millen.

Meanwhile, as the calendar turned to a new decade, the Montreal Canadiens' dynasty was unraveling. With a record of 18–14–6, they were, for once, actually on the same planet as the usual Norris Division bridesmaids, Los Angeles and Pittsburgh. The Pens welcomed Montreal to the Igloo on January 2, sitting only three points behind the formerly Flying Frenchmen. Goals by ex-Habs Rod Schutt and Pat Hughes lifted the Penguins to an impressive 5–3 win, pulling them to within one point of the Norris peak.

"It's obvious the only way to win the Norris Division is to beat Montreal. So we knew that's what we had to do," said Schutt afterward.[2]

Not since the NHL realigned itself into a four-division setup in 1974–75 had the Penguins owned first place in its division. A win on Long Island the following night would change that, with both the Canadiens and Kings, tied for first place, idle that evening. Three times during the first two periods, the Isles grabbed a one-goal lead, only to have the Penguins answer back and tie things up. Jim Hamilton, recently recalled from the farm team in Syracuse, tied it and Gary McAdam made it 4–3 in the third. Greg Millen repulsed the Islander attack the rest of the way, including a key pad stop on a Bob Bourne breakaway early in the third, and the Penguins left the Nassau County Coliseum with the two points needed to vaunt them to the Norris penthouse. An ecstatic coach Wilson saw the accomplishment as a sign of the Penguins' arrival, at last, in the club of the NHL's elite. "[The Stanley Cup] is up for grabs this year. There are seven, eight teams in there. We're one of them."[3]

The Penguins' new lofty perch also gave them a taste of the view that Pittsburgh's two other major sports teams were enjoying at the time. Baseball's Pirates had won the World Series in 1979, and football's Steelers were kings of the NFL, having won three Super Bowls since 1974. And just over two weeks after the Penguins' win on Long Island, the Steelers would claim their fourth title by winning Super Bowl XIV. Both championship franchises sported black and gold uniforms, and rumors had begun to circulate that the Penguins were looking to change their colors to that same scheme that now defined Pittsburgh professional sporting success. Black and gold are also the city's official colors.

"Our fans practically demand it," said Martha. "Anything we can do to make going to a hockey game more entertaining, we'll try."[4]

The players liked the idea. "I think everybody in Pittsburgh identifies with those colors, so why shouldn't the Penguins identify with them, too?" said Greg Malone.[5]

The idea had been floating around the Penguin offices since DeBartolo and Martha assumed control in 1978, but it wasn't until a formal notice was sent to the league in January 1980 that the idea took definite shape. Plans were submitted and approved, but the sartorial switch hit a snag when the Boston Bruins protested, claiming they had sole NHL rights to the black and gold colors. The hissy fit from the Hub was doomed to failure, though, what with no legal basis to support it. NHL president John Ziegler formally denied the challenge when he ruled that the Penguins' NHL predecessors, the Pirates of the 1920s, had worn black and gold eight years before the Bruins switched to the scheme.

The Pens debuted their new duds—ironically ordered from the Boston Bruins Pro Sports Shops in Boston Garden[6]—on January 30, 1980, at home versus St. Louis, who had agreed to wear their home whites so the Pens could show off their dark road uniforms to their fans. It was a gracious move by the Blues, but they were anything but cordial once the puck dropped, ruining the party by dealing the Penguins a 4–3 loss.

The Pens may have started to dress like their champion brethren but their play in their new colors was hardly similar to that of the Pirates and Steelers. In fact, the Penguins lost their first six games in black and gold, including a 9–0 embarrassment in Buffalo February 7. The streak was part of a larger slide that had begun after their climb to the top of the Norris on January 3, in which they won only three times in their next 20 games.

The downturn could in part be chalked up to injuries to their top two centers. Orest Kindrachuk's respectable production and solid leadership were removed from the lineup when he suffered a hip injury in mid–January, and Greg Malone was lost for the season when he tore knee ligaments in a win at Toronto February 13.

The signing of U.S. Olympic hero Mark Johnson, after he and his upstart American teammates had stunned the world by taking the gold medal at the Winter Olympics in Lake Placid, New York, caused a flurry of excitement in Penguin Country—even garnering the team a rare front-page story in the *Pittsburgh Post-Gazette*. But Johnson did little to help lift the Penguins and the slide into the all-too-familiar lower echelons of the NHL continued.

"I don't know what the hell the problem is," said a baffled and frustrated Ron Stackhouse after a 6–5 loss in Philadelphia February 17. "How can we be so different from one night to the next, look great one period and horrible the next? When it comes to the why, I just don't know."[7]

The Pens were not being helped by the shaky play of their youthful goaltending corps. Millen was fighting the puck and Holland was, well, a rookie. It was now, in hockey's dog days of January and February, when the true Cup contenders often separated themselves from the also-rans, that the Pens could have used a steady veteran presence in goal—someone like Denis Herron. But his hard-won experience, mostly gained behind woeful Penguin teams of the 70s, was now in Montreal. The 1979–80 Penguins would have to survive or perish with their goaltending kiddie corps.

Fortunately, Millen was able to regain his previous form and the team managed to steady the ship somewhat, going 10–10–2 from February 20 on. That was good for a 14th-place finish overall and a first-round date with a familiar foe, the Boston Bruins.

As with their playoff encounter the previous year, the Penguins entered the se-

Orest Kindrachuk was named Penguins captain before he even played a game for the club. He arrived in a trade with the Flyers in June 1978 (courtesy Mike Hanczar).

ries looking like easy fodder for the Bruins. Boston had ended the season strong, responding well to a coaching change that saw GM Harry Sinden take over from Fred Creighton. Pittsburgh had finished the season on a depressing note, having been pummeled by the Sabres 9–1. And the prospect of heading to the Boston Garden was never an inviting one. Aside from routinely having to face a strong Bruin team every visit, former Pens defenseman Dave Burrows remembered the visitors' dressing room as being equally uninviting. "It was a really old building and I used to hate going to the dressing room there," he said. "It had shag carpet, and it was always soaking wet. I didn't even want to walk around in there it was so bad. I don't know if they did that dressing room thing on purpose or what, but back then you did nothing for the visiting team. You'd make them feel as uncomfortable as possible, kind of thing."[8]

Nevertheless, the Penguins came into the old barn for game one with no intentions of rolling over and dying.

"We made up our minds as a team to go out and work hard and give it a damn good shot," said Gary McAdam.[9]

And work they did. After holding the Bruins scoreless in the first, thanks to three penalty kills, Mark Johnson struck at 8:25 of the second on a power play, depositing a Peter Lee rebound under the crossbar to stun the small Garden crowd of 9,725. McAdam made it 2–0 at 14:47 and Johnson added his second early in the third. Meanwhile, Greg Millen was stopping all the rubber coming at him—which was quite a lot, as the Bruins took control for the rest of the period. Terry O'Reilly got the B's on the board with a little over six minutes to play and Craig Mactavish placed a 15-foot wrist shot past Millen with 1:14 to go to make it a one-goal game. Former Bruin Gregg Sheppard, however, finished his old mates off with an empty-netter and the Penguins had completed the shocker of the young playoffs with a 4–2 win. Their effective execution of a game plan bent on clogging up the defensive zone, coupled with the spectacular goaltending of Millen, were the keys to victory. Sinden went so far as to call Millen's work "the best performance we've seen by a goaltender in this building all season."[10]

"The team played a super game in front of me," Millen said in typically humble fashion. "I was just trying to get my body in front of everything."[11]

He did the same in the first period of game two, stopping all 12 shots to keep the game scoreless after 20 minutes. There was no panic in the Bruins, however. They just kept coming at Millen, confident that their superior play would eventually pay off. And it did when "Nifty" Rick Middleton slipped behind the Pens' defense and bore in alone on Millen. The goalie came out to challenge him, but the swift-skating

Greg Millen's spectacular goaltending helped the Penguins come agonizingly close to upsetting the Bruins and Blues in first-round playoff series in 1980 and 1981, respectively (courtesy Mike Hanczar).

right winger deked Millen and sidestepped him, leaving a wide-open cage to deposit the puck into and give Boston a 1–0 lead. The shot was just one of a whopping 22 the Bruins took in the period, with two others going in as well to give them a commanding 3–0 lead after two. They cruised from there to a 4–1 win to tie the series. The final shots were an embarrassing 42–17.

"We just stopped skating and left everything to the goalie," Sheppard said. "He played another great game but I can't say the same thing about the guys in front of him."[12]

Boston had owned much of the play in the first two games and looked to take full command of the series as it shifted back to Pittsburgh for game three. Ross Lonsberry, however, had been through such playoff wars before with the championship Philadelphia Flyers clubs of the mid–70s, and he, like his Penguin teammates, had no intention of throwing in the towel. The 33-year-old left wing opened the scoring at 13:28 of the first and then doubled the lead only 1:17 into the second when he picked up a rebound in the Boston crease and put it past Cheevers. A Randy Carlyle blast from 35 feet made it 3–0 before the period was done. From there, the Pens went into a defensive shell, not getting a third-period shot until almost the 14:00 mark. The strategy worked, however, and the Pens walked off with a 4–1 win and a shocking 2–1 series lead. They were but one victory away from one of the biggest upsets in recent memory and a quarter-final date with the hated Flyers.

One key to the Pens' success to that point in the series was the defense's ability to keep the front of their net clear. Ron Stackhouse, Russ Anderson, Randy Carlyle and the rest of the blueline corps quickly swept any rebounds out of harm's way and made sure any Bruin who dared venture into the slot was not welcomed kindly. In game four, however, they stopped doing it— with disastrous results. Peter McNab was allowed to camp out in front early on and at 5:13 he deflected a shot from the point to give the Bruins a 1–0 lead. Rick Middleton also took up residence right in front of Millen and put a point-blank range wrist shot home at 6:42 to make it 2–0, and the rout was on. By the time the buzzer mercifully sounded to end the first period, Boston led 5–0, thanks in large part to a goal and two assists from dazzling rookie defenseman Ray Bourque. Boston cruised to an 8–3 win, sending the series to a deciding fifth game back in Boston.

Incredibly, the teams would be playing their third game in three days, a scheduling nightmare that would never happen today. The Penguins came out flying, buzzing the Bruin goal for the first minute and a half, but Boston regrouped and began taking the play to Pittsburgh. At 3:49, another Bourque shot from the point was deflected past Millen, again by McNab, to put Boston up 1–0. The Penguins must have felt as if the horror show that was game four had simply continued into a fourth period. By the midway point of the contest they were down 4–0 and all that was left to do was play out the final 30 minutes with as much pride as their tired legs could muster. In the end, the scoreboard read 6–2 Bruins and the Penguins' dreams of a major upset had evaporated into the steamy air of the Boston Garden rafters.

"I don't think they had the depth on defense to play so many games in a row. They went with four defensemen and the other two I don't think are good enough to play," said Bruins star Terry O'Reilly. "Plus, I think their goalie got a little tired."[13]

Millen didn't disagree. "I think everybody was a little tired. [The Bruins] showed their class by coming back."[14]

The end of the season also marked the end of Johnny Wilson's three-year contract. In early May, the Penguins announced it would not be renewed. Management was looking for a different type of coach than the old-school Wilson.

"We will be looking for someone who can motivate people," said Penguin president Vince Bartimo. "We need someone who is a little more volatile, more outspoken."[15]

After the names of some potential candidates were bandied about in the press for a few weeks, including Don Cherry, who had recently been fired as head coach of the Colorado Rockies, the Pens found their man in Eddie Johnston, the energetic and affable former Bruins goalie who had coached the Chicago Black Hawks during the previous season. In his only year behind the Black Hawk bench, "EJ" guided the team to a 14-point improvement over the previous season and a first-round playoff sweep of St. Louis before bowing to the powerful Buffalo Sabres in the quarter-finals. Johnston was fired because of his disagreements

Sniper Rick Kehoe came to Pittsburgh in a 1974 trade with the Maple Leafs and proceeded to average 31 goals over his next 10 seasons with the Penguins. In 1980–81, he exploded for a career-high 55 (courtesy Doug McLatchy).

with GM Bob Pulford, particularly the coach's refusal to rehire assistant coach Keith Magnuson.

Johnston appeared headed for the vacant head coaching position in Boston, but when another former Bruins netminder—Gerry Cheevers—got the job, the Penguins scooped him up.

"He strikes me as the type of fellow who's … going to get the most out of his players," said Paul Martha. "He's going to be able to take some of our kids and work them in with the older fellows. That's where I think he's going to do a masterly job."[16]

At a press conference announcing his hiring, Johnston identified his top two priorities: improving the Pens' penalty killing and their power play.

"I think the potential is there for the Penguins to have a very good hockey team," said the new coach.[17]

Like the many other previous press conferences held to introduce a new Penguin coach, an air of guarded optimism filled the room. Perhaps this new bench boss would be able to put Pittsburgh's flailing past in the rear-view mirror and finally get the club on the road to a Stanley Cup. Edward DeBartolo, Jr., was in attendance that day and summed up the dream every diehard Penguin fan held onto.

"Every time I fly into the city, I pass that billboard out by the airport that boasts of Pittsburgh as the 'City of Champions.' Someday, we're going to have a Penguin up there with the Pirates and Steelers."[18]

It would now be up to Johnston to help make that dream a reality.

16

The Rick and Randy Show: 1980–81

One of Eddie Johnston's first moves as coach was to call up an old hockey buddy and invite him to training camp for two days. He wouldn't be trying out for a spot with the Penguins, this old friend, but would instead be acting as an extra hand to help EJ run drills, and maybe impart a bit of advice along the way. It didn't hurt that this old pal of his had, during a 12-year NHL career, won eight consecutive Norris trophies as the league's best defenseman, two scoring championships (as a defenseman, mind you), two Stanley Cups and had revolutionized the blueliner position while coming to be considered by many as the greatest player in hockey history.

On September 29, the great Bobby Orr pulled on a bright gold sweat-shirt with a Penguin logo and the words "Property of Pittsburgh Penguins" emblazoned on it and stepped onto the ice at the Mt. Lebanon Recreation Center. Mainly working with the Pittsburgh defense corps, Orr helped out with drills, took shots on the goalies and provided a huge heaping of inspiration to a young club searching for a winning identity.

"He was going better than anyone on the ice," laughed Johnston after Orr's second day. "He's shooting and the goaltenders are trying to get set for it and before they can, the puck is by them."[1]

The players were awed by the presence of such a hockey deity, who joked and posed for pictures with them. "I just wish I could do what he could do," said defenseman Mario Faubert. "He can still skate circles around people. Around me, anyway."[2]

Orr had kind words to say about the team. "These kids can skate and they have lots of speed. Now, I'm not saying they're going to win the Stanley Cup this year, but the material is here to do it in a couple of years."[3]

Some of Orr's Norris-winning pedigree seemed to rub off on 24-year-old Randy Carlyle, who started the season strong and quickly established himself as one of the club's leaders. Regularly playing a whopping 40 to 45 minutes a game, Carlyle did it all: quarterback the power play, kill penalties, defend the Pens' zone and push the puck up ice to take the play to the other team's defenders. After 20 games, he had 20 points on one goal and 19 assists. By mid–December he had 30 assists, tops among all NHL defensemen. His 25 power play points had already shattered Ron Stackhouse's club record for an entire season.

Carlyle said much of his success stemmed from Johnston telling him in training camp that he would be getting lots of ice time. "That sort of allowed me to settle down and get comfortable. I found I could let things develop instead of being concerned about what I was accomplishing on each specific shift."[4]

Johnston attributed Carlyle's improved play to cutting down on his give-aways and moving the puck up the ice. "He sticks his nose into the play."[5]

Center Orest Kindrachuk, hampered by a hip injury that caused him to miss 28 games and the playoffs the previous year, also started the season strong. His eight points in the Pens' first three games helped earn the 30-year-old captain NHL Player of the Week honors. With such a fast personal start, "Kindy" had high hopes for his team.

"I've been here a couple of years now, and when you evaluate the franchise in Pittsburgh, it's been kind of stumbling and fumbling around for 13 years," he told the *Hockey News*. "People are waiting to see a contender. With EJ coming and if Mr. DeBartolo possibly acquires the [Civic Arena], you'll see a contender coming to the city. After 13 years of disappointment it would be great to be part of it and see the franchise turned around."[6]

Unfortunately for Kindrachuk and the Penguins, he wouldn't be a part of anything the Pens would do in the future. While the hip caused him no issues, a back problem that had plagued him for years flared up after only the ninth game of the season, sending him to the sidelines. He returned in early January, only to reinjure the back after four games. Kindrachuk could avoid the doctor's scalpel no longer and in February underwent successful surgery to remove a disc from his lower back. He would not play another game for the Penguins, finishing out his career a year later with four games for the Washington Capitals, where he scored his 118th and final NHL goal.

Kindrachuk's injury was but one of many that hampered the Pens' efforts in the early going. Particularly hard hit was the center position, which saw both Greg Malone and Gregg Sheppard go down in the second game of the year, a 5–4 win over Winnipeg.

"At the end of training camp, I said center was our deepest position. The minute I said it, we lost them all," lamented Johnston.[7]

With no farm system and few young prospects waiting in the wings—

thanks to so many draft picks having been traded away—Johnston was forced to temporarily transplant wingers George Ferguson and Pat Hughes to center to fill the voids. By the Pens' 20th game, Penguin players had missed a cumulative total of 100 games due to injuries, most in the league and nine more than their closest competitor. Johnston yearned for the day when he could deploy a full, healthy lineup and not have to depend on those who had been underperforming. When that day came, he told the *Pittsburgh Press* in early January 1981, "the guys who haven't been producing will find themselves in the stands or so far away it'll take a search warrant to find them."[8]

One of the coach's complaints was a lack of physical play. "Some of these guys, you don't have to get their jerseys cleaned, they never go into the corners. You save money there."[9]

Veteran Nick Libbett observed the same thing. "Unfortunately, we don't have that type of [physical] team. I wonder if some of the guys even know how to be physical. Maybe they never learned what they're capable of doing."[10]

Another item on Johnston's list of disappointments was the Penguin goaltenders. Both Greg Millen and Rob Holland were fighting the puck and letting in key goals at inopportune times. The result was that the Pens had the worst goaltending in the league throughout the first month of the season, sporting a collective 5.25 goals against average. Holland was eventually sent down to Syracuse and replaced by 21-year-old Nick Ricci, whose inconsistent play during his spot duty appearances did nothing to solve the crisis in the crease. Johnston desperately hoped one of his youngsters would get on a hot streak.

"We've got to get some consistent goaltending. In a stretch of 10 games, we can't go 5-and-5. We've got to get eight good games, one so-so game and maybe one bad game in there."[11]

Fortunately, some of the rubber burning holes in the Penguins' net was offset by a pair of Penguin sharpshooters operating at the other end of the ice. On November 18, Bastien swung one of his best deals as Pens GM when he acquired center Paul Gardner and former Pen rearguard Dave Burrows from Toronto in exchange for a pair of forward prospects, Kim Davis and Paul Marshall. The deal turned out to be yet another fleecing of the Maple Leafs by the crafty Penguins. Bastien was well aware of the 24-year-old Gardner, having been part of the Kansas City Scouts' management team that drafted him 11th overall in 1976. Gardner proceeded to put up a 30-goal season in each of his first three seasons, no small feat considering most of that time was spent with the woeful Colorado Rockies, whom the Scouts had morphed into shortly after Gardner had been drafted. The kid could clearly score, but the knock on him was that he didn't know what his own end of the rink looked like. Such supposed defensive weaknesses didn't bother Eddie Johnston, who had had Gardner on his radar for a few years and had tried, unsuccessfully, to obtain him while coaching the Black Hawks.

"He looked like he had a terrific scoring touch, and you don't teach that," said the coach. "If you find it, though, you had better take good advantage of it."[12]

Gardner put that scoring touch on display for Penguins fans as soon as he put on a Pittsburgh jersey. In his first 21 games he netted 13 goals and 12 assists for 25 points, earning NHL Player of the Week honors for one seven-game stretch in December—for which he was presented with a six-piece set of designer luggage during the first intermission of a game. Gardner also became the first Penguin to score four goals in one game during a 6–5 loss to the Flyers December 13. Much of Gardner's success came from camping out in front of the opponent's net and either banging home rebounds or deflecting incoming shots.

"On the power play, Eddie wants someone to stand in front of the net a lot, and that's right up my alley," said Gardner after his four-goal game. "I just try to get into the open spot and not get tied up. Sometimes I do, but that lets Rick [Kehoe] or Ross [Lonsberry] get free."[13]

Kehoe, in particular, was getting free a lot, and scoring at a pace like never before. A steady sniper who averaged 28 goals a year since coming into the league with Toronto in 1971–72, the Windsor, Ontario native netted four goals in the Pens' first three games and never looked back. By December 3 he had hit the 20-goal mark, thanks to a hat trick that helped Pittsburgh pull out a 4–4 tie against his former team at Maple Leaf Gardens. The next night in Montreal, it was Kehoe's goal at 5:08 of the third period that tied the game at two and spurred his teammates to think they could actually win in the vaunted Forum, a place no Penguins squad had taken two points from since 1969.

"That [goal] really got us going," said defenseman Dave Burrows. "Montreal had controlled the game for the first two periods but, for a change, we hadn't let them run away from us. We were still very much in the game and Kehoe's goal made us realize we could win it."[14]

And win it they did, when Pat Hughes scored shortly before the halfway point of the third and the defense managed to hold off a depleted Canadiens squad—missing were such old Penguin hope-killers Guy Lafleur, Larry Robinson and Guy Lapointe—for a 3–2 victory.

"Chico," as his teammates called him due to his resemblance to the mustachioed star of the hit 70s TV show *Chico and the Man*, earned NHL Player of the Week honors for the period of January 12 to 18, thanks to a hat trick against St. Louis January 14 and a last-minute, game-winning goal against Los Angeles three nights later.

"All he needs is three or four chances and he'll put the lamp on twice," said Johnston after the St. Louis game.[15] Added Blues coach Red Berensen,

"He's a natural goal-scorer. You give him chances and he'll put them in. He moves in for rebounds, he's always around the puck."

The humble Kehoe attributed part of his 1980–81 success to having been around the league long enough. "I guess maybe it comes a little easier for me," he told a Pittsburgh sports reporter with a smile. "It's being in the right place at the right time and a little experience, too. At times, it just happens. I can't pinpoint it."[16]

Penguin management realized how special both Kehoe's and Carlyle's seasons were becoming, and began promoting them to the rest of the league. Paul Martha and Baz Bastien started mentioning Carlyle in early Norris Trophy discussions, and Kehoe for the Lady Byng, awarded for gentlemanly play. Such boosterism was necessary because the Penguins, despite the heroics of Rick and Randy, were on no one's radar, thanks to a woeful 20–30–9 record by mid–February. Their 49 points had them clinging to 16th place overall (out of 21 teams), and the final playoff spot. (Since the addition of the four WHA teams in 1979, first-round playoff berths had been determined on overall league standings, with the first-place team playing number 16, second-place facing 15th, and so on.)

Despite the so-so goaltending, the lack of grit and absence of depth throughout the organization, Eddie Johnston made sure to infuse the Penguin dressing room with a sense of optimism.

"A lot of people have the idea that we'd be happy finishing 15th or 16th and just making the playoffs," said Greg Malone. "Well, that's just not true. We think we belong much higher up in the standings. Coach keeps talking about 10th or 11th, and that's probably a realistic position to strive for."[17]

Toward the end of February, the attitude finally started to bear fruit. With wins at home against Colorado and Winnipeg, followed by a 6–4 triumph in Washington and a 6–4 win back at the Igloo against the Rangers, the Penguins equaled the club record of four consecutive wins, which had been accomplished seven times previously. To set a new mark they'd have to do something they'd had trouble accomplishing all year: winning on the road, where the Pens sported a woeful 6–17–7 record. Specifically, they'd have to beat the Nordiques and their red-hot goaltender Dan Bouchard in Quebec. Since arriving in a trade with Calgary in late January, Bouchard had won 11 of his first 12 starts. Such an impressive record didn't seem to carry much weight with Rod Schutt, though, who deflected a Peter Lee blueline blast past Bouchard after only 10 seconds of play. Randy Carlyle picked up his 61st assist on the goal, thus breaking teammate Ron Stackhouse's team mark for defensemen set in 1975–76. Carlyle then put the puck in the net himself on a close-in slapshot at 2:24, and Rick Kehoe made it 3–0 only 15 seconds later. It was 4–0 by the end of the first, and the Pens held off the Nordiques the rest of the way to escape with a 5–4 win and a new team record.

The Penguins tacked on a sixth straight win for good measure, a 6–5 triumph over Los Angeles at home on March 4. But the winning streak turned out to be a mere aberration. Pittsburgh returned to its stumbling ways for the rest of the season, winning only four of their remaining 15 contests. They backed into the playoffs on the night they played their 79th game—a 5–2 loss to Boston at home—when Washington lost to the Islanders, eliminating the Caps from the playoff hunt. The only other highlight of the game was Rick Kehoe netting his 54th goal and thus breaking Pierre Larouche's mark set in 1975–76. Chico would finish with 55 tallies, while Randy Carlyle set the pace for all NHL defenseman by registering 83 points.

The luster of those impressive individual statistics was tarnished, however, by the stark team numbers: 30 wins, 37 losses and 13 ties—the exact same record as the year before. Their 73 points were good enough only for 15th spot overall and a first-round date with the St. Louis Blues.

On paper, the best-of-five series looked like a mismatch. The Blues, who had had been the surprise sensation of the regular season, had finished second overall in large part due to the standout goaltending of Mike Liut. Their impressive scoring attack was led by 104-point man Bernie Federko and Wayne Babych, who had quietly fired home 54 goals.

Despite the teams' huge difference in points, there was hope for Pittsburgh fans. The Blues had looked decidedly average down the stretch, going 4–5–3 over their last 12. Eddie Johnston was well-acquainted with his opponent, having swept the Blues the previous year as coach of the Black Hawks. The Penguins had nothing to lose and headed to St. Louis for the series opener feeling loose and relaxed.

Game one followed the expected script with the Blues winning 4–2 in a tight affair that was only sealed with an empty-net goal with one second left. Millen was outstanding, keeping the Pens alive in the face of a 48-shot barrage. The Penguins gave him some more support in game two, riding a four-goal second period outburst to a 6–4 win. Johnston's addition of rookie Mike Bullard to the lineup paid off, as the young gun's two assists sparked the middle-frame goal-fest. The crafty coaching move seemed to take the Blues by surprise.

"They didn't key on me at all," Bullard said. "They pretty much let me do what I wanted."[18]

Before a raucous game three Pittsburgh crowd that began cheering 45 minutes before the puck even dropped, Blues future Hall of Famer Bernie Federko spoiled the party by scoring the go-ahead goal with 4:06 left to give St. Louis a 5–4 win.

Things weren't looking good early in Game 4 when the Blues jumped out to a 2–0 lead. But the Pens weren't ready to start golfing yet.

"We came out flat in the first period but we didn't get our heads down. We just said, 'Let's get it together,'" Carlyle told the *Pittsburgh Press*.[19]

They fought back to tie the game and then pulled ahead on Carlyle's shorthanded blast halfway through the second period. Bullard continued his strong play by scoring the eventual game-winner 44 seconds into the third, taking a George Ferguson pass from the corner and banging a short three-footer past Liut. The Pens won 6–3 and were headed back to St. Louis for a fifth and deciding game.

In a steamy Checkerdome arena, the Penguins twice grabbed a one-goal lead but each time were unable to maintain it. Trailing 3–2 with less than 10 minutes to play, Paul Baxter carried the puck deep into the Blues zone and patiently held on to it as defenseman Ed Kea sprawled to knock it off his stick. Baxter, backed into the corner, sent a seeing-eye pass into the slot that Rod Schutt fired toward Liut, who made a spectacular skate save. The puck was loose, however, and Greg Malone backhanded it off the right post and in to tie things at three. With no further scoring in the third, the game headed to a winner-take-all overtime.

Throughout the series, Eddie Johnston had been doing his best to play with the mind of Liut by claiming he had seen a flaw in the goaltender's game. He would not, however, say exactly what it was. "When will I reveal the weakness? When I'm out of coaching," he said after game two.[20]

"Johnston does things like that in the playoffs," said Liut. "I don't know who made him the wizard." Added Blues coach Red Berenson: "They're scared to death of Liut. They'd like to break him psychologically."[21]

EJ must have been onto something because Liut was hardly playing up to the form he had displayed all season long, giving up a whopping 16 goals in games two through four. Unfortunately for the Penguins, though, as overtime began, it appeared Liut had worked out whatever flaw Johnston claimed to have noticed. After the teams played each other evenly for the first 10 minutes of the extra frame, the Penguins began to take over. Showing a bit more jump than the Blues, they dominated play and generated numerous scoring chances. The most glorious came with about four minutes to play. St. Louis defenseman Jack Brownschidle batted a Carlyle pass out of the air at center ice but it caromed toward his own blue line and on to Rick Kehoe's stick. Kehoe pushed it ahead to Mark Johnson, who was charging full-speed up the middle. Johnson split the Blues' defense and came in on a breakaway. "Magic," as his teammates called him, deked left, but the lanky Liut stayed with him all the way and stoned him. The play, however, didn't end there. Johnson picked up the rebound at the side of the net and fired it out to Gardner, who one-timed the puck inches wide of the right post.

The drama continued all the way into a second overtime. A St. Louis shot off the stick of Tony Currie beat Millen but clanged off the post. At the other end, Liut kept up his brick wall-like play, stopping five unanswered Penguin shots.

Just past the five-minute mark, with the Penguins having taken the game's last 12 shots, St. Louis's Rick LaPointe carried the puck deep into Penguin territory. Before being checked by Mario Faubert, he pushed the puck loose along the boards. Blues center Mike Zuke, who had played little during the game and had some fresh jump in his skates, got to it first. Randy Carlyle moved from the low slot to try to check him, but Zuke quickly flipped it out to an unguarded Mike Crombeen stationed in front of the net. As Carlyle looked over his shoulder, Crombeen one-timed a shot past Millen into the Pittsburgh net. The crowd erupted as the exhausted Penguins looked on in disbelief. Crombeen, a light-scoring right winger, had been sick all day and had been used sparingly throughout the game, but his fresh legs earned him more ice time as the battle dragged on.

Millen, who had faced 52 shots, lay on the ice for a good 15 seconds while the Blues celebrated beside his crease. "I would have played all night, all week," Millen said afterward. "I wasn't even thinking about being tired."[22]

"We spilled a lot of blood and guts out there," said a disappointed Carlyle.[23]

Both teams seemed to realize they'd just played a classic and weren't afraid to praise their opponents.

"This game will stick out in my mind for a long, long time because of the heart everybody showed. I'm including their guys, too," said Malone.[24]

"Those guys played great hockey," the Blues' Wayne Babych said, adding that Millen was "incredible."[25]

Back in his Civic Arena office a day later, Johnston was asked what the flaw he'd seen in Liut's game was. He revealed that the netminder had uncharacteristically been playing further back in his net until he broke the habit early in the third period of the deciding game.

"I wish he hadn't," said Johnston, "but he did, and in the overtime you could see what a tremendous difference it made."[26]

Nevertheless, Johnston later added, "the people of Pittsburgh should be very proud of this hockey club. I really felt we should have won it."[27]

Some of the sting of such a heartbreaking loss was offset at the NHL Awards a few weeks later, when Carlyle captured the Norris Trophy and Kehoe took home the Lady Byng. They were the first major individual league trophies ever captured by Penguin players and the first of any kind since Lowell MacDonald won the Masterton in 1973. Carlyle set another Penguin precedent when he was named to the NHL First All-Star Team.

Winning the Lady Byng "was an honor," Kehoe said, "because there were some pretty good players up for the award." He added that three factors combined to help he and Carlyle win the trophies. "It was our performance, naturally, but also EJ was promoting us. He had the connections with the media. Randy and I had also played in Toronto. That exposure was probably another thing that might've helped us." After all, he added, "Pittsburgh wasn't in the spotlight at the time. It wasn't like a lot of people were tuning in to watch the Penguins play."[28]

Things seemed to be looking up for the Pens on the ice, and off it, too: owner Edward DeBartolo had managed to secure his long sought-after lease of the Civic Arena, putting the franchise on its most solid footing ever.

"We're no longer an endangered species," Carlyle said later that year. "We know we're here to stay. And now it's up to us to get out there and play."[29]

17

One Bounce Short:
1981–82

The Penguins were on the move to start the 1981–82 season—not to another city, as had so often been rumored, but to a new division, as part of the NHL's long-discussed realignment. The teams were now grouped by geography in an effort to build or intensify seemingly natural rivalries. The Pens were placed in the Patrick Division, along with a formidable group of foes that included the Flyers, the two-time Stanley Cup champion Islanders, the always-contending Rangers and the ever-improving Capitals. Pittsburgh would get to know these clubs intimately, what with eight regular-season meetings with each now a part of their schedule. The top four teams of each division would make the playoffs and battle it out amongst themselves for the first two rounds. Any road to Stanley Cup glory for the Penguins, therefore, would now undoubtedly have to go through either Philly or Long Island.

If that didn't seem like a big enough challenge, the Pens learned early in the off-season that they'd have to make their way in the world without their starting goaltender from a season ago. Free agent Greg Millen, who had captured the hearts of Penguin fans with his acrobatic puckstopping and constant bopping to the arena organ music during stoppages, signed a deal with the Hartford Whalers in June worth $160,000 a year—four times as much as he had made the year just ended—to run three years and an option year. There was also a $75,000 signing bonus.

In 1980–81, Millen had played out his option year with the expectation that he'd eventually ink a new deal with Pittsburgh. But negotiations stalled, and by the time Mike Crombeen had ended the Pens' season in mid–April, the two sides had still not reached an agreement. Millen was reportedly upset that GM Baz Bastien refused to remove a clause that stipulated if Millen was ever sent down to the minors, he would earn a minor-league salary. When things got particularly frosty in early June, Paul Martha was brought in to replace Bastien at the negotiating table across from Millen's agent, but the effort was too little, too late. Millen opted for the Hartford offer, leaving the Penguins staring down another year of uncertainty in the crease.

Just before losing Millen, the Pens signed 27-year-old goaltender Michel Dion, whom Johnston had wanted to sign the year before. Dion had flashed moments of brilliance throughout his seven-year career that included stops with the Indianapolis Racers and Cincinnati Stingers of the WHA as well as Quebec and, most recently, Winnipeg in the NHL. But he was also a bit of a wildcard, sometimes letting his emotions get the better of him. His tenure with the Nordiques came to a dramatic conclusion during a game in December 1980 against the Bruins at Le Colisee. After giving up a weak goal on a shot from far out, the home fans started getting

Michel Dion arrived in Pittsburgh in 1981 and, with help from coach Eddie Johnston, a former goalie himself, regained his confidence and grabbed the Penguins' starting job (courtesy Ron Kerrigan).

on him. Dion grew increasingly agitated and distracted. When he gave up a second bad goal off a long shot, he stormed off the ice, throwing off various pieces of his equipment as he went. Ex-Pen Michel Plasse had to finish the game. The Nords put Dion on waivers eight days later and eventually traded him to Winnipeg for cash in February 1981.

Dion later said he regretted the incident, wishing it had never happened. He came to the Penguins with a smile on his face and a seemingly renewed focus. It would now be up to the old veteran of the nets, Eddie Johnston, to help take his game to a higher level. EJ had noted that Dion tended to give up a lot of goals off long shots, so he immediately sent him to an optometrist. Sure enough, it was discovered that Dion had an issue with depth perception and was fitted for contact lenses that would rectify the problem.

Johnston also noticed Dion moved around more than he had to in the crease. He worked with him on his footwork and helped get him more settled, literally, in the nets. By the time training camp ended, Dion had secured the starting job, easily outshining youngsters Nick Ricci and Paul Harrison. His

Michel Dion repels a Hartford Whalers attack during a 3–3 tie at the Igloo, February 10, 1982. In the first round of the playoffs that year, Dion's outstanding play helped the Penguins nearly upset the defending Stanley Cup champion New York Islanders (courtesy Ron Kerrigan).

strong play carried into the regular season and was the main reason behind the club's solid start.

Early on, the Pens were keeping up with the big boys in their new division, sitting second in the Patrick by late November, just ahead of the Flyers and just behind the Islanders. A 2–1 win at home against Montreal in front of a rare mid-week sellout crowd on November 26 gave the Penguins a 7–1–2 record in their previous 10 games and an overall mark of 11–8–4—which equated to the best start in team history. Attendance was up, with fans being drawn to the Igloo in large part by their new darling Dion, who heard the chants of "Dee-YON, Dee-YON" loud and clear. It seemed he'd finally found a home in the hockey world.

"I've never had such positive feelings about a team in my life. Playing for the Penguins beats 'em all."[1]

His club was also playing some of the toughest hockey of their history. Winger Gary Rissling was short on talent but big on getting under opponents'

Former Penguin 50-goal-scorer Pierre Larouche looks to score on his old team as a member of the Hartford Whalers, 1982 (courtesy Ron Kerrigan).

skin. Sporting a mug that only a mother could love, Rissling brought an agitator element to the Pens, the quality of which hadn't been seen since the days of Eddie Shack.

Newcomer Pat Boutette—yet another ex-Maple Leaf now wearing a Penguin uniform—took up residence on the Rick Kehoe-Paul Gardner line in the spot vacated by the now-retired Ross Lonsberry, and was proving to be every bit as tough as his predecessor.

"He's not scared of a thing in any building around the league," said Gardner. "He's good for Rick and me because if somebody tries to push us around, he steps right in and makes the other guys back off."[2] It also didn't hurt that Boutette could score, racking up six goals and 14 assists in the season's first two months, good for fourth in team scoring.

On defense, there was the hulking Paul Baxter who, after two months of the season, led the league in penalty minutes with 134. Pat Price was third with 117. The Pens' performance during a visit to Philadelphia in late October served notice to the league that they were not going to be pushed around. Rissling came out like a cannonball, hitting everything in sight and racking up 14 penalty minutes before the game was even seven minutes old. When

Baxter slugged Behn Wilson after a Mel Bridgman goal that gave the Flyers a 2–1 lead, a brawl erupted that resulted in 72 total penalty minutes. When the game-slash-boxing-card was finally finished, referee Denis Morel had dished out a whopping 222 penalty minutes combined. They Flyers emerged with a 6–4 win—Pittsburgh's 17th straight visit to the Spectrum without a win—but also a realization that the Penguins were no longer pushovers. Johnston was mightily pleased.

"I said before, we aren't going to be intimidated by this club any longer. I thought the effort by my club tonight was terrific."[3]

Pat Price summed up the Pens' new pugilistic identity in the locker room: "I guess everybody figures the Pittsburgh Penguins are doormats. Our reputation has been that way, I guess, but after tonight it won't be."[4]

On December 3, Penguin fans perusing their morning papers read about yet another triumph for their team—this time a solid 4–2 beating of the visiting Winnipeg Jets. They read of the hustle displayed by every player for all 60 minutes, and the fortress-like goaltending of Dion. Turning to the NHL standings, they saw their club sitting at 13–8–4, only two points behind the Islanders for first place in the Patrick Division, and three points up on the third-place Flyers. Times were indeed good for the Pittsburgh Penguins. But any fan who had followed the club for any stretch of time over their 15-year history, chock full as it was with disappointments and letdowns, knew that to grow optimistic about the Pens' future was to do so at their own peril. And sure enough, following that Winnipeg win, the 1981–82 edition stayed true to historic Penguin form.

For no apparent reason, the forwards stopped forechecking. The defensemen began giving the puck away in their own zone with alarming regularity. Michel Dion was knocked out of the lineup for three weeks with a pulled hamstring just before Christmas and struggled to regain his elite-level form after he returned. To make things even more frustrating, the Penguins would often play one period of dedicated, spirited hockey and then take the other two completely off. Many times, they'd play fast and loose, thinking they could win by getting into shootouts.

"We just don't have enough scorers or marksmen or enough speed to play that way," said Johnston. "We have to do what we do best, and that's grind it out, check by check, and make a few breaks along the way."[5]

That style wasn't displayed enough to stop the Penguins from sliding further down the Patrick standings. Veterans such as Greg Malone weren't producing. Carlyle's game had slipped from his heady Norris Trophy-winning form of a year earlier. And many of the team's rookies, including defensemen Mark Chorney and Tony Feltrin and forwards Doug Shedden and Steve Gatzos simply weren't ready for the big time and were shuffled between Pittsburgh and its new farm team in Erie, Pennsylvania.

Things hit rock-bottom February 3 at the Igloo when the Pens lost to Minnesota 9–6, blowing leads of two and three goals and at one point surrendering six consecutive markers. "That was disgraceful, absolutely disgraceful," said Johnston, who for the first time since coming to Pittsburgh heard boos from the hometown fans (all 7,271 of them). "We made a lot of stupid mistakes and let things get out of hand."[6]

To add injury to insult, the Pens were hit hard by the loss of some top players during this sobering stretch. Hard-shooting defenseman and power play specialist Mario Faubert suffered a season-ending broken leg in December and leading scorer Paul Gardner was knocked out of the lineup (literally) when he was sucker-punched by Winnipeg's Jimmy Mann January 14, resulting in a broken jaw that had to be wired shut for weeks. The Pens' loss that night knocked them into fourth place in the Patrick, where they would stay for the rest of the year. They'd finish with 75 points, a whopping 43 behind their first-round playoff opponent, the league-leading, two-time Stanley Cup champion Islanders.

Like the two previous years, the Pens headed into their first-round se-

The Penguins net once again under siege during the 1982–83 season. Embarking on a rebuild that year, the Pens surrendered a whopping 394 goals (courtesy Ron Kerrigan).

ries as massive underdogs. The Islanders boasted a star-studded lineup that included all-star forwards Mike Bossy and Bryan Trottier, perhaps the game's best defenseman in Denis Potvin, and "Battlin'" Billy Smith in goal, who stopped pucks as effectively as he kept his crease clean of opposing players with vicious hacks and slashes. New York was also deep with experienced warriors who knew what it took to win, like Bob Nystrom, John Tonelli and Clark Gillies. They'd racked up an incredible 118 points during the season, and during one stretch put together a new NHL record 15-game winning streak. They were particularly dominant on home ice, not having lost at the Nassau Coliseum since December 29, going 21–0–2. To advance, the Penguins would somehow have to take three of five games from this monster, including at least one game on Islander ice.

The task seemed impossible. In the face of such a formidable foe, most of the hockey world wondered why Pittsburgh should even bother showing up. The Penguins, however, could find motivation in a few rays of hope poking through the gloom. They were the club that ended New York's record winning streak, pulling out a 4–3 win on February 21 on a pair of third-period Mike Bullard goals. They also knew that if they could induce the Islanders into taking penalties they'd be able to trot out the league's most productive power play. Using a pick-play style that Johnston had learned from basketball's Boston Celtics coach Tommy Heiansohn during his days as a player with the Bruins, the Pens had set a new NHL record with 99 power play tallies.

"There were certain ways you could pick," remembered Rick Kehoe. "It wasn't like you just picked the guy off. EJ taught us how to turn your back to [an opponent] and let him run into you so it wasn't like you were standing there waiting for him."[7]

The Pesky Penguins could also hang their hat on an impressive 7–2 drubbing of the Islanders in the final game of the season. That night, they were in the face of the Islanders from the opening faceoff, hitting them hard, knocking them off their game, and goading them into stupid penalties which led to four power play goals. Former Islander Pat Price knew better than anyone that in the upcoming battle, it would take three similar efforts to simply give his team a chance of getting past such a juggernaut.

"We have to make them doubt themselves, and that's going to take total dedication and total sacrifice from everybody."[8]

Things got off to a bad start for the Pens even before the first puck was dropped when Mother Nature dropped a freak April snowstorm in the New York area the day before game one, making it impossible for them to fly in on that day as scheduled. Instead, they left Pittsburgh the morning of gameday and only arrived at their hotel at noon, leaving no time for their scheduled morning skate. They came out sluggish in the first period and the Islanders pounced. Goals by Bossy, Gillies and Trottier gave New York a 3–1 lead after 20 minutes. They added three more in the second and coasted to an 8–1 demolition.

"We were always a step behind," said Michel Dion. "I hate alibis, but I think the fact that we got up at seven this morning and spent five hours traveling up here to Long Island had a lot to do with it."[9]

Expressing disappointment at his forwards' lack of jump, Johnston planned to "try some different things in the second game and maybe we'll get back to a more physical style of play."[10]

The Penguins did just that as game two got underway the next night. They clogged up the middle of the rink and took the play to the Islanders, generating a number of great scoring chances. There were only two problems. First, Billy Smith showed why he was one of the finest goalkeepers of the day, making a number of spectacular saves to frustrate the Penguin shooters. Second, the more determined effort only lasted for the game's first eight minutes. Mike Bossy again opened the scoring, notching a power play goal at 7:57. Then, a couple of costly miscues by Pen defenders Paul Baxter, who fanned on a clearing attempt in the crease, and Pat Price, who mishandled a Randy Boyd pass, led to two more Islander tallies. When the buzzer sounded to end the first period, New York had built a commanding 4–0 lead.

By the end of the second, in which the Pittsburgh forwards suddenly forgot how to back-check and the Islander forwards cruised unmolested in on Dion time and again, the score was an embarrassing 6–1. The final tally read Islanders 7, Penguins 2. Pittsburgh departed Long Island battered, bruised and bewildered. They had so far failed to win even a period, let alone a game. The *coup de grace* and an ignominious end to the Penguins' season now seemed to be a mere formality.

The players, fans and everyone connected with the team were upset with their showing in New York, but perhaps no one more so than team owner Edward DeBartolo, Sr. A champion in the business world, he apparently could not stomach watching his hockey team play like chumps. The day between games two and three, DeBartolo issued a terse statement from his empire's headquarters in Youngstown, Ohio, in which he offered a refund to anyone who had bought a ticket for the third game at the Civic Arena.

The bizarre offer caught everyone off-guard, including Johnston.

"He's the boss and he has every right to make that statement."[11] But, the coach added, "we are playing the best team in hockey and there was enough pressure on us by being down two games to none, but this will make things even rougher on us."[12]

The players certainly didn't appreciate the statement. Said defenseman and vocal leader Pat Price later, "We were pretty upset at that statement. We're a pretty proud bunch of guys."[13]

The refund offer was yet another strange chapter in the Penguins' thus-far tortured history. Traditionally, when the team had laid the kind of eggs they had on Long Island, Pittsburgh fans would express their disappointment by staying away from their games. Now, the owner himself was going to take a pass—a rarity in professional sports, to be sure. Rather than join DeBartolo in his game-three boycott, the fans used it as a rallying cry for their struggling team. By game time, only about 200 tickets were submitted for refund, all of which were quickly gobbled up by other fans. A crowd of 14,310—about 1,000 more than had been expected—came out and gave the Penguins a roaring standing ovation when they emerged for the warmup.

Pittsburgh Post-Gazette columnist Dan Donovan accurately compared the fans to the Penguins' big brothers, in that they can scold their hockey team, but watch out if anybody else does. "The fans … were saying, in effect, no matter who owns the team, this is the fans' hockey team. We'll decide who to boo."[14]

The Pens gave none of their fans a reason to boo on this night. They came out skating, shooting and checking and didn't let up as they had in game two. The Islanders played just as well, but both Billy Smith and Michel Dion stopped almost everything that came their way, often with acrobatic and unbelievable saves. Each netminder allowed only one goal through regulation, Smith having made 33 saves to Dion's 30.

Looking down the Penguin lineup as overtime loomed, fans wondering who might play the hero for their team could be forgiven for discounting Rick Kehoe. Despite being a prolific regular-season scorer, Kehoe had managed a grand total of two markers in 32 post-season games. Just before the five-minute mark, though, Kehoe had a chance to make everyone forget about that underwhelming statistic. Taking a pass from Pat Boutette along the right boards in the Islander zone, Kehoe carried the puck deeper toward the corner. After considering a pass back to Boutette, who had ventured in front of Smith, Kehoe decided to rip a sharp-angle shot as hard as he could at the net. Smith, distracted by Boutette enough to take his stick off the ice, felt the shot hit his skate. It caromed into the net, causing the Igloo to explode in celebration and the Penguins to cascade over the boards to mob Kehoe.

Fortunately for the Penguins, game four would be played the very next night, giving them no time to come down from the high of their dramatic win. As in game three, the Isles jumped out to a 1–0 lead, but a 40-foot slapshot off the stick of Andre St. Laurent at 12:44 tied things at one. Paul Gardner knocked in his first of the playoffs at 14:13 to give the Pens the lead after one period.

Playing at home gave Johnston the advantage of having the final line change, and he used it constantly to send out his checking line of St. Laurent, Kevin McLelland and Rod Schutt against the Isles' top line centered by Bryan Trottier. Not only did they shut "Trotts" down for the second night in a row, they also contributed at the other end, with St. Laurent notching his second goal to put the Pens up 4–1 in the second, and Schutt adding an additional insurance marker late in the third to make the final 5–2. Incredibly, the Penguins had come back from the brink and evened the series.

"Who would have ever thought that we'd be two-and-two with the Islanders?" asked a smiling Johnston in his cramped office as the sound of the lingering fans chanting Dion's name wafted into the jubilant Pens' dressing room.[15]

Dion basked in the cheers and his team's turnaround as reporters surrounded him in his stall. "There were a lot of things said about us [after game two] and a lot of people, I guess, threw in the towel. But we sucked up our guts and said, 'Let's show everybody we can play.'"[16]

Bob Grove was a young Penguins beat reporter working for the *Washington Observer-Reporter* at the time. Game four "was a little shocking because there was not much response from the Cup champs," he remembered. "It was a 5–2 game and the Penguins were every bit 5–2 winners. If you're the Islanders, you can rationalize losing game three. It was very tight. But you expect a big pushback from them in the next game, and it never happened."[17]

At their last practice before heading back to New York, the Penguins were a loose bunch. "We're going up there relaxed and ready to have some fun," said Dion. "All the pressure right now is on the Islanders." The goaltender couldn't help but think about what things would be like if they succeeded in pulling off their own miracle on ice. "It'll be an unbelievable night for every guy on this team and for this whole franchise."[18]

Penguins fans who remembered the heartbreaking playoff loss to the Islanders in 1975, when New York snatched the series away from the Pens by winning four straight after Pittsburgh had led the series 3–0, also couldn't help but think about how sweet this bit of revenge would be. Indeed, blowing this series would no doubt hurt the Isles even more than the 1975 loss did the Pens. That matchup was relatively even, and no one was realistically expecting Pittsburgh to win the Stanley Cup. The 1982 Islanders, by comparison, came into the series as heavy favorites and were expected to win yet another championship. Penguin fans could practically taste the delight of such a victory. But they also knew that it would have to be won in an arena where their opponent—incredibly—had not lost a single game to a Patrick Division foe all year. Many Islanders, however, knew that such a feat didn't count for anything now.

"I'm scared to death. It's do or die," admitted John Tonelli.

"It's scary," added Bob Bourne. "The Penguins have everybody going and we haven't had the whole team going, but I feel we can regroup."[19]

The Islanders appeared to be doing just that in the early going, outplaying the Penguins in the first period and outshooting them 13–4. Dion, however, turned everything away and the frame ended scoreless. The tension continued into the second until Bob Nystrom, returning from two weeks off with a pulled groin, put the Isles up 1–0 when he fired a loose puck in the crease by Dion. Only 43 seconds later, however, Kevin McClelland deflected Greg Hotham's point shot off a faceoff past Smith to tie things at one. Five minutes later, Mike Bullard received a pass at full speed from Rick MacLeish, entered the Islander zone, blew past defenseman Mike McEwan, deftly deked Smith to the left, pulled the puck back to his right, and backhanded it into the open cage. Penguins 2, Islanders 1.

Murmurs of disbelief spread through the Nassau Coliseum crowd. The game was going seriously off-script. Disbelief turned to outright horror three minutes later when Paul Gardner stole the puck from Ken Morrow deep in the Islanders zone and fed the puck back to Carlyle, who one-timed a blistering slap shot over Smith's shoulder, giving the Penguins a 3–1 lead. The buzzer sounded, and incredibly, the Penguins were only 20 minutes away from one of hockey's biggest-ever upsets.

The Islanders were hardly ready to give up, however. They kept skating and shooting, firing 16 times at the Penguin goal in the first 14 minutes of the third, only to have Dion stop each one.

"With about eight minutes to go, the Nassau Coliseum was completely quiet," remembered Grove. "You talk about a fan base that was shocked. They sat there and they watched their team losing to the Pittsburgh Penguins and they were in complete disbelief. The Penguins were in firm control. Michel Dion was playing the game of his life."[20]

There were still those eight minutes to play, though. A hooking call on Carlyle with 7:04 left gave the Islanders a power play. To give his top unit a breather, New York coach Al Arbour replaced Smith with backup Roland Melanson, which meant Melanson could be warmed up for a few minutes before play would resume. Melanson was then quickly exchanged back for Smith. The ploy must have helped, because with time winding down in the penalty, McEwan slammed a Mike Bossy rebound into a half-empty net to make the score 3–2.

The Pens nursed their slim lead until, with just over two minutes remaining, Carlyle went into the left corner of his own zone to retrieve a routine shoot-in. There was nothing routine, though, about the bad hop the puck took over his stick. The disc went right on to the blade of an onrushing John Tonelli, who fired it past a surprised Dion to tie things at three. Time ran out on the period and, for the second year in a row, Pittsburgh was going to overtime in the deciding game of a first-round series.

After four minutes of tense hockey, Bullard found some open ice at center and sped in on a two-on-one with MacLeish. Showing the poise of a veteran, Bullard faked a shot, causing defenseman Ken Morrow to go down.

Bullard sidestepped him and moved into the slot, where he let a hard, point-blank wrist shot go. As the crowd held its breath, Smith came up with a clutch save to keep the Islanders alive.

Two minutes later, Tonelli broke in on Dion on a partial breakaway. Defenseman Paul Baxter took him out, sending the puck behind the net. Tonelli got to his feet and reached the puck first, sending it out to Bob Nystrom in front. Randy Carlyle checked him off the puck, but the puck sat there long enough for Tonelli to move in and put it past Dion, ending the game and the Penguins' dream of taking out the defending champions.

Sudden death indeed.

As the Islanders mobbed Tonelli and the Coliseum erupted in joy and relief, the stunned Penguins could only stand in exhaustion and disbelief. In a rare show of post-game sportsmanship, Billy Smith—who usually refused to join the customary post-series handshake line—came down the ice to console Dion, who had won the respect and admiration of the Islanders and the entire hockey world with his performance in the series.

"If the Penguins had've been able to hold on for another six minutes," Grove said, "it would have been one of the biggest playoff upsets in NHL history, at that time for sure and I think today it would still stand as one of the more improbable results. But I just wasn't to be."[21]

Said Dion after the game, "Everyone, deep down, is disappointed because we know we should have won." But, he added, "everyone on this team has a joy we can't explain. Because we almost beat the Stanley Cup champions. Everyone on this team can walk with his head up. This is something nobody can take away from us."[22]

The Islanders would go on to win their third consecutive Stanley Cup, losing only two more games along the way. The Penguins would head into the offseason knowing they'd won some new respect and wondering if they'd be able to carry the momentum of their inspired performance into the next season.

PART FIVE

Bottoming Out
(1982–83 Through 1983–84)

18

Paying the Piper: 1982–83

Six games into the 1982–83 season, Edward J. DeBartolo Sr.'s hockey team sported a sorry record of one win, four losses and one tie—and he wanted to know why. Accordingly, he summoned the Penguin braintrust to his Youngstown, Ohio, headquarters to get an explanation, and to solicit opinions on how to fix things. Unanimously, Paul Martha, Baz Bastien and Eddie Johnston told him the only way to build a winner was to go with their youth. DeBartolo looked at his hired hands and, like the Godfather granting his approval to Michael Corleone, replied, "Then that's the way we're going to go."[1]

Finally, after 15 years of avoiding the unavoidable reality that the surest path to building a winning team is one paved with draft picks and patience, the Pittsburgh Penguins were going to embark on a youth movement—and all the growing pains such a trip entails. The Flyers and Islanders had done it, with resounding Stanley Cup-winning success. The Sabres had done it too, establishing themselves as one of the most respected teams in the league.

Now, it was the Penguins' turn. It was time to pay the piper. Time to take a deep breath and absorb the inevitable pain that results from trade after trade after trade of high draft picks for aging stars with but a year or two of good hockey left in their skates. Gone were such greybeards as Ron Stackhouse (retired), George Ferguson (traded to Minnesota) and Gregg Sheppard (contract bought out).

By mid–November, however, with the Penguins owning a dismal 5–11–2 record and sitting dead last in goals against with 88 in only 18 games, fans and the media began to wonder whether the kids the Pens were committing to were the right ones. Philadelphia had built around young superstar Bobby Clarke and a supporting cast that featured the likes of Rick MacLeish and Bill Barber. The Islanders had grown with Bryan Trottier, Denis Potvin and

Mike Bossy, while the Sabres had the great Gilbert Perreault and his French Connection linemates, Rick Martin and René Robert.

Simply put, there were no Bobby Clarkes or Bryan Trottiers on the 1982–83 Penguins roster. Since 1976, the franchise had had a grand total of three first-round draft picks. The future of the franchise would instead depend on a few "scraps" that had still been on the table during the later rounds of those drafts. This cast included, from 1980, forward Kevin McClelland and defenseman Tony Feltrin, both picked in the fourth round; forward Doug Shedden (fifth round); forward Pat Graham (sixth round); from 1981, forward Steve Gatzos (second round); defenseman Rod Buskas (sixth round); forward Dave Hannan (tenth round); and from 1982, forward Tim Hrynewich (second round).

Apart from the jewel in the crown—Mike Bullard, drafted ninth overall in 1980 and coming off a 36-goal effort in his first full NHL season—any experienced hockey observer would have to know that the Penguins would be lucky to develop a few solid second-, third- or fourth-line players out of this

Montreal's Guy Lafleur dashes up ice during a game at the Igloo. The Penguins usually had a tough time against Lafleur and the Canadiens, winning only 13 games against them in their first 15 seasons (courtesy Ron Kerrigan).

lot. But it was the hand the Penguins had dealt themselves, and it was what they'd have to play. Compounding the Pens' early-season woes was the absence of Bullard, who missed the first 20 games while recovering from a bout of mononucleosis, which he contracted during the summer.

Amongst the fans, "There was just a complete sense of hopelessness," recalled Pens beat reporter Bob Grove. "If [the Penguins] were rebuilding in a sensible way, I think some of the fans could have lived with the losing on the ice because, 'Hey, the future's coming.'" Had the team not traded away so many first-round picks, they would have been able to build around young players who would have been in the league for four or five years by that point. "But there was none of that. So there was a hopelessness on the ice and there was just not a lot of confidence that the Penguins had it figured out how to rebuild the right way."[2]

Nevertheless, a resilient core of Penguin diehards continued to come out. Numbering no more than about 5,000, this group had kept turning up at the Civic Arena, year after year, in the hope that one day, just maybe, these Penguins would start to fly.

Paul Gardner keeps former Penguin Pierre Larouche in check. Gardner's great hands around the net helped him score 98 goals in 207 games with the Pens in the early 1980s (courtesy Ron Kerrigan).

"Win or lose, there weren't many of us, but we would be there no matter what, weekday games or whatever," said long-time season ticket holder Mike Hanczar, who estimated he had been to about 1,000 Penguin games. "We were rabid fans, just waiting for a winner to show up. I think there was always a hope that we would get good. We'd have one good year, and you'd say, 'Well, maybe this is the year they're going to start getting better.' But it never happened."[3]

Bill Peduto, who would one day go on to become mayor of Pittsburgh, grew up a Penguins fan during the 70s. "You have those fans who were in that arena [back then], and there aren't that many. It's a cherished club of people who really were the devout fans during the early years, years that were some of the toughest." Peduto added that, while the losing was hard to take, identifying as a Penguins fan during an era that saw the Steelers and Pirates regularly win championships created a strangely positive feeling amongst those who were part of the resilient, core base—and it's one that endures.

"It was like enjoying the obscure band that few people had heard of. You wore your Penguins gear, you had your tassel hat, you proudly stated that hockey was your sport, and it was a self-identifier which has branded itself on those who were the Penguins fans in the seventies. It's like a tattoo: it doesn't wash out."[4]

As the season ground on, Johnston and Bastien hoped that the goaltending tandem of Dion and Denis Herron, who had been reacquired from the Canadiens in September for his third tour of duty in Pittsburgh, would be a saving grace and, for the most part, the netminders came through. The coach and GM were also counting on the roster's few remaining veterans to steady the youngsters enough to keep the team competitive in the tough Patrick Division. Unfortunately, it was the kids who seemed to be rubbing off on the vets, with many of the older players performing well below the standard that was expected of them. A December 16 4–4 tie at home versus Detroit was typical, with Pat Price's failure to clear the Penguin zone leading to a Red Wing go-ahead goal and Randy Carlyle's ill-advised pinch in the Detroit zone with the Pens up by a goal in the third leading to Mark Osborne's tying goal off a three-on-one rush. It was a mistake that resulted from the Pens captain forgetting a basic hockey principle.

"You don't gamble when you're leading," said Johnston. "You wait for the other team to gamble because they're the ones behind."[5]

Price in particular was slogging through a nightmarish season in which nothing seemed to be going right. By late December he had scored only one goal and was a team-worst minus-17. Price's play drew the ire of both the Igloo boo birds, who adopted him as their chief whipping boy now that Stackhouse was gone, and with Johnston, who was growing increasingly impatient with Price's poor play. Things came to a head between the two after a tough 6–5

Michel Dion makes a kick save while captain Randy Carlyle defends the Penguin crease from a Flyer attack (courtesy Ron Kerrigan).

loss to the Blues at home on December 29. They had a long, loud shouting match in the dressing room, in which Johnston called out Price on a conversation the defenseman had recently had with assistant coach Mike Corrigan. EJ heard that Price had commented that there was no way the Penguins were going to make the playoffs with as many youngsters as they currently had in the lineup. To Johnston, this smacked of a defeatist attitude that had no place in his dressing room. The next day, Price was put on waivers.

Price, however, claimed Corrigan had misrepresented his comments when he relayed them to Johnston. He said he meant that the Penguins would not be able to make the playoffs with the amount of pressure Johnston was putting on all the kids in the lineup. "So, rather than the young guys take the blame, I suggested the pressure be put on the veterans, myself included."[6]

Price and his underachieving play was gone, but so too was one of the team's veteran voices that could help steady the youngsters. The Pens put up a surprising 2–1 win over the Islanders in their first game after the Price fiasco. But it turned out to be just a mirage at the edge of the widest desert of

Penguin hockey ever traversed, where wins were as scarce as water. A 5–1 pasting from the Canadiens the next night marked the first stop on a horrific 18-game winless skid that included a whopping 17 losses and one tie. The Penguins found new ways to lose every night. They were blown out 7–2 in Edmonton. They lost a tight one in Winnipeg when their own Dave Hannan scored the winning goal for the Jets, his attempt to clear a rebound misfiring and trickling past Dion.

Three nights later on home ice, it was a hot Minnesota goalie who did them in. The Penguins stormed the North Star zone throughout the first period, firing 13 shots at Marcus Mattsson, only to have each one of them stopped. The Stars offense eventually woke up in the third, as one goal quickly became two, then three, then four. When the collapse was mercifully ended by the game's final buzzer, the score read 7–0 North Stars.

"In the third period there, everything kind of came down on us and we got into a spot where a lot of guys more or less gave up," said Greg Malone afterward.[7]

With the streak standing at seven games on January 22, the Penguins appeared to be putting an end to it when they charged out to a 3–0 lead against the Quebec Nordiques before one of the larger home crowds of the season, 10,633. But as was so often the case with the 1982–83 Pens, they didn't know what to do with a lead and squandered it in the second half, giving up four Nordique goals on four straight shots, en route to a 7–3 loss.

They tied the club record winless streak at 10 with a 6–2 loss to Washington on home ice, in which they gave up five goals in the first 15 minutes. Desperate for a solution, Paul Martha suggested assistant coach Mike Corrigan take over the in-game coaching duties for a stretch while EJ move to the press box. Johnston was strongly opposed to the idea, and the two worked out a compromise whereby both coaches would work behind the bench.

It didn't help. Two more losses followed, and when they blew a 2–0 lead in New Jersey late in the third by giving up three goals in two minutes and 37 seconds, the Pittsburgh Penguins found themselves alone in the NHL's basement.

The team was losing badly on the ice, but the off-ice numbers were perhaps even worse. As the team fell in the standings, so too did attendances at the Civic Arena. A January 19 game against New Jersey drew only 5,213 diehards, and four fewer came out for a visit by the Capitals a week later. Those who did come out became increasingly bitter and vocal about their local team's sorry performance. Boos, groans and curses were commonplace. The proverbial bag over the head was often seen. As the streak dragged on, fans took up a cynical chant of "We want thir-ty!" a reference to the NHL record of 30 straight games without a win set two seasons earlier by the Winnipeg Jets.

To rookie Troy Loney, the scene in Pittsburgh was not exactly what he had pictured the NHL experience to be.

"My first NHL game, I played in front of 5,000 fans in Pittsburgh. You're in the NHL but it didn't feel like an NHL atmosphere with so few fans in the seats. So in one sense you're honored to be in the NHL, but your expectations might be a little higher. I had come from a junior franchise [Lethbridge Broncos] that was very successful and winning was part of it. And we were losing quite a bit those first few years."[8]

What was playing out was the nightmare scenario previous Pens management teams had done their best to avoid by selling off draft picks for past-their-prime veterans who could help the team stay respectable in the short term. Through it all, however, owner Edward DeBartolo, Sr., maintained that the franchise would not be moving anywhere. The Penguin faithful could at least take solace in knowing their team's owner seemed willing to take it on the financial chin, this year to the tune of a $3.4 million loss.[9]

Five more losses following the New Jersey collapse—in which the Pens surrendered a whopping 33 goals—convinced Johnston to vacate his post behind the bench for a February 12 game against Los Angeles and watch from the Igloo rafters while Corrigan did the coaching all by himself. The switch paid off, with the Penguins coming out on top, 6–4—their first win in 41 days. Both Andre St. Laurent and Peter Lee scored two goals, and rookie goalie Nick Ricci turned in a sparkling 15-save third-period effort to preserve the win.

There would, however, be no big turnaround for the Penguins this season. The winless streak decimated the campaign, leaving them 23 points out of the last Patrick Division playoff spot. The losing continued through February and into March. And just when things seemed like they couldn't get any worse for 82–83 Penguins, their storyline took a truly tragic turn. On the night of March 15, while returning home along a highway just south of the city after attending a banquet hosted by the Pittsburgh chapter of the Professional Hockey Writers Association, General Manager Baz Bastien collided with a motorcycle carrying two people. He then hit the guardrail and suffered a heart attack and a fractured skull. He was pronounced dead after being taken to a local hospital. He was 62. Miraculously, the motorcyclists were not seriously injured. Toxicology tests revealed that Bastien had a blood-alcohol content of 0.27, nearly three times the 0.10 mark that indicated intoxication.

The news hit the Penguin organization hard. Eddie Johnston, who had had a friction-filled relationship with Bastien since joining the organization, sometimes not even being on speaking terms with the GM, had been at the dinner. The two, ironically, had begun to bury the hatchet that night.

"It was the first time in a long time that things were positive, with him and I on the same wavelength. To have something like this happen is terrible."[10]

Michel Dion summed up the players' feelings: "He had such a heart and he cared so much for the game. He was so emotional and into it. And that to us was his expression of love to us."[11]

Paul Martha indicated there would be no announcement made about a successor for Bastien until after the season.

With only eight games left in the most miserable of seasons for the Penguins, the only thing left to decide was which of the league's three bottom-feeders would finish last overall: the Pens, the Devils or the Whalers. After a surprise 3–2 win at home over Montreal in their third-to-last game, the Pens dropped their final two to claim the dubious distinction for the first time in the team's history. Hartford finished with the same total of 45 points, but took the 20th spot by virtue of having one more victory that Pittsburgh.

"This is the first time in years I've finished at the bottom and that's not a very nice thought," commented Johnston.[12]

To add insult to injury, the Penguins would not even be able to reap the reward that was automatically accorded the league's worst team at the time: the first overall pick in the NHL entry draft. That's because they had traded it to Minnesota back in October for the North Stars' first-round pick as part of the George Ferguson deal. Instead of having the opportunity to select a gem like Pat LaFontaine, Steve Yzerman or Cam Neely, the Pens would be left to make their first pick way down at spot number 15. It was the final punch to the gut the Penguins would have to endure in a season that had left them more beat up than any other in their less-than-glorious history. And things weren't looking any better for the season ahead.

19

The Mario Miracle:
1983–84

The Penguins made Eddie Johnston their GM shortly after the 1983–84 season ended, but he wasn't their first choice. The DeBartolos had targeted Philadelphia coach Bob McCammon to fill the vacancy left after Baz Bastien's death. The Flyers wanted to make McCammon their own GM, however. McCammon used the Penguins' interest as a bargaining chip and ended up re-signing with Philly in the dual role of coach and GM. Johnston was the only other realistic choice the Pens' management team was considering and they inked him on May 27, 1983.

"I have to admit there were a lot of ups and downs the last few days," Johnston said about management's courtship of McCammon. "I never gave up, though, because I felt in my heart I was the right man for the job."[1]

Johnston was given "complete autonomy" over the team's hockey operations, according to vice-president Paul Martha, which meant it was EJ's decision to either hire a new coach or stay behind the bench himself. Johnston eventually tapped Lou Angotti, a former Penguin player and coach of their AHL Baltimore affiliate the previous year, to take over the head coaching reins. Just as the 45-year-old skipper was set to lead his new charges into training camp, however, tragedy once again hit the Penguin organization. On September 18, Angotti's 21-year-old son Jeffrey was killed in a car crash near Toronto. A stunned Angotti headed north to lay his boy to rest, with Johnston and Randy Carlyle also attending the funeral. A somber group of Penguins continued preparations for the upcoming campaign.

Their coach returned four days later, preaching discipline and a system that emphasized a simple game of hockey, with reckless rushes from the defense a thing of the past. "We're aiming to bring our goals against average down by playing a defensive-oriented game. Last year, we gave up too many goals and didn't have the offense to keep pace."[2]

His players were apparently hard of hearing, because they proceeded to give up at least 40 shots in each of their first four games. They lost them all, by a combined score of 22–8. Angotti's pledge to keep his lines intact for at least a month went out the window before they even played their fifth game. The shuffling did little good. After six outings, Penguin centermen had collectively generated a grand total of zero goals and three assists. In their own end, veteran goalies Michel Dion and Denis Herron were again doing their best each night to keep the dam from bursting, but they could only do so much under such repeated barrages.

By the end of October the Pens were a miserable 3–9–0, with all three victories coming on the road. It wasn't until November 23, in fact, that the team won its first home game—its 12th try on Igloo ice. The 4–1 win over the even more inept New Jersey Devils provided a narrow ray of hope that the season would turn around.

"Now the [winless-at-home] monkey is off our back, and I think you'll see us put together some kind of a winning streak before long. You can't do that when you don't win at home," said winger Mark Taylor, acquired in a multi-player deal with Philadelphia that saw speedy center Ron Flockhart also join the Pens.[3]

The Penguins did put together a streak, but it wasn't of the winning variety. Following the New Jersey win, they went winless in their next seven games. After squeaking out a 3–2 victory over Hartford on December 13 to momentarily stop the bleeding, the Penguins endured another five-game winless skid that included a disastrous trip through New York, where they were blown out 11–3 by the still-champion Islanders and 6–1 by the Rangers the following night. To provide extra help in keeping Angotti and Johnston up at night, Denis Herron had to leave the Islander game with a pinched nerve in his back. Michel Dion came in and gave up the last eight goals, clearly rattling the emotional goaltender's fragile psyche. "I spent the last three weeks building up my confidence. I just hope that tonight doesn't destroy it," he said after the game. "If I struggle all year restoring my confidence and can't get it back, we're in trouble."[4]

Sadly, the team was in trouble before the season's first puck dropped. One look at the roster would show that this miserable struggle they were enduring came as no surprise. The quick-strike approach over the years of trading draft picks for aging stars was still having its disastrous effect. Most of the faded stars who had kept the Penguins competitive in the late 70s and early 80s were now long gone, replaced largely by a squad of inexperienced youngsters who, on a team with more depth, would be spending another year or two in the minors until they were ready to make a successful jump to the NHL. The roster was littered with players 21 or under who fit this category: Bob Errey, Tom Thornbury, Marty McSorley, Troy Loney, Norm Schmidt, Phil Bourque and Andy Brickley. These "Boys of Winter," as the Pens' 1983–84 marketing campaign dubbed them, were unreasonably being called upon to form the core of an NHL team. The results were predictably horrendous.

"I can honestly say we were a minor-league team playing in the NHL," reflected Mike Bullard years later in a TSN documentary about the 1983–84 Pens. "We were the comical team of the NHL. We were a joke. Us and New Jersey."[5]

Angotti and Johnston seemed to try every last combination of players they had at their disposal, with troops being called up from the minors and others sent down in a seemingly endless cycle. By Christmas, the Penguins were 15 points out of the final Patrick Division playoff spot. It was abundantly clear that they were not going to make up that kind of ground. The losses kept piling up as the young club sunk deeper into a depressing funk that they couldn't seem to get out of. They lost 17 of 20 contests between the start of January and mid–February, many of them soul-crushing. A 5–4 loss at home against Winnipeg on January 18 was one of the harder ones to bear. Leading 4–2 with only 1:19 left in the third period, they surrendered a screened-shot

Mike Bullard was a rare shining light for the Penguins in 1983–84, scoring 51 goals for the last-place club (courtesy Ron Kerrigan).

goal off the stick of Paul MacLean that made it 4–3. With their goalie pulled, the Jets swarmed the crease of the suddenly panicking Pens. With only two seconds left, defenseman Moe Mantha's slap shot found its way behind Dion for the tying score. In overtime, MacLean broke free on Dion, who tried to poke-check the puck off his stick. He did, but the disc took an unfavorable path through the air and eventually settled in the back of the net.

"That goal was a typical play for me this year," said Dion. "By that I mean, it went wrong, even though it was the right play."[6]

A February 17 blowout loss at Calgary by the score of 10–3, coupled with a New Jersey win against Hartford, landed the Penguins in a familiar spot— the NHL basement. The Penguins' season had gone from bad, to worse, to absolutely horrific, and even their head coach couldn't help but be a realist.

"We honestly don't have much talent," Angotti told the *Pittsburgh Post-Gazette.* "We've got three good goaltenders and six or seven other guys who have the kind of talent and work habits it takes to make it in the NHL. That's not enough. We're trying to rebuild with 19-year-old free agents instead of a lot of first- and second-round picks. Most of the draft choices we've had lately are mid- and late-round picks, and you don't get too many good players there."[7]

Pittsburghers' interest in the Penguins was falling as low as the team was in the standings. Articles about them were becoming harder to find in the local papers. There either were none or they were buried on the back pages of the sports sections. Late in the season, they were booted off the flagship radio station of their small network for two games, their broadcasts replaced with those of the city's new indoor soccer team, the Pittsburgh Spirit.

Nowhere, however, was the city's apathy toward the Penguins more evident than at the team's home games. Three times toward the end of the year, the team drew less than 4,000 fans to

Fan favorite defenseman Paul Baxter kept opponents honest, racking up 851 penalty minutes during his three years in Pittsburgh, 1981–82 to 1983–84 (courtesy Ron Kerrigan).

a game. By mid–March the average was just below 6,900, the second-worst showing of any Penguin club, "bested" only by the 1968–69 club that attracted a mere 6,008 per game. Fans with paper bags over their heads were a frequent sight. There were no sellouts. The closest they came was a turnout of 15,838 on February 22 against Edmonton, but that sudden inflation occurred only because people wanted to get a glimpse of record-breaking scoring sensation Wayne Gretzky. With such sad attendance numbers, owner Edward J. DeBartolo figured to lose a whopping $5 million on the 1983–84 Penguins.

The franchise had hit a wall. They were out of solutions. There were no quick-fix options left to even contemplate. Years of mismanagement had left the cupboard bare of talent. Season after season of losing had left the city's sports fans apathetic and tuned out when it came to the Penguins. They were, quite simply, an embarrassment. Even the most optimistic of those fans who did still care about the team had to wonder just how long DeBartolo would continue to keep his money-losing investment afloat and choose not to sell it to outside interests or simply declare the ailing franchise dead. An indication of just how tenuous a grasp the Penguins had on the cliff from which they were hanging was evident in comments team vice-president Paul Martha gave to the *Pittsburgh Press* regarding DeBartolo's expectations around how long the rebuilding effort would take to produce a contender.

"I don't think there was ever a set time limit, although you never know. If Mr. DeBartolo doesn't like the results, he could pull the plug. The decision is up to him."[8]

The sad, 17-year saga of the Pittsburgh Penguins had reached the hopeless point where, if they were going to keep skating in Pittsburgh, some sort of miracle was going to have to happen. Fortunately for this eternally luckless franchise, such a miracle actually existed, roughly 500 miles northeast of the Civic Arena. It took the form of an 18-year-old scoring superstar who was rewriting the offensive record books of the Quebec Major Junior Hockey League.

This miracle's name was Mario Lemieux.

Standing 6'4" and weighing 200 pounds, Lemieux was a graceful giant who was utterly dominating the QMJHL with pinpoint passes, laser-like shots, silky smooth hands and an indomitable drive to live up to his name: "The Best." All of this super-sized talent and determination had translated into the finest offensive performance the league had ever seen. When it was over, Lemieux had racked up a mind-boggling 133 goals and 149 assists for 282 points—in only 70 games. His goal total broke the QMJHL record of 130 held by his idol, Guy Lafleur, and his points total surpassed the old mark of 251 set by former Penguin Pierre Larouche. Such numbers drew comparisons to Wayne Gretzky, who was rewriting the NHL record books after putting up stratospheric point totals at every stage of his hockey career. Such comparisons were given yet more fuel by Mario's decision to adopt a form of Gretzky's famous number 99, turning it upside down to a 66. Lemieux's size, grace and talent also drew comparisons to Montreal Canadiens legend Jean Beliveau.

"He is like him: tall, a good skater and a good passer," said Claude Carrier, assistant general director of the QMJHL. "But he is really more quick with his hands than Beliveau. Mario has long arms and the best hands I've seen in this league."[9]

In a strong draft year that included the likes of Kirk Muller, Ed Olczyk and Al Iafrate, Lemieux was still easily the consensus number one pick. He was exactly the type of savior the Penguins were in desperate need of to get the franchise off life support and give them a fighting chance of remaining in the Steel City.

"This kid is marketable," observed Bob Perno, Quebec representative for Lemieux's agent, Gus Badali. "When he walks into a room, everyone turns around. He will sell hockey in any city he plays."[10]

The only thing standing in the way of the Penguins and their chance to pick the prodigal Lemieux were the New Jersey Devils. They were the only team other than the Penguins with a chance to finish last overall, a position that at the time guaranteed the cellar-dwelling team the first overall draft pick. As the season moved into its final month, with Pittsburgh and New Jersey tied for last with 32 points, the next-closest clubs, Toronto and Los Angeles, were light years away with 50 points each.

The battle for Lemieux was down to the disastrous Devils and the pathetic Pens. Although neither team would admit to trying to lose in order to secure the top pick, the hockey world quickly came to view this "battle" as a race to the bottom, with the reward being the chance to nab Lemieux and let him fill all their empty seats.

Neither team had to try too hard to lose. The Devils roster was filled with marginal veterans like leading scorer Mel Bridgman and Don Lever, along with some promising young talent that had yet to hit its stride, such as 19-year-olds Pat Verbeek and Ken Daneyko. Veteran goalkeepers Ron Low and Glenn Resch could not make up for a porous defense that, by season's end, had allowed a whopping 350 goals. Things were so bad in the swamps of East Rutherford that Wayne Gretzky famously called the organization a "Mickey Mouse operation" after his Oilers and manhandled the Devils 13–4 on November 19 at the Meadowlands.

Despite the glittering end-of-season prize that was certainly within the Devils' grasp, there is little evidence that the club's management took any measures to help it lose games to get the first overall pick. Under the direction of no-nonsense coach Tom McVie, the Devils played the same style of gritty, talentless and ultimately unsuccessful hockey down the stretch as they'd played all season long. Their winning percentage in the season's final month (0.264) was better than both October (0.100) and November (0.200), and comparable to February (0.269).

Such cannot be said about the Penguins. A series of eyebrow-raising personnel moves by Johnston in the season's final weeks left little doubt in the minds of most hockey observers that the Penguins were flat-out tanking in order to claim Lemieux.

First was the banishing of goalie Roberto Romano to Baltimore on February 24, even though the 21-year-old had looked the sharpest of all three Penguin goalies for weeks, having been in the nets for each of the team's six victories since mid–December. Johnston and Angotti justified the move by claiming that a temporary replacement was needed in Baltimore after Skipjacks' goalie Vincent Tremblay was suspended for three games for being the first player off the bench in a brawl in Hershey. But observers couldn't help but wonder: if the Pens were still interested in winning, why was their top-performing goalie the one chosen for demotion?

Second was the trading of defenseman Randy Carlyle to the Winnipeg Jets on March 5 for no immediate return. The shipping of Carlyle out of town

Randy Carlyle's daring up-ice rushes and fearless defending electrified Penguin fans and earned him the 1980–81 Norris Trophy for top NHL defenseman (courtesy Ron Kerrigan).

was not the issue. The 27-year-old captain had not regained his Norris trophy-winning form of 1980–81 and the fans were getting on him. Carlyle's relationship with management had soured, and it had been rumored for months that he'd be traded for younger talent to feed into the Pens' ongoing youth movement. But by receiving Winnipeg's first-round choice in the upcoming draft and future considerations, the Penguins were conveniently left with a gaping hole on defense, their most circumspect position—which was saying something indeed. That hole would do little to help the team gain any points the rest of the way.

Third, Johnston called up the aforementioned Tremblay from Baltimore, owner of the farm club's worst goals against average. If the intention was to put a team with the best chance of winning on the ice, the choice of Tremblay was one of the worst ones that the GM could have made. The Penguins threw the 24-year-old in net for their last meeting of the season against New Jersey, a "must-lose" affair on March 6 that Devils coach McVie jokingly dubbed the "Lemieux Bowl." Tremblay was burned only 18 seconds in by Paul Gagne and gave up just enough the rest of the way to offset a rare offensive outburst by his teammates and send the Pens to a 6–5 loss. Tremblay would play in three more games, losing them all. The four losses would be his last appearances in the NHL.

Some in the Devils organization began to publicly question the Penguins' will to win. "We're trying to win every game and I hope Pittsburgh is, too," team president Bob Butera said in early March. "I'm not being accusatory, but I think Pittsburgh's talent is better than they're showing."[11]

The Penguins denied the allegations, none more heatedly than Angotti, who called the statement "the most hypocritical thing I've ever heard." Added the livid coach, "We went all out to win the hockey game [on March 6 versus the Devils], even though Butera makes a statement like that."[12]

Many years later, however, a repentant Angotti had dropped the charade of indignity and come clean, admitting that he and Johnston had indeed done their utmost to cause their team to lose in order to land Lemieux.

"There were about 30-plus games left, and Eddie said, 'You know, we have to make a conscious decision as to what we can do, and the only thing we can do is, we gotta get Mario Lemieux.'"[13]

It was a decidedly different outlook in the locker room, where the only thing on the players' minds was winning, said Rick Kehoe. "When you tie up your skates as a player, you're going out there to win. You might not be as talented as the other team, but you're still going out there to win. The only thing that could change that would be management making personnel moves, so they called up different guys or did whatever they were doing. But that's the management end of it, not the players."[14]

Dave Hannan remembered it the same way. "From a player's standpoint, there was never anything said. We were trying to win every game." When a team is out of the playoff picture before the regular season ends, he added, organizations will say, "OK, let's give this guy a little more opportunity because we want to find out if he will be ready to play next year and be a regular part of the team.' Every team does that, but in our minds, we just wanted to go out and win every game."[15]

Reporter Bob Grove saw nothing but pride and determination in the locker room during the season's tough last weeks, with draft picks being the furthest things from their minds. "I don't think any of the players cared one way or the other about any number one pick. This was their professional lives, their professional careers, that were on the line. They weren't very good but that doesn't mean they weren't all trying."[16]

As the season moved into its final two weeks, the Devils threatened to steal the prized pick out from under Johnston's nose by losing their last eight games. The inept Pens, however, were up to the challenge, losing their last six. On March 29, they "clinched" last overall with a 6–4 loss to the Rangers. The first pick, and their potential savior in his 66 jersey, would at last be theirs.

Or would he?

The Penguins left little doubt that they would indeed make Lemieux the first choice in the draft, to be held June 9 in Mario's hometown of Montreal, with Johnston all but confirming it in late March. In the weeks following the end of the regular season, the two sides began contract negotiations. As May turned to June, however, they still hadn't reached an agreement. A key sticking point was the Lemieux camp's insistence on a clause that would guarantee a set amount of bonus money should the Penguins attendance reach 10,000. Johnston countered that that figure was too low.

"We already averaged that many a few years ago," he said. "We think we're going to average over 10,000 again right away. Winning will take care of that."[17]

Badali was suggesting that, due to the stalled contract talks, his client may not even show up at the Montreal Forum where the draft was to take place. When the proceedings got under way at 3 p.m., however, Mario was in attendance. It was still unclear whether, when his name was called, he would make his way to the Penguins' table and perform the usual draft pick ritual of donning the team's jersey, shaking hands with the brass and smiling for photos. An air of nervous anticipation filled the steamy building.

Soon, Eddie Johnston was at the mike. His moment was finally at hand, after weeks of weathering accusations of tanking and resisting countless lucrative offers from other GMs for the right to select Lemieux. Some of the more notable ones that came to light included Quebec offering all three Stastny brothers and Minnesota willing to give up all of its picks in exchange for the

Pens' coveted first overall. Montreal also tried hard to make a deal with John-ston in an effort to add Mario to its long line of superstar French-Canadian heroes. Johnston even had to fend off suggestions from within the Penguins organization that they should unload the pick. EJ resisted them all, and now, at long last, his moment had arrived.

"Pittsburgh ... le premier choix.... Pittsburgh ... numero soixante-six.... Mario Lemieux!"

An anything-but-overjoyed Lemieux rose from his seat, waved to the crowd ... and sat back down. He was not going to the Penguins' table. John-ston and the rest of the Penguin draft team could do nothing but sit and feel the embarrassment. The draft continued.

Later, Johnston was photographed with the other two first-round picks he had craftily attained (defenseman Doug Bodger [number nine overall] and forward Roger Belanger [number 16]), each proudly wearing their new home white Penguin jerseys. But no Mario. Lemieux was also photographed, still wearing only his suit, smiling between the number two pick, Kirk Muller in his Devils jersey, and number three overall, Ed Olczyk, resplendent in his new Chicago colors.

For diehard Pens fans, such pictures were nothing less than stakes through the heart. After two seasons of watching their team wallow in the depths of the NHL, even the elation they were hoping to feel by seeing the most exciting junior player in years put on a Penguin jersey was, on this day, denied them. A few thousand of them had gathered at a draft event the Pen-guins hosted at the Civic Arena for season-ticket holders, where a big screen broadcast the proceedings.

"Right away, the feeling was that Mario was a bit of a primadonna," said long-time fan Mike Hanczar, who was in attendance. "They walked out dis-gusted, saying, 'Who is this? Who does he think he is?'"[18]

In the days after the draft, however, the two sides kept talking. After conferring with Lemieux and his father the day after the draft, Perno brought a new offer to Badali, who sent it to Johnston. Significantly, the attendance clause had been taken off the table in return for a sweeter base salary. John-ston brought the proposal to Martha and the elder DeBartolo, who gave it their stamp of approval. The contract was for about $700,000 over two years, plus an option in year three. The deal was announced the next day, and on June 19, Mario Lemieux came to Pittsburgh for the first time in his life and pulled on a crisp, home white Penguin jersey with his name and now-signa-ture "66" emblazoned on the back.

"This is the biggest thing that's ever happened to the Pittsburgh Pen-guins franchise," Martha said.[19]

"We expect him to be here a long time," added Johnston. "This is the rebirth of the Pittsburgh Penguins, a beginning for our organization."[20]

For the first time in years, everyone associated with the Penguins was smiling. But no one seemed to have a bigger smile than the prodigy himself.

"I can't tell you how happy I am to be in Pittsburgh," said Lemieux. "The team's going to be a super hockey team in a couple of years. I'm looking forward to next season."[21]

With the bitter contract negotiations behind them, it was now time for Lemieux and the Penguins' management team to start working together to try to, at long last, build a winner in Pittsburgh.

PART SIX

Mario
(1984–85 Through 1987–88)

20

Getting on Route 66:
1984–85

The Penguins' Mario Lemieux Era began on October 11, 1984, in the Boston Garden, a building that had played host to countless examples of the franchise's futility in its first 17 seasons. Penguin squads had emerged victorious from the cramped and decrepit cathedral on Causeway Street only four times in 39 tries.

On his very first NHL shift, however, big Number 66 seemed hell-bent on showing the hockey world that those days were over. On his very first shift, Lemieux stripped the puck from Boston defenseman Mats Thelin behind the Bruin net and quickly fed a lurking Rick Kehoe in the slot, whose hard shot required a nice save from goalie Pete Peeters to keep the puck out of the net. Less than a minute later, Lemieux intercepted a pass from all-star defenseman Raymond Bourque at the Penguin blue line. Lemieux pushed the puck by Bourque and, in an instant, was past the defender, gathering the puck and skating away with massive strides that turned everyone else on the ice into spectators. Bearing down alone on Peeters, the rookie flicked his wrists back ever so slightly to fake a forehand wrist shot, only to just as deftly take the puck over to his backhand. Peeters, having bit on the fake, was left far out of position. He could only watch helplessly as Lemieux slipped the puck easily into the empty net.

First shift.

First shot.

First goal.

Lemieux leapt off his skates and upon landing punched the air in jubilation, a massive smile on his face that reflected all of his 19-year-old joy, pride and relief. A disgruntled murmur spread through the stunned Garden crowd, every member of which seemed to be asking, "Did you see that?"

Lemieux's goal sent a charge of excitement through his teammates, including veteran Denis Herron, who watched the goal from his crease at the other end of the rink.

"We said, 'Well, maybe this is the superstar. Maybe this is the guy that will put us forward a step higher.' The mood on the team was just great."[1]

"[The goal] took a lot of pressure from me," said Lemieux afterward. "Now that it's over, it's over, and I'll be more relaxed on the ice."[2]

The Penguins would eventually fall to the Bruins that night 4–3, squandering 2–0 and 3–1 leads. But with his incredible goal, "Le Savior," as some Pittsburgh papers were calling Lemieux, displayed a flash of brilliance that was enough to excite long-suffering Penguins fans with the prospect of what magic lay ahead.

Under the stern eye of new head coach Bob Berry, a disciplinarian who had enjoyed a respectable eight-year playing career spent mainly with the Los Angeles Kings before moving into the coaching ranks, the Penguins got off to a good start, going 5–4–0 in October. They rode their momentum into early November, which included a visit from the player Lemieux was so often being compared to, the great Wayne Gretzky and his high-flying Edmonton Oilers. Despite taking place on a U.S. election night that would see Ronald

Mario Lemieux's arrival in Pittsburgh in 1984 marked the biggest turning point in franchise history (courtesy Doug McLatchy).

Reagan elected to a second term, the showdown of superstars attracted a sellout crowd—the first at the Igloo in more than two calendar years. Midway through the third period, Lemieux fed a perfect pass across the slot to linemate Warren Young, who merely had to tap it behind Grant Fuhr to give the upstart Pens a 3–2 lead. Gretzky answered back in typical Number 99 fashion, batting a Jari Kurri rebound past Denis Herron with less than four minutes to go. The game ended in a 3–3 draw, the squandered second point the only thing missing in an otherwise rousing success of a night for the Penguin organization.

"[Lemieux] did things on the ice that brought people out of their seats," said Gretzky. "That's what this city needs, and that's what the National Hockey League needs."[3]

The goal by Young was his 11th of the season, an impressive total for a 28-year-old career minor-leaguer who was finally getting a prolonged chance on hockey's main stage. After Penguin mainstay Rick Kehoe, who had been placed alongside Lemieux to start the season, suffered a recurrence of a neck injury only six games in—one that would ultimately end his career—Berry moved Young on to Mario's left wing and put former St. Louis Blue Wayne Babych on his right. Receiving impossible tape-to-tape passes from Lemieux soon became routine for his linemates.

"Sometimes, I just don't see how he can get the puck through," said an amazed Babych after tapping home one such pass for a goal against Detroit October 30.[4]

The respectable start was also made possible by the fruits of Johnston's trade of Randy Carlyle to the Jets the previous season, which turned out to be a big boost to the Penguin blue line. The first-round pick they received was converted into Doug Bodger, and the future considerations turned out to be Moe Mantha, a 6'2", 195-pound four-year veteran just entering his prime. Both were smooth skaters and highly adept at moving the puck up the ice. They quickly became the team's two highest-scoring defensemen.

"Mantha reads plays well. He moves up on the play," Johnston said. "He's a big guy and he moves the puck exceptionally well coming out of our own end."[5]

But Rome, as they say, was not built in a day, and neither would the new Pittsburgh Penguins. This was still a club woefully short on depth, skill and experience. Its threadbare roster still showed ample evidence of the raw, self-inflicted wounds that had come from trading so many draft picks over the years for the short-term gain of squeaking into the playoffs. Much like those of the previous two basement-dwelling years, this was a roster full of youth, some of it too inexperienced to merit being in the big leagues. And with such a lineup came the roller-coaster of emotional highs and lows typical of a young team. The month of November, for instance, produced but one victory and featured a dreadful nine-game winless stretch, but was followed by a miraculous five-game winning streak, only one short of the franchise record. By mid–January the Penguins were only four games under .500 and tied with the New York Rangers for the final Patrick Division playoff spot. By comparison, a year earlier the pitiful Pens were 22 games under .500 and 26 points out of the playoffs.

These brash young Penguins could flash signs of greatness, like the January night against visiting Chicago, when they spotted the Black Hawks a

4–0 lead after one and then roared back with five of their own in the second period and held on for a stunning 5–4 triumph.

The win, however, proved to be but a crest in a season of highs and lows. A fragile confidence could seemingly evaporate with one or two losses, which was the case when they followed the big Chicago win with a 7–6 shootout loss to the Jets on January 21 and a tight 4–3 defeat at the hands of the Minnesota North Stars two nights later. The losses marked the start of a 12-game winless streak that sent the season hurtling downward and out of control. The streak reached rock bottom in—where else?—Philadelphia, where the Flyers obliterated the Pens 8–2, setting the tone early by outshooting Pittsburgh 19–1 in the first period.

"It seems like we're saying we don't want to do anything to win," commented center John Chabot after the game. "We have no confidence in ourselves, that's the main thing."6

The Penguins were suffering from the lack of a veteran voice or two to help steady the ship in these kinds of rough waters. "We need that 26- or 27-year-old player who can go in the locker room and settle things down when things are going bad," said GM Eddie Johnston. "A tough guy who has the respect of his teammates. But we're such a young club, we don't have that type of guy."7

Troy Loney remembered the Penguins of that era being "a team that had bits and pieces, but … we didn't have that strong leader guy. So that fell to some of the older guys, and some of them might not have been playing so much for the logo on the front but more for just trying to extend their careers. That's a little sad, but that's the reality of what we had at the time."8

Despite such shortcomings, the Penguins were still in contention for the final Patrick Division playoff spot, thanks to the equally bad New York Rangers and New Jersey Devils. A big 5–4 win over the fourth-place Blueshirts on March 2 before a near-sellout crowd at the Igloo brought the Pens to within two points of New York, but that was as close as this Penguin team would get to Lord Stanley's annual springtime dance. They would enjoy only three more wins the rest of the way, as the young defense corps crumbled most nights during the typically more intense games of the season's home stretch.

Compounding their on-ice misery were some disconcerting events off of it. On March 14, news broke that two Canadian concert promoters had offered to buy the Penguins from Edward DeBartolo, Sr., and move them to Hamilton, Ontario, where a new arena was being built.9

DeBartolo issued no confirmations or denials regarding the offer, which helped fan the flames of panic amongst Penguin fans. DeBartolo's son, Edward Jr., threw some gasoline on them by telling the press that "there has been a lot of money lost by the [DeBartolo] corporation and the family in

Michel Dion takes a rare breather in the Penguin net. Pittsburgh gave up 385 goals in 1984–85 (courtesy of Ron Kerrigan)

Pittsburgh, and if it was my decision—which it isn't right now—I'd have to look closely at the situation."[10]

What was known for certain was that the elder DeBartolo was miffed at the city and its mayor, Richard Caligiuri, over a $2-million lawsuit the city had launched over DeBartolo's disbanding of the local United States Football League franchise he owned, the Pittsburgh Maulers. The city claimed DeBartolo had violated a four-year lease agreement by pulling out of their home field, Three Rivers Stadium. As winter turned to spring, the suit and the relocation rumors lingered in the Western Pennsylvania air like old steel smoke. With no one yet saying yay or nay, everyone was left to wonder whether the Penguins would be back in the fall or residing in another city.

The Penguins were officially eliminated from playoff contention when they lost 4–3 to the Islanders on April 2. They finished the season at 24–51–5, which landed them in 20th spot, second-last overall. The hopes spurred by a respectable first half had been obliterated by a 7–32–1 mark over the second half. That 40-game performance equated to a miserable .186 winning percentage—worse than the .238 mark they'd managed during their previous 38-point season.

The reasons for the rancid record were many: a futile power play that generated the least amount of man-advantage goals in the league; a porous, mistake-prone defense that surrendered 385 goals, second-worst overall; an inability to win on the road (.200 winning percentage, worst mark in the league). The root cause of most of these problems was a lack of big-league bodies on the roster. In Berry's estimation, there were probably only "five or six guys on our team that are solid, sound National Hockey Leaguers."[11]

Through all this doom and gloom, however, there was one intensely shining beacon of hope: Mario Lemieux. His immense talents earned him an even 100 points on the season, only the third rookie in NHL history to reach the three-figure plateau. With the entire hockey world watching, he earned MVP honors at the NHL All-Star Game in Calgary by scoring two goals and an assist. He helped the Penguins improve by 15 points in the standings and helped attract 125,823 more fans to the Igloo than the year before. That represented the biggest improvement in attendance in the NHL and equated to an average of just over 10,000 per game. He was the runaway winner of the Calder Trophy for Rookie of the Year.

"He's proven himself game after game," said Johnston. Added Berry, "He has the ability to be a great player in this league. Not just an offensive player, but a great all-around player. I think everybody realizes what he can do offensively. It's awesome."[12]

Despite missing the playoffs, Lemieux himself could draw significant satisfaction from his first NHL season.

"I had to prove to Pittsburgh that they didn't make a mistake by making me the first choice. I think the fans in Pittsburgh helped me a lot. I think they know that I was worth the price."[13]

In Number 66, the Penguins clearly had their foundation in place. It was also clear, however, that there was a huge amount of work still needed to be done to build a winning team on top of it.

21

March Sadness: 1985–86

Since buying an ownership stake in the Penguins in 1977, Edward J. DeBartolo, Sr., had lost an estimated $19 million on his eternally waddling Penguins.[1] That represented but a small dent in his fantastically large fortune, which had been reported to be at least $600 million.[2] However, the shopping mall magnate had not amassed such riches by betting on losers—and that's exactly what the Penguins had been the whole time DeBartolo had been involved with them.

A good chunk of the blame could be attributed to "the Godfather" himself, for hiring an overseer of the operation—Paul Martha—who was an ex-football player with little hockey knowledge, and then pulling him away from his Penguin duties by assigning him similar roles with other DeBartolo sports holdings, including the Pittsburgh Maulers of the United States Football League and the Pittsburgh Spirit indoor soccer team.

Through all the losing, embarrassment and wounded personal pride, however, DeBartolo had kept the Penguins afloat in a sea of his own red ink. He'd usually done so with an extreme amount of patience, but by the spring of 1985, that patience was wearing thin.

At an April 25 press conference, held amidst the aromas of spaghetti, meatballs and lasagna wafting through the air of Antone's Italian restaurant in suburban Youngstown, the owner issued an ultimatum to the city and its hockey fans: the Penguins would have to sell 400,000 tickets—an average of 10,000 per game—by July 15 or he would have to "exercise our other alternative."[3] Although the specific words weren't uttered, this was the most clearly worded threat to move the Pens out of Pittsburgh ever issued by the DeBartolo empire.

And that ticket demand was just the appetizer.

DeBartolo also called for the elimination of a local amusement tax that was bludgeoning his bottom line, as well as a reduction in the city's parking tax. Further, he wanted the city to cough up money to help him make capital improvements to the Civic Arena and help him with debt-servicing costs related to the facility. And, of course, the USFL Maulers lawsuit would have to be dropped.

The city quickly acquiesced on the last issue, while the Penguins marketing department immediately went into high gear in promoting their golden attraction, Mario Lemieux, to meet the ticket ransom. The campaign culminated in a TV telethon—in which Lemieux, Gary Rissling and other Penguins answered the phones—that took place during breaks of a WPGH-TV showing of the wild frathouse movie *Animal House*. Given the craziness of the Penguins' predicament, the choice of film was indeed fitting.

The sales efforts worked. On July 22, Penguins fans, players and employees—not to mention a few politicians—breathed a collective sigh of relief when Martha announced that his boss was sufficiently satisfied with the strides made to accommodate his demands. The city and county reduced DeBartolo's annual rent at the Igloo from $700,000 to $275,000; agreed to subsidize his operating expenses by $550,000; gave up $50,000 in parking revenues DeBartolo had been paying; and committed to financing $11.4 million in Civic Arena improvements.

The agreement bound DeBartolo to keep the Penguins in Pittsburgh only through the upcoming season, and then let the city know in May 1986 if he planned to commit, at the city's request, to keeping the Pens put for a further five years. But the franchise had, at least for the present, survived yet another very real threat of extinction. Pens fans could now get back to thinking about pucks, not bucks.

While the team's future in Pittsburgh had remained up in the air, Eddie Johnston soldiered on in his attempts to build a playoff-caliber squad around Lemieux. He had been left with a significant hole on left wing when surprise 40-goal scorer Warren Young, a free agent, bolted to Detroit when the Red Wings made the aging left winger an impossible-to-decline four-year, $1-million contract. Johnston compensated for the loss by inking veteran forward Terry Ruskowski, the type of experienced player with the leadership capabilities EJ knew his team had lacked in 1984–85.

"He's a real enthusiastic guy and we've been interested in him for quite a while," said Johnston, who had coached the 30-year-old Ruskowski during his time behind the Chicago Black Hawk bench. Said Pat Quinn, coach of Ruskowski's most recent team, the L.A. Kings, "Terry might not rank skill-wise in the top 50 percentage in the league. But in intangibles, he's in the top 10 percent."[4]

The crafty Johnston then turned to the waiver draft in search of any hidden gems. He found a few: veteran left wing Willie Lindstrom, who had scored 30 points the previous year playing on Edmonton's checking line; a big, up-and-coming winger in Dan Frawley; and former first-round pick Mike Blaisdell. Just before training camp, Johnston gained more leadership and a still-solid goalie when he signed Gilles Meloche, whose resume stretched all the way back to the California Golden Seals.

"We're looking not only for him to win some games for us, but for on-ice and off-ice leadership," coach Bob Berry said.[5]

That kind of steadying presence would be dearly needed on a team that still included only six players over the age of 24. It would be up to this kiddie corps to get the franchise into the playoffs for the first time in four seasons. To help them, Penguin management submitted a formal request to the NHL to move the team from the tough Patrick Division to the Norris, perennially the weakest of the NHL's four divisions. The move made sense geographically, with Pittsburgh located close enough to clubs in the centrally-oriented Norris. A two-thirds majority vote was needed at the June NHL Board of Governors meeting, but it was decided the balloting wouldn't even take place because the schedule for the upcoming season had already been worked out. There was no appetite for tinkering with it just to accommodate the Pens' request. The matter would instead be held over until the December governors' meetings.

The youthful Penguins stumbled their way through the first two months before hitting their stride in late November. An impressive 7–1 win over Toronto, without Mario Lemieux in the lineup, no less, on November 27 sparked a five-game winning streak. The run included a home-and-home sweep of the New York Rangers, who were realistically the most likely candidate for Pittsburgh to beat out for a playoff spot.

The winning streak brought the Pens to within a victory of .500, a mark they flirted with but never quite reached until they bested the Blues 5–2 in St. Louis on January 18. Two nights later, they marched into the home of the two-time defending Stanley Cup champion Edmonton Oilers and thrashed them 7–4 on the strength of four assists from Lemieux and a hat trick from Mike Bullard. The win vaulted the Pens to the giddy heights of third place in the Patrick, tied with the Islanders, but still only two ahead of the fifth-place Rangers in the ultra-tight playoff race.

Clearly, this was a new Penguin team, and the reasons for their improvement were many. One was a determination to prove the critics wrong and show them they were no longer the league laughingstock.

"Everybody picked us [to finish] last in the division," Bullard said. "Everybody always picks us last. It's a matter of respect. We have a lot to prove to some people in this league."[6]

Looking back on the period today, winger Troy Loney remembered the Penguins of the mid–80s having to overcome pessimism not only from outside the organization, but also from within it.

"The franchise just had this [sense of] non-expectation hanging around it. I think there was a hangover from the 1975 Islanders coming back and sweeping them. There was just this heavy fog hanging around the team, so expectations weren't high."

After so many years of losing, respect for the Penguins was not high, Loney added, "from games, to referees, to everything…. I would honestly say we got hosed a lot of times just because 'Ah, it's the Penguins.' That was just the mentality of the league at the time amongst some of the referees and the other teams."[7]

Bob Berry was doing his utmost to change things. A belief in his tight-checking system that made up for the lack of depth and talent was taking hold in the dressing room. That buy-in, Berry said, was made possible in large part by the presence of a few veterans who recognized the value of his approach and who spread the word to their younger teammates.

"One of the big differences in this team this year is that we've got some allies in the dressing room," Berry said. "Those two or three can turn around four or five others who aren't so committed to winning."[8]

Another big reason was the rebound of captain Mike Bullard, who the year previous had struggled through injuries, a drunk-driving charge, rumors of his captaincy being stripped, and a drop-off of 19 goals, from 51 to 32. Now, halfway through the 1985–86 season, "The Bullet" was back on track for another 50-goal year. Bullard chalked up his resurgence to getting married, showing up to camp in better shape, and coming to grips with the presence of his superstar teammate Mario Lemieux.

"I'd be kidding people if I said there maybe wasn't a little jealousy," he said of his thoughts of Lemieux the previous season. "I was a little upset at management at first because they seemed to be building everything around him. But Mario and I are really good friends now."[9]

There could be no doubt, however, that the top reason for the Pens' improvement was Number 66 himself. With a year of NHL experience under his belt and a comfort level with the Penguins and Pittsburgh that was as high as his point totals, Le Magnifique proceeded to put on the kinds of dazzling offensive displays of which only Wayne Gretzky seemed capable. Multi-point games were becoming the norm as he toyed with opposing defensemen and goalies, using his long reach, big stride and smooth hands to regularly make them look like amateurs. On New Year's Eve he pumped in four goals for his first career hat trick and added two assists in an 8–4 pounding of the Blues. His first marker that night, as described by the *Pittsburgh Post-Gazette's* David Fink, was a fairly typical example of Lemieux's awe-inspiring abilities: "Breaking down the left side of the slot, Lemieux faked to his right, then moved to his left. Then, he faked to his right, slid the puck to his left,

Wayne Gretzky warms up before a game at the Civic Arena. Only The Great One scored more points (215) in 1985–86 than Mario Lemieux, who had 141 in only his second year in the NHL (courtesy of Ron Kerrigan).

made a half-turn and slapped the puck past goalie Rick Wamsley, who was helpless to stop it."[10]

"Mario is a franchise player—the type who comes around once every 10 years or so," observed GM Eddie Johnston. "He can do it all: He has great hands like Phil Esposito. He sees everything like Gretzky. His anticipation is so good. And when he's gone, you don't catch him."[11]

Lemieux was driving the Penguins' point total up, but also the all-important Civic Arena attendance numbers. Mario's presence was largely responsible for the jump in average attendance during his rookie year, which rose to 10,018 over a dismal 6,839 in 1983–84. By the mid-way mark of the current campaign, that average was up even further, to 10,749. For all of his efforts, Lemieux was rewarded with a new five-year contract in January 1986, worth about $650,000 per year. That put him in the top five highest-paid NHLers—in only his second year.

"We had to sign Mario," Johnston said. "I can't think of anything more important to our franchise."[12]

With the contract out of the way, Lemieux could now "just think about hockey. I wanted to sign and get this thing over with. I like the city, I like the way the team is playing. I think we are going to do well the next few years, so I just want to stay and help this team build."[13]

The next major step in that building effort, as the second half of the season got underway, was to get the Penguins into the playoffs for the first time in four years. A strong February helped them build a healthy five-point cushion on the fifth-place Rangers by the first week of March. With only 16 games remaining, the Pens embarked on a four-game road trip that began with three games in western Canada.

The strong play they had displayed of late, however, seemed to have been detained at the Canadian border.

Midway through the trip opener in Calgary, a shot caromed off goalie Roberto Romano and trickled toward the goal line of his net. The play was initially whistled dead but, after some deliberation by the officials, was later ruled a goal. Romano, who said the puck hit his pad and never went in, and coach Bob Berry went crazy on referee Bill McCreary, but to no avail. The controversial marker proved to be the winner in a 6–3 Pens loss.

Three nights later in Edmonton, Oiler defenseman Paul Coffey blew by Pens blueliners Moe Mantha and Doug Bodger while killing a Penguin power play, deked Penguin goaltender Gilles Meloche and deposited the puck into an empty net, giving the Oilers a 2–0 lead en route to a 5–3 win. The Coffey goal rattled the young Bodger, shattering his confidence and sending him into a long slump.

The shorthanded goal parade continued two nights later in Winnipeg, when the suddenly powerless Penguin power play surrendered two of them during one five-minute man-advantage.

"Right there, everything went up in smoke," center John Chabot reflected after the season was done. "From then on, we were tentative, edgy and lacking in confidence, especially on the power play. That was our season right there."[14]

The Penguins would win only two more games the rest of the way. A trade with Detroit for flashy winger Ron Duguay and the signing of highly touted college forward Dwight Mathiasen did little to stem the tide. The Penguins saw their playoff dreams dashed on the second-last night of the season when they fell 4–3 in overtime to the Flyers at the Igloo. They ended the season a mere two points behind the fourth-place Rangers.

Many factors contributed to the collapse, including fatigue. "I think we're a little bit tired because we don't have a lot of natural talent on the team and all the games we won this year were by hard work," said Mario Lemieux. "Maybe some of the guys are exhausted right now."[15]

Berry put part of the blame on a few veterans who he felt didn't give anything close to their full effort down the stretch. Although he didn't name names, it was clear Mike Bullard was one. After a promising start, the captain showed little leadership on the ice and even less off of it, having been hit with a fine for missing a team curfew in Montreal late in the season.

Other factors were Roberto Romano picking the worst time to go into a slump, losing seven of his final eight appearances. And a season-ending knee injury to inspirational leader Terry Ruskowski March 26 sapped the Pens of considerable steam.

No doubt, the nightmare finish was hard to take. But it overshadowed the many positives that revealed just how far the team—and franchise—had moved in the right direction in 1985–86. The Penguins were the most improved team in the league, going from 53 to 76 points. In only two years, they'd improved on their embarrassing total of 38 points in 1983–84 by a whopping 100 percent. For the first time in seven years, they scored more goals (313) than they allowed (303).

No edition of the Pittsburgh Penguins had attracted more fans to the Civic Arena than the 1985–86 one. Records were set for total attendance (503,020), average attendance (12,575) and sellouts (13).

And then there was Mario Lemieux. The 20-year-old's breathtaking skills resulted in the kind of play and statistics (141 points) that elevated him to the consensus second-best player in the NHL, behind only the great Wayne Gretzky, in only his second year in the league. His 93 helpers made him only the fourth player in NHL history to break the 90-assist mark. He put together a 28-game point scoring streak, fourth-best of all-time.

Still, Number 66 knew the Penguins needed more, even from himself, if they were going to reach the playoffs in 1987.

"We need a good defenseman, a guy like Paul Coffey or Ray Bourque, and one of those players who can take care of everything that goes on out there on the ice. And maybe I can help by [talking in the locker room]. This year, I just stayed in my corner and said nothing. Next year will be my third year."[16]

Pens fans could only hope it would be a charm.

22

Fast Start, Hard Crash: 1986–87

If the Penguins were feeling any hangover from their March meltdown when the puck dropped on the 1986–87 season, they weren't showing it. Before a sold-out Civic Arena for the season opener, they spotted the Washington Capitals a 3–0 lead, but a hat trick from winger Randy Cunneyworth turned the tide and propelled them to an impressive 5–4 victory. Two nights later, defenseman Doug Bodger ripped a 60-foot howitzer past John Vanbiesbrouck in overtime to beat the Rangers 6–5. Bodger followed that up with two goals the next night in the intimidating Chicago Stadium and, together with goalie Roberto Romano's 39 saves, the Penguins won 4–1 to move to 3–0. "This should give the guys a little confidence," said winger Warren Young, who had been re-acquired from the Red Wings just before the start of the season. "This was a big win in not an easy place."[1]

The Pens rode that confidence to three more wins against the Kings, Sabres and Devils to tie the then-franchise record of most consecutive wins at six. To set a new mark, they'd have to beat Buffalo again on Igloo ice. Stung by their 7–3 drubbing at the hands of the Penguins five nights earlier, the Sabres came out with a fire in their bellies, roughing up the Pens at every turn and building a 4–2 lead through the first 55 minutes. But when Buffalo rookie Jim Hofford took a late five-minute slashing major, Mario Lemieux went to work. After only a minute and a half of the ensuing power play, Number 66 had put two pucks past goalie Jacques Cloutier to tie the game. In overtime, Cunneyworth tapped home the winner midway through the frame and the Pens had a new team record winning streak.

"We're making believers out of everybody with this team, that it's never over until it's over," said Bob Berry.[2]

His charges were now only one win shy of tying the league record for most consecutive wins to start a season. To get there, though, they'd have to win the next one in Philadelphia, where they hadn't come away with two points since January 1974. As sweet as such a victory would have tasted, it wasn't to be. Mark Howe notched a goal and three assists as the Flyers came out on top 5–3. The first loss of the season was tough for many Pens to take, including defenseman Moe Mantha. "We had a lot of momentum and a great attitude coming in here," he told the *Pittsburgh Post-Gazette* after the game. "That's why it hurts so much."[3]

Nevertheless, the blistering start had finally put the Penguins in the hockey world spotlight after lingering for so long largely as a comical afterthought. They were suddenly appearing on the covers of hockey magazines ("Penguin Power," read the front-page headline of *The Hockey News*, while *Hockey Stars* magazine trumpeted, "The Penguins: New Power in the East"). The *Pittsburgh Press* ran a rare front-page feature describing how Penguin Fever was sweeping through the city's sporting scene, with the Pens becoming the city's new darling while the traditional powerhouse Steelers and Pirates were faltering. At sporting good stores, Penguin gear was, incredibly,

A seven-game winning streak to start the 1986–87 season made the Penguins the toast of the town in Pittsburgh. The Pens took a rare turn in the city's sporting spotlight as the Steelers and Pirates suffered downturns (courtesy City Planning Department Records, City Archives, Office of the City Clerk, City of Pittsburgh).

outselling Steelers merchandise. As one store manager put it, "Penguin stuff is hot. It's Penguins. Period. Everything. They're hot now."[4]

Finally, in their 20th season, it seemed that the Penguins had at long last arrived. The franchise appeared to be on solid ground. Encouraged by the rapidly clicking turnstiles and city officials' willingness to accommodate his financial demands, owner Edward J. DeBartolo had committed, before the season began, to keeping the Penguins in Pittsburgh for at least five more years. And now they were sitting on top of the NHL standings. Mario Lemieux had quickly become the city's favorite athlete.

The Penguins were booming, but as the team's diehard fans had witnessed so many times before, a bust was just around the corner.

The team cooled down over the next few weeks, playing mere .500 hockey during a stretch that featured lackadaisical efforts against lower-rung opponents like Hartford and New Jersey. A notable non-contributor throughout the young season was captain Mike Bullard, who had tallied only one goal over the entire first month. The former 50-goal-scorer was demoted to the fourth line. His frustrations boiled over during a November 11 practice in which he was giving a considerably less-than-full-out effort. He quickly got into an argument with Berry, who kicked him off the ice. Later, Berry stripped Bullard of his captaincy and handed it to Terry Ruskowski. By mid-afternoon the following day, Bullard had been traded to the Calgary Flames for center Dan Quinn.

"We have built a team here with a lot of character and a terrific attitude," said GM Eddie Johnston. "We didn't want that to backslide, and we were afraid it might if we kept Mike here."[5]

The debacle marked the end to a controversial but promising career for Bullard in Pittsburgh. After being the club's lone shining star during the pitiful 1983–84 season, the Bullet never seemed entirely comfortable living in the shadow of Mario Lemieux.

"I'm leaving here bitter," he said the day of the trade.[6] Less than a week later, however, Bullard had come to see the deal as a fresh start. "In the long run, coming to Calgary and getting out of Pittsburgh might be the best thing that ever happened to me."[7]

For Quinn, coming to an organization like Pittsburgh from Calgary, a team that had made the Stanley Cup Final the previous year, was "a big step back." He remembered the conditions of the suburban Pittsburgh rink where the Penguins practiced being decidedly more spartan than the gleaming new Saddledome in Calgary.

"We practiced in Mt. Lebanon at the high school arena. It was a good rink, but we dressed in a locker room for the swimming pool. So we had to walk through snow to get to the ice, as [the rink] was a separate building. We did that for a couple of years." By contrast, "We had a brand new building in

Calgary, with a modern dressing room. To go down to that, I was like, 'Oh my God.'"[8]

Beset by a suddenly cold power play, which plummeted from third-best to 14th by late November, and a rash of injuries, particularly to the defensive ranks, the Pens' slide grew more intense through December. By the end of the calendar year they were a mere .500 hockey team at 15–15–7, and a New Year's Day overtime loss to Washington sunk them back into losing-record territory.

A big reason for the Pens' woes was the lack of offense beyond Mario Lemieux. The 55 points he had amassed by late December accounted for a whopping 44 percent of all Penguin scoring. Berry desperately shuffled his lines to see who might be able to click with him, but each experiment met a dead end. Dwight Mathiasen, Dan Frawley, Ron Duguay, and even Lemieux's old beneficiary, Warren Young, all failed to make a mark.

"I think too many of the guys are thinking about why they aren't scoring and forgetting the other things," observed Berry. "Sometimes if you hit people and play aggressively, the scoring will take care of itself. I reminded them of that, and hopefully it sinks in."[9]

Unfortunately, it was the Penguins who got hit hard when Lemieux suffered a sprained right knee against Philadelphia on December 20. Attempting to avoid a Ron Sutter check along the boards, Lemieux's skate caught a rut in the Igloo ice. The injury would keep him sidelined for 14 games. The Penguins would win only two of them. By the time he returned on January 22 in Los Angeles, the Penguins had fallen back into a familiar position: fifth place in the Patrick. The heady days of early October were now long forgotten. The Penguins' disappointing play had landed them in yet another dogfight for fourth place and the division's final playoff ticket—this time against their familiar New York Rangers foe and the regressing Washington Capitals.

If the Penguins' effort wasn't guaranteed to be entertaining every night, Pens fans could at least depend on the team's radio and TV play-by-play man to keep things interesting. Save for a one-year hiatus, Mike Lange had been calling Penguin games since 1974, developing a loyal following along the way and becoming recognized league-wide as one of the game's most distinctive voices. The Sacramento, California, native developed a trove of hilarious one-liners that he bellowed after Penguin goals and victories. "Scratch my back with a hacksaw!"; "She wants to sell my monkey!"; and, after a Penguin win, "Ladies and gentlemen, Elvis has just left the building" were just a few of Lange's signature calls. Viewers and listeners loved them, and they represented another magnet to help draw more Pittsburghers toward the Penguins and hockey.

"Nobody calls a game like Mike Lange," said local broadcaster and Pens fan Jim Mirobella. "He has so much energy. He can convey the excitement, and you know exactly what's happening. Sometimes, I think it's more exciting to sit home and listen to him than to go to the game."[10]

Fortunately for the Penguins' bottom line, Lange's beloved broadcasting didn't stop the Civic Arena from being filled like it had never been before for Penguin hockey. Despite the slide and the extended absence of Lemieux, the fans kept showing up, to the tune of nearly 600,000 by season's end and an average of 14,965—good for ninth in the 21-team NHL.

What they saw was a club still short on talent and willingness to play the physical kind of game required to offset their lack of natural ability. Rare was the night all players seemed to be giving it their all. Lemieux's heroics were often nullified by a porous defense or shaky goaltending, such as a 6–5 loss to Boston in which Lemieux scored five points. Solid efforts were followed up with stinkers, such as the loosey-goosey 6–5 loss in New Jersey after a hard-fought 4–4 tie in the Pens' traditional house of horrors, the Philadelphia Spectrum. Of the Devils game, Berry said, "It was disgraceful. I don't think we could do anything that was more disappointing than this game."[11]

Rumors of Berry's imminent firing sprang up in late January when Paul Martha said he couldn't guarantee that the coach would still be around by the end of the season.[12] A solid 4–2–1 start to March, however, had kept Berry in place behind the Penguin bench. Their first playoff spot in five years was there for the taking, but the Penguins once again fell flat on their beaks. A 7–2 drubbing at the hands of the struggling Maple Leafs in Toronto, which had followed a huge 8–1 Penguin win in Quebec two nights earlier, caused Berry to unleash a vicious, expletive-ridden post-game rant in which he questioned the players' professionalism and commitment.

"Big shots. Performers. In the back door, put the show on, back out on the bus, go somewhere else. Just like a circus performer. Good show, bad show, good crowd, bad crowd, it doesn't matter. They get paid, anyway."[13]

A win in a crucial showdown with the Rangers at home on March 14 would move them to within one point of New York. They quickly fell behind 2–0 but rallied late in the third to send the game to overtime tied 2–2. Tomas Sandstrom's marker at 1:08 of the extra frame, though, silenced the sellout crowd and knocked Pittsburgh five points back of the Broadway Blueshirts.

"It's devastating." whispered forward Dave Hannan in the solemn Penguin locker room after the game. "There's not much to say except we have to work hard for the last nine games and hopefully we'll get some points."[14]

Two more crucial losses, one to Washington by a 4–3 score, and yet another defeat in Philadelphia—the 37th straight time the Pens left the Spectrum without a victory—pushed them to the brink of elimination. A year that had seen the Pens get off to the best start in team history was officially given its last rites a week later when they fell at home to Montreal, 4–1. They finished with a 30–38–12 record, four points back of the Rangers.

"It's tough to be finished this early all the time," said Doug Bodger. "It's getting tougher and tougher—but there's nothing we can do about it now."[15]

Despite the setback, however, the Penguins remained confident about their team's future.

"The feeling was one of hope," remembered Dan Quinn. "It wasn't like it was devastating because we missed [the playoffs] by a few points. We knew that once we got in, we were going to be a very tough team to beat."[16]

Added Dave Hannan, "We found out that the league doesn't sit still. All organizations try to get better, and I think we probably didn't have the depth that other teams had…. At the same time, we all knew we were going to continue to get better. We all knew that as they're building with Mario, as an individual you have to say, 'OK, I want to be here. I want to be part of this team getting better and better every year.'"[17]

The inevitable firing of Berry took place eight days after the season ended. Assistant Jimmy Roberts was also given the heave-ho.

"After three years, this team hasn't made the playoffs and we need changes somewhere," said Lemieux. "And when they make changes, it's always the coaches who get fired. But they did a good job with the players we have."[18]

Lemieux's insinuation that the Penguin roster was critically short of talent had a considerable degree of merit. But those players who did possess adequate or above-average skill could not be excused for another playoff-less season in Pittsburgh. Some writers even opined that Lemieux, despite his stratospheric point totals, had another level of commitment still to display.

Unbeknownst to Lemieux or anyone else during those dark days of early April, the young superstar would soon have a golden opportunity to take his game to that extra level, on a stage far removed from Pittsburgh's Civic Arena, and to do so alongside none other than the man he was chasing to be the best in the game: the Great Wayne Gretzky himself.

23

Sour Cream:
1987–88

The fourth installment of the Canada Cup tournament, a two-week showdown to determine the world's best hockey nation, was set to be held before the start of the 1987–88 season. Defending champion Team Canada, winners of the last title in 1984, once again boasted an incredibly deep lineup of proven veterans and emerging NHL superstars. The talent pool was so deep that when Mario Lemieux arrived in his hometown of Montreal on August 3 for the team's training camp, he was not guaranteed a roster spot. Looking around the dressing room that day, he saw the likes of Wayne Gretzky, Mark Messier, Dale Hawerchuk, Brent Sutter and Paul Coffey. He also saw such leadership-laden, heart-and-soul guys as Rick Tochett, Dave Poulin and Kevin Dineen. By reason of simple mathematics, some of these names would not be penciled onto the final roster once the tournament got under way. Lemieux would have to work harder than ever to earn his place on demanding coach Mike Keenan's star-studded squad.

And work he did, not only securing a roster spot but proceeding to put up enough points in the team's first few games to move near the top of its scoring list, behind only Gretzky himself. He did so by playing on lines that did not include Gretzky. To most everyone's surprise, Keenan resisted the urge to put Number 66 on Number 99's wing and create a super line, preferring instead to spread their talents across two lines and only put them out together on power plays.

The approach worked well enough to get Canada into the tournament's best-of-three final round against their traditional nemesis the Soviet Union. But after dropping the first game 6–5, Keenan finally caved to the pressure during the make-or-break second game and paired the two superstars.

The result was a lightning bolt of scoring prowess that electrified the hockey world.

Sweeping over the ice in dazzling rushes nearly every shift, the dynamic duo combined for eight points, Gretzky getting five assists and Lemieux a natural hat trick, including the dramatic game-winner half-way through double overtime.

There was more Mario–Wayne magic in the deciding game three, which was another wild, back-and-forth affair that saw the two superpowers deadlocked at five late in the third period. With just over a minute to play, Gretzky, Lemieux and defenseman Larry Murphy broke up ice on a three-on-two rush. Although Murphy was wide open in the slot, Gretzky fed it back to the trailing Lemieux, who moved into the slot and made no mistake, burying a hard wrist shot over the glove of goalie Sergei Mylnikov to give Canada the lead. They held on for a 6–5 win and the tournament title.

With the goal, Mario Lemieux instantly became a Canadian hockey legend. His effort throughout the tournament had left no doubt in anyone's mind what he was capable of.

"This is my greatest thrill ever, scoring the last two game-winning goals," he said. "I think I've answered a few questions in this tournament."[1]

Perhaps most importantly for his employers back in Pittsburgh, the experience of proving himself at the game's highest level marked a new, more mature stage of Mario Lemieux's career.

"I've learned how to win. What to do when you're down in certain situations, how to react and what to say."[2]

Observed GM Eddie Johnston a few days later as he watched Lemieux fly around the ice at the Penguins' training camp, "I think he's on a high. And I think he wants to stay on that high."[3]

At that training camp, Lemieux saw the usual batch of new faces that Johnston had brought in to try to help finally get the Pens into the playoffs after what was now a five-year absence. The biggest one was behind the bench, in the form of Pierre Creamer, hired in June to replace the fired Bob Berry. The hiring was somewhat of a head-scratcher to many observers, considering Creamer was not mentioned on any shortlists prior to his signing, and also that his command of English was somewhat shaky. But the 42-year-old possessed many of the qualities EJ and Paul Martha were looking for: effective communication skills, teaching abilities, and a track record of winning. Creamer had enjoyed a long career in Quebec, where he had steadily rose through the ranks from minor midget hockey up to the American Hockey League. Everywhere he went, his teams took home titles, including the 1984–85 AHL Calder Cup-winning Sherbrooke Canadiens.

"I think he will help the team and help myself to give more than they want sometimes," said Lemieux. "He's a guy that can understand the young guys."[4]

There were a number of on-ice changes as well. Gone were wingers Terry Ruskowski, Warren Young and Ron Duguay, replaced by aging stars

Wilf Paiement and Charlie Simmer, hoping to latch on as one of Mario's wingers and recapture some of their rapidly fading glory. The defense corps had become younger but more talented, with the infusion of the club's two most recent first-round draft choices, Zarley Zalapski and Chris Joseph. With such youth on the blueline, mistakes could be expected. Youth was hardly the problem in goal, where 28-year-old Pat Riggin would be backed up by the oldest player in the league, 37-year-old Gilles Meloche, while youngsters Frank Pietrangelo Steve Guenette waited in the wings.

The stakes had never been higher for Johnston since his arrival in Pittsburgh seven years earlier. After five straight years of missing the playoffs, the unstated ultimatum coming from Youngstown was clear: make the post-season or you're fired. Edward DeBartolo, Sr., had even gone so far as to guarantee a rebate of one dollar per ticket for those fans purchasing multi-game ticket packages, should the Penguins fail to qualify for post-season play. The "Playoffs or Payoffs" marketing campaign meant upwards of $200,000 of De-Bartolo money was on the line.

Fortunately for Johnston, his patient stockpiling of high-end draft picks now allowed him to think about making trades for top-level players who weren't past their prime. And in late November, with the Penguins plodding along with a typical 7–10–4 record, EJ did just that, pulling off the most dramatic trade in franchise history.

Coming to Pittsburgh was all-star defenseman Paul Coffey, a cornerstone of the high-powered Edmonton Oiler squad that had captured three Stanley Cups in the past four years. A contract dispute with Oiler GM Glen Sather had kept the 26-year-old superstar on the sidelines all season, and Slats was looking to move him. Coffey had emerged as the smoothest-skating blueliner in the league, taking the puck up ice on breathtaking rushes and racking up points at a rate that was breaking records previously set by the great Bobby Orr. The two-time Norris trophy winner was the master of the outlet pass, routinely springing Wayne Gretzky, Mark Messier and Jarri Kurri on breakaways with his long, tape-to-tape dishes. Now, Coffey would be springing Mario Lemieux. With the arrival of Coffey, number 66 finally had a bona fide superstar to join him in his quest to get the Pens into the playoffs—and beyond.

"I think we can complement each other very well," said Coffey. "When you get a guy like Mario, who's so good with the puck, mostly from the red line in … if you get a guy who can move the puck up to him quick, it takes an enormous amount of pressure off him."[5]

With the acquisition of Coffey, a large amount of pressure had seemed to come off Johnston as well. "How many times do you get a guy who's scored 140 points? We needed a guy back there on our power play. We needed a guy to run our ship."[6]

Paul Coffey's arrival in November 1987 added a new dimension of speed, skill and leadership to the Penguins' lineup (courtesy Ron Kerrigan).

The price of this particular cup of Coffey was steep, however. Going to Edmonton were promising youngsters Craig Simpson and Chris Joseph, along with vets Moe Mantha and Dave Hannan. The Pens also received forward Dave Hunter and tough guy Wayne Van Dorp.

Coffey, switching from his traditional number 7 to a new 77, was in a Penguins uniform the day after the trade when his new team took on Quebec at the Civic Arena. Coffey wasted no time electrifying the hometown fans, dashing all over the ice and earning three assists in a 6–4 come-from-behind Penguin victory. Coffey instantly supercharged the slumbering Penguin power play, earning all his points during man-advantage situations to help the Pens overcome a 4–0 Quebec lead.

"A team that comes back from a deficit like that shows a lot of character," he said afterward. "We just have to keep going from here."[7]

The Penguins' benefited from being a tight-knit group away from the rink, recalled Dan Quinn.

"We had a really good, fun locker room. Everybody was their own guy, but pulling for each other, supporting each other. We'd have married guys go out with the single guys. We'd all be at the same spot having a good time because that's the way it was back in the day. We'd be in New York City four times a year each with the Devils, Rangers and Islanders [in our division], so we could all go out on a Sunday night and have fun."[8]

The Pens rode the enthusiasm of the Coffey deal through December, losing only four of their next 15 games. But a knee injury to Coffey just before Christmas, suffered while colliding with referee Don Koharski, helped send the Penguins into an ugly 10-game winless streak. The stretch marked the beginning of a wild roller coaster ride of a season. They followed the 10-game winless streak with four straight wins, then three losses, then another four-game winning streak, then seven losses in eight games, and then a rebound with three straight wins. No one really knew which team was the real Pittsburgh Penguins.

Some chalked the streakiness up to youth. "It's one of the problems," said veteran Gilles Meloche. "You win a couple and you think it's going to come easy. Then all of a sudden you lose two games and you realize you haven't been working as hard as you should. In this league, you can't take a period off or a shift off or you'll be behind the eight ball."[9]

Another problem was coach Pierre Creamer, who emerged as a polarizing figure in the dressing room as the season went on. Many players, including Mario Lemieux, said they felt he was an open and approachable bench boss who was doing the best he could despite being a rookie NHL coach adjusting to a new language and culture. Others, however, voiced their displeasure with Creamer, often in the form of off-the-record discussions with reporters. Many of his decisions were questioned openly in the press. These curiosities included giving the captaincy not to Lemieux, the team's obvious leader, but to hard-working but marginal journeyman winger Dan Frawley, scorer of a whopping 28 goals in 180 career games; keeping talented right winger Rob Brown in the press box for many games despite Brown's impressive production whenever he was in the lineup; doing the same with young goalie Frank Pietrangelo, whose reward for three stellar efforts in October was a demotion to the Pens' Muskegon farm team; stripping alternate captain Dan Quinn of his "A" and not being able to fully explain his rationale due to his faulty English; and physically wearing down Lemieux by double-shifting him late in games that were already decided. Reporters following the team lambasted Creamer for rarely speaking to his troops before games and his inability to communicate tactical adjustments between periods.[10]

"Creamer was not suited for the job," said beat reporter Bob Grove. "His English wasn't good enough to get the job done." On the Frawley captaincy, Grove remembered being puzzled. "I love Dan Frawley. Dan Frawley was a hardnose player. But the day he was named the captain I said, 'What are they thinking?' That whole year kind of turned out to be a head-shaker."[11]

The Creamer situation reached new levels of absurdity in early March when Edward DeBartolo, Jr., called five Penguin players to his offices in Ohio for a discussion about the coach and his tactics. The unconventional meeting—rarely did NHL owners sit down with players with no GMs or coaches present—was part of Junior's sudden decision to take a more active role in the Penguins, a part of the DeBartolo empire traditionally handled by his father while Junior was busy overseeing his San Francisco 49er football team. The discussion—which included Lemieux, Coffey, Frawley, Quinn and Dave Hunter—ended up focusing more on the Civic Arena's dilapidated dressing rooms than on Creamer. While the exercise accomplishing nothing, it was Junior's next piece of meddling into Penguin affairs that proved the most costly.

GM Eddie Johnston, a former Stanley Cup winning goalie, knew from before the season had started that his team was lacking a top-notch performer between the posts. Pat Riggin's best years were behind him and youngsters Frank Pietrangelo and Steve Guenette needed more seasoning before assuming a starter's role. Johnston had set his sights on free agent Andy Moog, a talented puck-stopper who had demanded a trade from Edmonton after growing tired of playing second-fiddle to Grant Fuhr. EJ waited patiently all season while Moog chose to play for Canada at the 1988 Winter Olympics. Finally, after the Games were done in early March, Johnston was set to pull the trigger on a deal that would have sent a first-round choice in the 1988 draft and Guenette to the Oilers. DeBartolo Junior, however, stepped in and quashed it.

"I had a gut feeling. I didn't like the trade," Junior told the *Pittsburgh Post-Gazette* the next day. "I don't think we should do anything stop-gap just to make the playoffs."[12]

Adding Moog would have been anything but a stop-gap measure, something veteran hockey men who knew the game—such as Johnston—knew all too well. Having just turned 28, Moog was in the prime of his career, one which had seen him compile an impressive 143–53–21 record. In all likelihood, he would have given the inconsistent Penguins the foundation they needed in goal and an infinitely better chance of finally getting into the post-season.

The veto marked another slap in the face to Johnston and his authority. EJ uttered some politically correct statements in the aftermath, but some of his GM peers couldn't believe what they'd witnessed.

"Where is [DeBartolo] going to find a good goaltender like Moog who's chomping at the bit to play?" wondered Oilers GM Glen Sather, who ended up shipping Moog to the Boston Bruins.[13]

"Any time a goalie like Andy comes along, you have to take a chance," said Boston GM Harry Sinden. "It's the one position you can't afford to fool around with."[14]

Through all the ups and downs on the ice and all the turmoil off it, one person who wasn't fooling around was Mario Lemieux. Piggybacking off his Canada Cup experience, Lemieux had just kept scoring, all season long. With

Paul Coffey now routinely feeding him breakaway passes and working magic with him on the power play, Lemieux had managed to stay within hailing distance of the Great Wayne Gretzky in the NHL scoring race. Such a battle hadn't been seen since 1979–80, the last year Number 99 hadn't won the Art Ross Trophy. A knee injury that put Gretzky on the sidelines for three weeks in January allowed Mario to pull ahead by 15 points by the time Wayne returned, a lead he maintained as the season moved into its final weeks.

The Pens were needing every last point they could get from Lemieux, just to keep them in the three-way dogfight that had developed for the fourth and final Patrick Division playoff spot. Joining in this year's usual battle between the Penguins and Rangers were the improved New Jersey Devils, who finally had some top young talent, including Kirk Muller and rookie goalie Sean Burke, to match their abundant grit. With four games remaining for each club, the Pens sat three points up on New Jersey as the teams prepared for a crucial home-and-home series. The Penguins, for once, controlled their own fate, needing three wins in their final four games to get in, regardless of what Jersey or the Rangers did. New York was tied with Pittsburgh but had only three games left.

After a scoreless opening period in the first game in East Rutherford, the Devils exploded for three unanswered goals in the second. The shots in the middle frame were a ridiculous 16–2. The Devils' tight checking and some hot goaltending from Burke carried them the rest of the way to a 4–0 victory.

"We just weren't playing together," lamented Coffey. "Maybe we just weren't prepared."[15]

In the second game back in Pittsburgh, with the Pens holding a 2–1 lead in the second period, the Devils exposed a weakness that had plagued Pittsburgh all season long: the penalty-killing unit, which was the worst in the league. New Jersey shredded it for three goals, taking full control of the game. They maintained their chokehold the rest of the way and humiliated the Pens, 7–2.

A Mario Lemieux overtime goal in their next game against Washington kept the Pens' fading playoff hopes alive. According to reports coming from the Penguin dressing room after the game, coach Pierre Creamer was oblivious to the Pens' need for a win that night to keep their playoffs hopes alive. Playing for a tie would take them out of the race, but this was apparently news to the head coach.

"He didn't know. He absolutely didn't," said Bob Grove. "I've talked to people who were there, including players, and he didn't know they needed to win."[16]

The Penguins went into the last night of the season one point back of both New York and New Jersey, meaning they would need help from the Rangers' and Devils' opponents if they were to somehow squeak into fourth place. The Pens beat Hartford, but the out-of-town help never came. New York's 3–0 win over Quebec officially ended the Penguins' season, and a dramatic Devils overtime win in Chicago ended the Rangers. New Jersey would ride their momentum all the way to the Wales Conference final, where they finally lost in seven games to the Boston Bruins.

The Penguins could merely hit the golf course early for the sixth straight season and ask themselves a thousand "what-ifs." They could also, however, console themselves with the many positives that came out of the season. Mario Lemieux had put up an incredible 168 points to become the first Penguin to capture the NHL scoring championship. He would later win the Hart Trophy for league MVP, also the first time a Penguin had taken home that coveted hardware. Additionally, a 36–35–9 record gave the franchise its first winning season in nine years.

But the prize everyone wanted—a playoff ticket—had once again eluded the organization. An angry thunder could be heard coming all the way from the DeBartolo headquarters in Ohio. As Penguin office staffers began writing refund cheques to those season ticket holders who qualified under the "Playoffs or Payoffs" campaign, it was clear to everyone throughout the organization that changes were on their way.

PART SEVEN

Building a Champion
(1988–89 Through 1991–92)

24

Enter Espo:
1988–89

In 1977, a group of Chicago boxing aficionados founded the Italian American Boxing Hall of Fame to help raise funds for youth boxing programs in that city. The idea proved such as success that a year later it was expanded to include standout Italian-American athletes in all sports. A decade later, the hall welcomed all-star NHL goalie Tony Esposito into its ranks. He was a natural choice, considering he had been one of the sport's greatest netminders of the 1970s and early 80s, with most of his career spent in the crease of the hometown Black Hawks.

Always a great raconteur, Esposito made many friends while attending the Hall's dinners and functions. One frequent attendee who took a particular shine to "Tony-O" was none other than Edward J. DeBartolo, Jr. The two hit it off immediately. Anxious to continue putting his stamp on the Pittsburgh Penguin hockey club he'd recently been entrusted by his father to run, DeBartolo saw in Esposito just the man he needed to manage the team on a day-to-day basis.

DeBartolo invited Esposito to his Ohio offices for what turned into a five-hour discussion. By the time the two men bid each other good day, DeBartolo's mind was made up: Tony Esposito would be the Penguins' next general manager.

The move, formally announced at an April 15, 1988, press conference, raised a number of eyebrows. For all his on-ice success, Esposito had gained zero hockey managerial experience since hanging up his pads in 1984. Nevertheless, Espo was not only given the GM duties held for the past five years by Eddie Johnston, he also would take over Paul Martha's responsibilities as vice-president. Both Martha, as governor and president of the Civic Arena Corp., and Johnston, as assistant GM, would remain with the club.

Coach Pierre Creamer, to no one's surprise, was accorded no such stay of execution. He was fired in June and replaced later than month by Gene

Ubriaco, a former Penguin player from the franchise's earliest days and, more recently, coach of the club's American Hockey League farm team in Baltimore. Many fans and sportswriters saw Ubriaco's life-long friendship with Esposito—the two had grown up together in Sault Ste. Marie, Ontario—as being his biggest credential for the job. It certainly wasn't his NHL coaching experience, of which he had none. In announcing the hiring, Esposito instead chose to highlight Ubriaco's 11 years of minor-league coaching experience and his reputation as an enthusiastic and patient teacher of younger players, which the Pens still had in abundance. Esposito downplayed the pair's personal connection.

"There's a six-year difference in our ages, so we didn't really grow up together. That had nothing to do with my decision. Nothing." He added defiantly, "I know I'm taking some heat for hiring a guy I know, but I don't consider him failing. He won't fail."[1]

When the puck dropped on the new season, it was clear to everyone that Mario Lemieux was going to do everything in his prodigious powers to ensure Ubriaco did not fail. At long last, Le Magnifique had some top-notch talent to work with on his wings. With sharpshooter Rob Brown finally given all the ice time he could handle on Lemieux's right wing, and hard-working Bob Errey digging pucks out of the corners on his left side, Mario exploded out of the gate like no other player had before in NHL history. After only 12 games, he had amassed an incredible 41 points, easily putting him on pace to break Wayne Gretzky's all-time single-season scoring mark of 215. Against St. Louis on October 15, Lemieux burned the Blues for eight points, becoming only the tenth player in NHL history to score that many points in one game. Rob Brown, beneficiary of three of Mario's six assists, marveled at his teammate's passing display. "It doesn't matter if there are six guys between us. You know he'll get you the puck."[2]

Mario Lemieux scored a career high 199 points in 1988–89. That total included 13 shorthanded goals—an NHL record to this day (courtesy Ron Kerrigan).

From writer Bob Grove's point of view, Brown's ability to grasp the way Mario played the game was integral to both players' success that year.

"Robbie Brown was a fourth-round pick. He wasn't a good skater, so nobody really felt he was big-time NHL material. Mario had had a long laundry list of linemates [during his time in Pittsburgh]. It wasn't like they had always been trying to find someone to score 60 goals beside him; they were trying to find somebody who *gets* the way he plays and can learn to anticipate a little bit what he might do. And Robbie Brown was that guy. He had a great sense for the game and he was an incredible finisher."[3]

The Penguin offense had become one of the league's best. By mid–November, only Wayne Gretzky's L.A. Kings had scored more goals than Pittsburgh. Unfortunately, the Pens were surrendering goals at nearly the same blistering pace. The 82 red lights that had come on behind their net represented the league's third-worst total. While crippling defensive lapses by Penguin skaters, fueled by lackluster backchecking by the forwards and costly giveaways by the blueliners, were a major factor, GM Esposito knew things were not going to improve without a proven, top-caliber starting goalie. With only 56 games of NHL experience between them at the start of the season, the duo of Frank Pietrangelo and Wendell Young was proving too inexperienced for a team that now had a legitimate shot at a Patrick Division championship—and perhaps even more.

Espo spied the answer in the form of Buffalo's Tom Barrasso. The 23-year-old Massachusetts native had burst on to the NHL scene five years earlier when, as an 18-year-old rookie straight out of high school, he captured both the Calder trophy for rookie of the year and the Vezina for best goalie. But a 2–7 start to the 1988–89 season, and the emergence of Darren Puppa as a legitimate starter, made Barrasso expendable. The Penguins sent Doug Bodger and their first-round pick in the 1988 draft, promising forward Darrin Shannon, to the Sabres for Barrasso on November 11.

That the notoriously private Barrasso had been labeled as arrogant and aloof at every stage of his career was of no concern to Esposito. The addition of Barrasso now gave the Penguins one of finest "down-the-middle" foundations in all of hockey: Lemieux at center, Coffey on defense, and now Barrasso in net. These Penguins were finally for real, and the hockey world took notice. No lesser an observer than the legendary Scotty Bowman, who coached Barrasso in Buffalo, noted simply that "[Barrasso] wins games. His goals against average might be high on [the Penguins], but it won't matter. He makes saves at the right time. There are certain times in every game when a team needs good goaltending and he can do it when it counts."[4]

Barrasso's arrival sparked a 12–1–3 run that pushed the Pens to the top of the Patrick Division and essentially removed all doubt that they would end their six-year playoff-less drought. Their lone loss during that stretch came at the place where Penguin teams never won, the Philadelphia Spectrum. The 4–3 defeat stretched the franchise's incredible winless streak in Philly to 42 games (0–39–3), one which had started when Mario Lemieux was a mere eight years old. They returned to their house of horrors on February 2 for another crack at getting the now-geriatric monkey off their backs.

"It would be nice to get [the media] to stop talking about it, to make us carry the burden of many teams gone by," said center Dan Quinn.[5]

Reflecting on the game years later, Quinn noted that while the streak represented a long history of losing, "none of us had played for 10 years [with the Penguins], so we didn't feel like that was such an incredible streak. But that particular night, we felt like 'Enough's enough.'"[6]

Ubriaco decided the best way to accomplish that was to simply go in and play their own game. "We decided to forget about playing tight. We decided to run-and-gun."[7]

The approach paid off in the early going. John Cullen opened the scoring at 10:45 of the first period, and Phil Bourque, Bob Errey and Rob Brown followed with tallies that gave Pittsburgh a commanding 4–1 lead after two. Ex-Pen Mike Bullard narrowed the gap to 4–2 with a goal early in the third.

"We got concerned, but we didn't panic," said Quinn.[8] His poise was on full display when he beat Ron Hextall on a breakaway at 6:36 to make it 5–2.

"It was back and forth early in the third," Quinn remembered. "I snuck away on a little break when Davey Hannan fed me and I beat Hexy. The whole bench went nuts because we knew it was going to be hard for us to blow a three-goal lead."[9]

Some outstanding saves by former Flyer Wendell Young carried the Pens the rest of the way to a momentous 5–3 victory. The run of futility in Philly was finally finished.

"It's a great thing for the organization," said long-time Pen Troy Loney, "especially the guys who have been around here four or five years and put up with this."[10]

Things were changing around the organization, and not just on the ice. Upon taking over the Penguin reins, Esposito soon realized the players needed a more professional workplace, one that befitted a National Hockey League team.

"Tony was the first person who made that change in the organization that said 'Hey, we're going to treat you as class players. We're going to treat the team as a class team, and we're gonna change things. We're going to change this attitude,'" reflected Loney. "It was Tony who decided they needed to renovate the locker room and to treat the players differently than in the past. He was basically saying, 'We're going to show you respect. You'll get respect, and the team will get better.'"[11]

As late as February 9, the Penguins sat atop the Patrick Division, with the Rangers in hot pursuit, one point back. How times had changed. The traditional Patrick powerhouses of the 80s had lost a step, with the Flyers languishing in fourth place and the Islanders taking up residence in the Penguins' old basement apartment, well out of the playoff race. With the Spectrum jinx confined to the history books, the Penguins looked to erase another franchise-long embarrassment: the lack of a championship banner hanging from the Igloo rafters. Never had the team finished first in any division, let alone conference or the entire league. Their closest brush with a banner came in their first season, when they finished six points back of St. Louis in the expansion West Division. And they had finished second only twice, in 1969–70 in the West and 1978–79 in the Norris Division.

The Patrick title was well within their grasp, but an extended swoon through February and March scuttled such dreams. The once-potent power play suddenly dried up, defensive collapses became commonplace, and general disarray reigned on the ice. In Detroit on February 23, the Penguins built a commanding 6–0 lead and then proceeded to blow it and settle for a 6–6 tie. Humiliating losses such as an 8–1 whipping in Quebec and a 10–3 pasting in Calgary brought back painful memories of 1983.

A big 6–4 win at Madison Square Garden to start the season's final week, however, lifted their spirits and helped them finish the season strong, landing in second place with 87 points, five back of Washington. The total was but two short of the franchise record set in 1974–75. The Penguins' top two forwards also fell agonizingly short of personal milestones, with Rob Brown finishing up with 49 goals and Mario Lemieux falling but one point of the stratospheric 200-point plateau. His 199 points represented the fifth-highest single-season total in NHL history, with Wayne Gretzky holding down the top four spots. A close examination of Lemieux's numbers was sure to leave anyone dizzy. There were seven hat tricks and two four-goal games. In 35 games he scored at least three points. Twice he scored eight. He established an NHL record with 13 shorthanded tallies. And in his most memorable performance of the year against New Jersey on December 31, Le Magnifique score five goals, each one in a different manner: even-strength, power play, shorthanded, penalty shot and empty net, which came with one second left. Interestingly, the rest of the Penguins, perhaps thinking more about the post-game New Year's Eve parties they'd be attending, didn't play all that well on the night, with the team's final shot tally reading 18. The stage was Mario's and no one else's.

"Even when he wasn't scoring goals, he was putting the puck through his legs, making twirls," said Rob Brown. "It was a classic example of the best hockey player in the world teaching us how to play."[12]

With their first playoff spot in seven years now secured, the Penguins set their sights on their first-round opponent, the New York Rangers. The matchup pitted the legendary Esposito brothers—Tony in the Pens' GM box and Phil behind the Ranger bench—against each other. Phil, also the Blueshirts' GM, had only recently taken over the team's coaching reins, after having fired Michel Bergeron with only two games left in the season. To many, the Rangers seemed in disarray, having lost their final five games of the season, but they showed none of it as they hunkered down into a tight, defensive struggle in game one before a sold-out and raucous Civic Arena crowd, finally relieved of their seven-year starvation for playoff hockey.

The first career playoff game for many Penguins made for some jittery nerves, remembered Dan Quinn.

"It was Mario's first playoff game and he didn't have his best—a little bit of standing around, looking around," he said. "It was evident that the guys who hadn't played in the playoffs before weren't used to having to step it up."[13]

With Jan Erixon and Lucien DeBlois keeping Lemieux in check for much of the game, it was left to three-time Cup winner Paul Coffey to fill the scoring void, which he did with two goals, including the winner on a power play marker midway through the third, leading the Pens to a 3–1 victory. Coffey's experience proved every bit as valuable as his shooting, often serving as a calming influence for the many Pens who were finally tasting their first post-season action.

Said winger Bob Errey: "He's on the bench talking to us. We're tied 1–1

Veteran Paul Coffey provided key leadership for the young Pens when they took on the New York Rangers and Philadelphia Flyers in the 1989 playoffs. It was the franchise's first post-season appearance in six years (courtesy Ron Kerrigan).

and he yells, 'Just relax boys, we're all right.' We're up 3–1, he says 'Keep fore-checking.' He doesn't get caught up in it. He takes it all in stride."[14]

The Ranger strategy to concentrate on Lemieux succeeded in containing the NHL scoring leader again in Game Two—but few other Penguins. Benefiting from more room than they were used to, Kevin Stevens, Rob Brown, Jock Callander, Phil Bourque and Randy Cunneyworth all scored their first career playoff goals in a first-period blitz that chased Ranger goalie Bob Froese to the bench and helped build a commanding 5–2 lead after one. Pittsburgh rode the explosion to a 7–4 win and a 2–0 series lead heading back to New York for Game Three.

The Rangers came out flying, racking up a 7–1 shots advantage in the first four and a half minutes, but each time Tom Barrasso was there to stop them. The big goalie routinely got his pads in front of pucks and flashed his hot glove hand to stymie the Blueshirts. While sweeping pucks clear from his crease, Barrasso was also sweeping aside his reputation for crumbling when it counted most.

"In the playoffs, if you're going to go far you need strong goaltending," said center John Cullen, "and Tommy is playing up to his potential."[15]

Barrasso held the fort long enough for Lemieux to open the scoring at 7:24 of the first. Tony Granato answered a minute later, but three in a row from Stevens, Cullen and Dan Quinn put the Penguins out of the Rangers' reach. Final score: 5–3 Pens and a 3–0 series stranglehold.

"It was kind of cool how silent that Garden was," said Quinn.

Lemieux again opened the scoring in game four, and two more markers from Phil Bourque before the frame was finished sent the Penguins on their way to a 4–3 win and a satisfying sweep of the Rangers, the first playoff series victory for the Penguins in a decade. Finally, the team had given the city and its fans—and themselves—something to be proud of.

"Every year I've been fortunate to be around the organization and see it get a little better and a little better and a little better," said Troy Loney, who first arrived in Pittsburgh in 1983. "From that, I've been gradually prouder and prouder and prouder. That's what you play for, to be proud of your team."[16]

The Penguins' round two opponent would be the Philadelphia Flyers, who had upset the Patrick Division champion Washington Capitals in six games. It would be the first time the cross-state rivals had met in post-season play. The rust of the Pens' eight-day layoff showed early in game one, as they fell behind 3–1. Goals by Dan Quinn and John Cullen only 33 seconds apart tied things up before the second period was over, though, and left wing Kevin Stevens' power rush around defenseman Mark Howe and nifty pass over to Rob Brown, who tapped the puck past goalie Ron Hextall, put the Pens up 4–3, which turned out to be the final score.

Two nights later, another rock-solid power forward—this one wearing an orange and black jersey—single-handedly evened the series for the Flyers. Tim Kerr answered an early Dan Quinn goal with a natural hat trick that gave the Flyers a 3–1 first-period lead en route to a 4–2 win.

Heading back to Philly for games three and four, the Pens were forced to deal with their first dose of adversity in the young playoffs. Somehow, they had to get past the disappointment of their first defeat. Questions around Tom Barrasso's big-game ability surfaced again, after the goaltender had had to remove himself from game two complaining of vision problems that caused him to see double. And, not to mention the pressure of having to win at least one game in a building that, despite a pair of regular season wins, still had to be an intimidating place for anyone wearing a penguin on their chest. Heading into game three, "we didn't know what to expect. We didn't know how we were going to respond," said Quinn.[17]

Barrasso provided an answer to one question, at least, by returning to his usual rock-solid play and helping his team get to the end of regulation tied at three. He robbed Scott Mellanby only 21 seconds into overtime and later stopped a Brian Propp breakaway a few moments later.

"Without Tom Barrasso, this game is over very quickly [in overtime]," said defenseman Zarley Zalapski.[18]

With eight minutes to go in the extra frame, Rob Brown showed a rare burst of speed, blowing past Mark Howe along the left side and dishing a perfect pass to Phil Bourque, who went in on Hextall and beat him through the five-hole. The Penguins poured off the bench and mobbed Bourque at center ice in celebration of one of the most dramatic victories in franchise history.

"Robbie's not known as the fastest guy," said Bourque later in the jubilant Pens locker room, "but he must've had the turbo-chargers kicked in. I just went to the net and he made an unbelievable pass. I'm numb. I'm still numb."[19]

The gritty Flyers showed their mettle in game four, rebounding with a dominating performance that resulted in a 4–1 win to even the series at two. In losing the game, the Pens also lost Lemieux for most of the third period after he collided with teammate Randy Cunneyworth in the neutral zone, banging his head off Cunneyworth's shoulder and crumpling to the ice. Lemieux did not return and was labeled questionable/doubtful for game five by trainer Skip Thayer.

True to form, Lemieux had thus far put up impressive point totals in his first Stanley Cup playoff experience. His 10 points on six goals and four assists led the Penguins. That total, however, seemed sub-par for the man who had registered an incredible 199 points in the regular season. He sat an unusual nine points back of his familiar rival, Wayne Gretzky, in the playoff scoring race. Observers noted that the "Mario Magic" that had resulted in performances such as his eight-point New Year's Eve outburst, or his routine potting of hat tricks, hadn't yet been seen in this post-season. Coach Gene

Ubriaco, however, felt it was only a matter of time before Lemieux put on a show of magnificence.

"It'll be there, and he'll be there."[20]

Mario was there, in the lineup for game five, and it was clear to all early on that "it" was also there. At 2:15 of the first, Lemieux snuck behind the Philly D, deked Ron Hextall with the slightest of fakes and backhanded the puck into an empty net to make it 1–0. Ninety seconds later, standing completely unmolested at the side of the Flyer net, Mario took a Bob Errey pass and directed it home for a 2–0 Pens lead. Just before the seven-minute mark, Lemieux again gained a step on the suddenly slothful Flyers' defense and, fading to his right side, rifled a pinpoint wrist shot to the far side of Hextall's net, beating him cleanly.

The Igloo exploded in joy. Lemieux had clearly taken his game to that next level and the Flyers seemed helpless to stop him. After Errey made it 4–0 only 12 seconds after Lemieux's hat trick goal and ex-Pen Mike Bullard answered back for the Flyers, Mario scored perhaps his craftiest goal on the night. Seeing Hextall venture behind his net for a loose puck, Lemieux swooped in and, with his long reach, stick-checked the big goalie, took the puck around the net and swept it into the open cage.

Lemieux would add three assists and an empty-net goal to tie the NHL single-game playoff records for goals with five and points with eight, leading the Pens to a 10–7 win. He also tied a few single-period NHL post-season records: most goals (four), most points (four), and assists (three). His final goal also set a new Penguin mark for career playoff goals at 10, one more than Jean Pronovost. Incredibly, it had taken Lemieux less than two playoff rounds to accomplish the feat!

"He elevated his game to the point where he just showed everybody else how much better than us he can be," observed Tom Barrasso.[21]

Even the Flyers were in awe of the display.

"I've never seen an individual performance like that," said coach Paul Holmgren. "We just got in front of that snowball with the Number 66 on it early, and when he gets rolling, it's a scary thing."[22]

The Penguins were now just one win away from advancing to the semi-finals for only the second time in their history, and one win away from extracting a measure of revenge against a team that had inflicted some of the worst pain on them during their 21 years of existence.

But the Flyers were not ready to relinquish their villainous role just yet. They had seemed to regain a measure of confidence in the third period of game five, outshooting Pittsburgh 21–7 and outscoring them 4–1. Clearly, there was some fight left in these Philadelphians and they showed it in game six back at the Spectrum. Two more goals from the hulking Tim Kerr in the first period set the tone and the Flyers coasted to an easy 6–2 win against a suddenly powerless Penguin squad. To the surprise of no one, this first-ever Battle of Pennsylvania would need a seventh game to decide a winner.

Just prior to puck drop, the Penguins learned of a bombshell emanating from the Flyers' dressing room: starting goalie Ron Hextall was out of the lineup with a sprained right knee, injured in the second period of game six. Backup Ken Wregget would be his replacement. The former Toronto Maple Leaf had looked sharp in the fifth game, shutting out the Pens during his 29 total minutes of relief work. He looked just as sharp in the first period of game seven, stopping all 11 Penguin shots. Brian Propp gave Philly the lead late in the frame. Lemieux answered at 4:21 of the second with a howitzer from the right faceoff circle that beat Wregget cleanly.

A Jeff Chychrun cross-checking penalty less than a minute later brought the vaunted Penguin power play back on to the ice, and Mario and Co. looked ready to take command of the game. But when Propp took defenseman Jim Johnson out of the play at the Flyer blue line, Mark Howe grabbed the puck and broke out on a two-on-one with Dave Poulin. Howe waited until defender Paul Coffey went to his knees and shoveled the puck over to Poulin, who ripped a 25-footer past Barrasso.

"It was a crusher for the Penguins," wrote Bill Lyon in the *Philadelphia Inquirer* the next day. "You could see them deflate, doubling over like a fighter hurt by a left hook to the kidneys."[23]

The Pens recovered enough to pepper Wregget with 24 more shots, but the backup stopped them all. Old Penguin favorite Mike Bullard delivered another dagger 40 seconds into the third to make it 3–1, and Scott Mellanby finished the Penguins' season for good with an empty-netter to make the final 4–1.

"We had a great opportunity in front of us, and unfortunately it slipped through our hands," said Tom Barrasso in the solemn Penguin locker room.[24]

"Kenny Wregget stood on his head," Quinn remembered 30 years later. "I remember we pumped a lot of shots at him in the first period but we were down 1–0. It was just deflating. I had some point blanks on him myself on the power play and he made some great saves. He was energetic and acrobatic and fresh. He was the difference in that game."[25]

Despite the disappointment, it was clear to all that the season represented a gigantic step forward for the team and the franchise. This was a group that looked to have a promising future ahead of it.

"It's tough to accept right now, but we have to learn from this," said Lemieux. "Hopefully, we can regroup from this and go as far as the finals. I think we have the potential to do that. It's just a matter of getting a couple more players and building from there."[26]

25

Backaches and Heartaches: 1989–90

Expectations had never been higher for a Pittsburgh Penguin squad than they were for the 1989–90 edition. With a lineup featuring 199-point scorer Mario Lemieux, the game's top offensive defenseman in Paul Coffey, and elite puckstopper Tom Barrasso, who was set to play his first full season as a Penguin, many observers felt Pittsburgh was poised to capture the franchise's first division crown—and maybe much more.

What's more, General Manager Tony Esposito had made off-season moves that promised to firm up two weak spots on the previous year's roster, adding Andrew McBain, a right winger who had scored 37 goals in 1988–89, and monstrous defenseman Jim Kyte from Winnipeg in a trade that sent Randy Cunneyworth, Dave McLlwain and goalie Rick Tabaracci to the Jets.

The Penguins, however, were soon to be reminded that nothing is a certainty in pro sports. A number of unexpected roadblocks appeared on their path to prosperity, most notably an uncharacteristically slow start by Lemieux. Of course, "slow" was a relative term. After eight games, Le Magnifique had posted four goals and 10 assists, good enough for a spot on the NHL's top 10 scoring list and a pace that would see him collect 140 points on the season—spectacular for most players, but decidedly underwhelming for the league's two-time defending scoring champion. The "slump" continued into November, with Lemieux chalking it up to a lack of concentration and his not moving his feet as effectively as in the past. Mario's malaise spread to the rest of the offense as well, with the Pens averaging only 3.5 goals per game in October, down from 5.3 in October of the previous year.

"We're not scoring in bunches like we did last year," said Rob Brown, the 49-goal-getter a season earlier who collected a mere four in October. "Last year, we were winning games 7–1 and 9–2, winning big at home. This year we haven't."[1]

Other observers thought the Pens' slower-than-expected start was the result of the players' discontent with coach Gene Ubriaco. Colorful Hockey Night in Canada commentator and former Bruins coach Don Cherry went so far as to say the Pens were playing poorly to get Ubriaco fired. The most common complaints centered on Ubriaco's constant shuffling of lines, his inability to get the power play going, the lack of any systems to set up the attack, and his oft-displayed refusal to capitalize on the last-change advantage given to the home team before faceoffs.[2]

Players were also upset with how some of their peers were pushed out of the lineup and ultimately shipped out of town. When popular defenseman Rod Buskas was dealt to Vancouver after spending the season watching from the press box, some players displayed their disapproval by wearing black armbands at the next practice. Dave Hannan, who claimed he had not been informed by Penguins management when he was claimed in the NHL waiver draft by Toronto before the season, confirmed there was discontent in the Pittsburgh locker room.

"There's a little bit of frustration over there right now," he told a Toronto newspaper. "They have some guys who aren't happy."[3]

Esposito denied reports of any dissention and continually stated his belief that the players would eventually play their way out of the slump. As the team continued to turn in uninspired efforts throughout November, however, rumors of Ubriaco's firing persisted. By early December, the DeBartolos had seen enough and pulled the trigger on sweeping changes that saw both Ubriaco and Esposito given the heave-ho and replaced by 43-year-old Craig Patrick, the former Rangers general manager considered by many to be one of the most astute young minds in hockey. The arrival of the calm yet focused and determined Patrick immediately injected a breath of fresh air into the organization and pricked the boil of tension that had plagued it for months.

Finally, it seemed, the DeBartolos had hired the right man.

"I think [Patrick]'s got a lot of respect from everybody around the league, and I'm sure he's going to have a lot of respect in this [dressing] room," said Lemieux. "I think it was a good change, a good choice. The attitude's going to change."[4]

Patrick was born into hockey royalty. His grandfather, Lester Patrick, had been a standout at all levels of the sport. He was one of the game's first great defensemen, helping the Montreal Wanderers capture back-to-back Stanley Cups in 1906 and 1907, and was also one of its top innovators. Along with brother Frank, he introduced rules and features that helped define the game as we know it today, such as bluelines, penalty shots and assists. While coaching the Rangers in 1928, the 44-year-old Patrick famously filled in as goalie in game two of the Stanley Cup final, sparking the Blueshirts to their first ever NHL championship.

Lester's sons, Muzz and Lynn (Craig's father) played in the NHL. Muzz was a solid defenseman and Lynn was a Hall of Fame forward. It was therefore not much of a surprise when Craig also made it to the big show, debuting with the California Golden Seals in 1971. A dependable yet unspectacular right winger, Patrick played 401 games over the next eight years for some horrible teams: the Seals, Kansas City Scouts and Washington Capitals. It was during a brief stop in St. Louis in 1974–75 that Patrick tasted his only post-season action: two losses in a quick preliminary round sweep at the hands of—ironically—the Penguins.

Patrick may not have had the on-ice talent of his father or grandfather, but it was clear to all who knew him that he had their hockey brains. Shortly after retiring as a player, Patrick was named as an assistant coach under Herb Brooks on the 1980 U.S. Olympic team, playing a crucial role in getting the most out of a roster of castoff amateurs and taking them all the way to a stunning gold medal win.

With his stock higher than ever, it wasn't long before the team that his grandfather had helped build came knocking on Craig's door. The Rangers hired him as their assistant general manager in 1980 and removed the first word in that title a year later, making him the youngest GM in league history at the time. He guided the Rangers to the playoffs every year he was at the helm, but with no Stanley Cup final appearances by 1986, Patrick was let go.

He'd been serving for three years as director of recreation and athletics at the University of Denver when the DeBartolos came calling. Patrick had received some solid offers to return to the NHL's management ranks, but resisted all of them. The situation in Pittsburgh, however, seemed just right. "I've missed the NHL since July 15, 1986," he said the day he was introduced as Pittsburgh's GM and interim coach, the date of his Ranger firing clearly burned into his memory. "I've missed it terribly."[5]

With the Penguins, Patrick saw a team with enough offensive talent to take care of the task of scoring goals. What he didn't see was an effective defensive system, which he got to work instilling as soon as he arrived. The players welcomed it with open arms.

"It's going to take time to get Craig's system into our team, but I think you've got 20 hockey players here who are really willing to learn," said Coffey.[6]

Slowly but surely, the Penguins came back to life under Patrick's guidance, returning to the .500 mark 20 games into his tenure. Mario Lemieux, who had felt so sluggish and out of sorts that he had undergone medical tests in November to see what might be wrong (the tests all came back negative), was scoring consistently. On January 4 at home against Vancouver, Lemieux's assist on a Zarley Zalapski goal at 7:50 of the first period gave him at least one point in 29 consecutive games, making him only the second player in league history to amass that long a streak (Wayne Gretzky had done it three times).

Throughout January, Lemieux kept scoring on a regular basis and extending his incredible streak, but it was a few points he put up that didn't count in the standings that received the most attention. On January 21, the NHL All-Star Game came to Pittsburgh for the first time, and expectations were high for a grand performance by the Penguins' captain. On a worldwide stage, Mario the Magnificent didn't disappoint. He scored on a wraparound only 21 seconds into the game, causing the roof to nearly blow off the venerable Igloo. At the 13-minute mark, he rifled a slap shot past Mike Vernon for his second goal. Later, he took a feed from familiar partner Paul Coffey along the right boards and cut in on Vernon. Not taking his eyes off the net, he pulled the puck back, sending an incoming Al Iafrate sliding off to the corner. With defenseman Doug Wilson hooking him from behind, Lemieux confused Vernon by deftly transferring the puck to his backhand before easily depositing the puck into the empty cage. As the Civic Arena erupted again, even the greatest players in the game could do nothing but shake their heads. "It was just phenomenal," said teammate-for-a-day Ray Bourque. "The guys [on the bench] were looking at each other in awe. It was like, 'Wow!'"[7]

Lemieux capped his day with a fourth goal in the third period, leading the Wales Conference to a 12–7 win and taking home his third All-Star MVP award in only his fifth appearance.

"It was special," Lemieux said after the game. "I wanted to do something for the fans of Pittsburgh."[8]

Lemieux kept doing special things following the All-Star Game, namely scoring at least one point in every game he played. As the streak hit 40 games and beyond, it seemed a certainty that he would break Gretzky's record of 51. There was, in fact, really only one thing standing in the way of setting a new record, and it wasn't any of the Penguins' opponents. Lemieux's back, which had been a source of pain for him since his junior days, was getting worse than ever. The problem was a herniated disk in his lower spine that caused him constant pain. On some game days, he could barely walk into the arena. Once on the ice, however, he'd incredibly go out and get his required point, and often many more. The weight of having to lead his team every night, in what had become another dogfight for a Patrick Division playoff spot, did little to alleviate his condition.

On February 14 at Madison Square Garden, with only five games separating him from equaling the record, Lemieux finally succumbed to the pain and reluctantly pulled himself after a pointless first period. The streak was over at 46.

"You hate to see it end because of an injury," winger Troy Loney said.

"That's what's sad. If the guy had been able to give it his all tonight, he'd still have that streak going. We all know that."[9]

Patrick offered no timetable for Lemieux's return. His teammates would have to soldier on without him, and they'd also have to do so without Tom Barrasso. Six days before the streak ended, Craig Patrick revealed that Barrasso's two-and-a-half-year-old daughter Ashley had been fighting a form of pediatric cancer known as neuroblastoma since the previous summer. Barrasso would be taking a leave of absence to be with his wife and their daughter in Los Angeles, where Ashley was scheduled for a bone marrow transplant, radiation and chemotherapy.

"Tom's been living with this for a long time," said Wendell Young, who would now share the goaltending load with Frank Pietrangelo. "His family needs him now. That's all there is to it."[10]

Stunned by the loss of two of their biggest stars, the Pens managed to keep it together in the immediate aftermath of their departures. A 4–3 overtime win against the Islanders on February 22 put them into a tie for first place in the Patrick with the Rangers. Two nights later in Montreal, however, the fragile Penguin house began to crumble. Surrendering a whopping 62 shots—a new Canadiens team record—the Penguins were utterly blown out of the Forum by the score of 11–1. As the home team's goal total mounted, the Penguins' confidence plummeted. It was clear to everyone just how much they were missing Lemieux in particular.

"Even though Pittsburgh is playing well, you can't afford to lose a player like that for a long time," said Montreal forward Guy Carbonneau. "It took a lot of pressure off us, not having to play against [Lemieux]. You don't have to look where he is all the time."[11]

Said an exhausted Pietrangelo, who was in net for all 60 excruciating minutes, "Obviously, there were a lot of breakdowns. Everybody had an off-night. I'm just glad it's over. We've got to move on now."[12]

The only direction the Penguins would move over the next month, however, would be further down in the Patrick standings. They would win only three of their next 16 games. A solution to the club's porous team defense—which would eventually surrender the second-most goals against in the league with 359—had not been found. Quite simply, the 1989–90 Penguins were a team that liked to score goals and wasn't too keen on spending much effort on preventing them. It was easy to ease off on a backchecking effort when you had the insurance policies of Lemieux, Coffey and Barrasso in your hip pocket. But without Numbers 66 and 35, that approach simply didn't work.

The Penguin twine continued to bulge and the losses continued to mount. A saving grace was that the once-rugged Patrick Division wasn't what it had been in past years. Heading into the season's final week, the Rangers led it with a mere 81 points. Former giants Philadelphia and the Islanders were both well below .500 and trailing the fourth-place Penguins by two points. The final playoff spot was there for the Penguins' taking.

They scored a somewhat impressive 3–3 tie at home against the Stanley Cup Champion Calgary Flames, but followed that with a loss and a tie in a home-and-home with the Hartford Whalers, who had clinched a playoff spot and knew they would finish no higher or lower than fourth in the Adams Division.

The club got a morale boost when Barrasso returned to the lineup for their second-last game in St. Louis, but again the Pens fell short, losing 5–4. The Penguins' season would therefore come down to the last game, a do-or-die affair at home against the Buffalo Sabres. If the Penguins won, they were in the playoffs. Lose, and they'd need the Islanders to drop their final game against the Flyers and have Philly then lose their last game against Detroit.

It was a complex mess they'd put themselves in, but at least the Penguins still had their destiny on their own sticks. And they'd also have their best player back in the lineup for the Buffalo game. Lemieux, who had been undergoing special treatments and training in Los Angeles since he'd been forced to the sidelines, had improved enough to gain doctors' approval to come back for this all-important regular season finale.

"I'm here, and I'm going to play," said Lemieux. "It's important for myself, for the Pittsburgh Penguins, for my teammates, and for the fans in Pittsburgh that we make the playoffs."[13]

Mario's presence sent a charge through the Penguin dressing room. "There was a lot of confidence, just with him being here, just being on the bench," said winger Phil Bourque.

The game was a tight one from the opening faceoff, with the fans sitting on the edge of their seats through a scoreless first period. Pens center Doug Smith relieved some of the tension when he scored at 4:02 of the second, but Buffalo countered with a power play goal from Alexander Mogilny and a howitzer from Rick Vaive that knocked the water bottle off Tom Barrasso's net to give Buffalo a 2–1 lead.

But, as had been so often the case, it was Number 66 to the rescue. Lemieux rifled a long slap shot past Sabres goalie Clint Malarchuk 3:38 into the third to even the score at two.

A glance at the out-of-town scoreboard revealed that the Islanders had a comfortable 5–1 lead on the Flyers and were well on their way to victory, which meant all the Penguins now needed to clinch the final playoff spot was a tie. The score remained 2–2 through the third period and the first minute of overtime. (Unlike those of later years, regular season overtime rules at the time did not award a point to a team that lost in the extra frame.)

With less than four minutes separating them from a second-straight playoff appearance and the hope of salvaging a season that had gone horribly off-script, one of the unlikeliest scoring threats on the ice stepped into the spotlight for Buffalo and added yet another volume of heartbreak to the Penguin franchise's well-stocked library. In a seemingly innocent play, low-scoring defenseman Uwe Krupp corralled the puck near the boards just inside the Pittsburgh blueline and fired a hard shot toward the goal. Somehow, it found its way past a stunned Barrasso.

Game over.

Season over.

As the Sabres rejoiced, the Penguin players could merely drift off the ice toward the dressing room before a disbelieving Igloo audience.

"I didn't really see [Krupp's shot] until the last 10 or 15 feet," Barrasso said in the locker room. "That's when it hit something. That's my responsibility."[14] The always-frank goalie was not assigning blame for the night's result to anyone but the players themselves. "We put ourselves in the position where a bad break could beat us."[15]

A quiet Lemieux offered that the loss was "tough to accept."[16]

Phil Bourque was more direct. "This is an awful feeling. It's like getting kicked in the gut with an iron boot."[17]

The players, management and fans now had all spring and summer to feel the pain of that kick, and to ponder the many uncertainties that now faced the team. Lemieux, the very foundation of the franchise, was facing the possibility of back surgery, a procedure that, worst-case scenario, could prove to be career-threatening. The book was still out on whether Barrasso could fully overcome his personal challenges to fill the role of an elite goaltender the Penguins needed to become a true Stanley Cup contender. On the ice, the Penguins were a mess defensively and they needed more depth on offense if they were going to take things to the next level.

With Craig Patrick committed to handing the coaching reins to someone else for the 1990–91 season, the Penguins would also have to adjust to a new coach, the club's fifth in five years.

As the players headed off for yet another early visit to the golf course, Patrick went back to his Civic Arena office and got to work. His job of building this eternally underachieving franchise into a winner was just beginning.

26

Top of the Mountain:
1990–91

As the Penguins began yet another premature beginning to their summer, the second-biggest question surrounding the team (after the one about Mario Lemieux's health) was "Who will the next coach be?" Since his hiring as general manager in December 1990, Craig Patrick had repeatedly said his time behind the bench as interim coach would be temporary. After joining the organization, he wanted to use the remainder of the 1989–90 campaign to get a close-up view of his new charges from ice level, but once that was done, so too would his time as coach be.

The names of a few qualified and available candidates were bandied about in the press, including ex-Capitals coach Bryan Murray, Darryl Sutter, Blair MacDonald, coach of the Pens' Muskegon farm team, former Penguins defenseman Paul Baxter, and ex-NHLer Barry Melrose. Patrick, however, was looking for more than just a new coach. He wanted to rebuild whatever parts of the organization he felt needed an overhaul—and it seemed there were many. "What we need to do is put together a staff that's going to take us in the direction of success. We need to look at the bigger picture, not just focus on the coach."[1]

On June 12, Patrick brought that picture into clear focus when he announced the signing of two of the most respected minds in hockey. Scotty Bowman, the winningest coach in NHL history, would be the Pens' director of player development, and legendary U.S. college and former Calgary Flames coach "Badger" Bob Johnson was brought aboard as the team's new bench boss.

"To me, this develops the best management team in hockey," Patrick said at the press conference introducing his two new employees. "I've always been taught to surround yourself with good people, and I can't think of any better."[2]

Few were arguing. "With Patrick, Bowman and Johnson, that's a pretty impressive front-end team they've put together in Pittsburgh," said Edmonton GM Glen Sather.[3]

Johnson, a three-time NCAA champion as coach of the Wisconsin Badgers (from whence he got his nickname) who had also led the Flames to a Stanley Cup final appearance in 1986, had been growing restless in his role as executive director of USA Hockey in Colorado. He was itching to get back behind an NHL bench. Patrick had known Johnson since 1975 through their USA Hockey connections. His Penguins were in desperate need of the type of system-oriented, positive-thinking brand of direction he knew Johnson would bring.

"He's the best person for our particular situation," said Patrick. "He's a person who encourages performance as opposed to demanding it."[4]

The players enthusiastically welcomed the news of Johnson's hiring.

"He doesn't yell and scream. He's very knowledgeable," said Mario Lemieux. "He'll have more systems than they've had here in Penguins history. He's a great teacher."[5]

Added Tom Barrasso, "[Johnson] has proven himself. Now the players need to prove themselves to him."[6]

Bowman came to the Penguins with perhaps the most impressive resume in all of hockey. After coaching the expansion St. Louis Blues to the Stanley Cup final in each of their first three years, Bowman moved to Montreal, where he guided the powerhouse Canadiens to five Stanley Cup wins in seven years. After being rebuffed for the Montreal general manager's post in 1979, Bowman shuffled off to Buffalo, an organization that was more than willing to give him that title. He never did attain the same kind of success with the Sabres as he had in Montreal, however, and was let go during the 1986–87 season. He had been doing color commentary for *Hockey Night in Canada* for three years when Patrick approached him about a role with the Penguins. The timing was perfect because Bowman, like Johnson, was eager to get back into the competitive fray.

"I haven't lost a game in three and half years on TV, but I was always thinking that maybe someday I'd get back in hockey," he said. "This affords me an opportunity to get back into the NHL on a level I was seeking."[7]

As director of player personnel, Bowman's chief responsibility would be assessing the organization's talent at all levels. He'd be evaluating potential draft choices, trade candidates and players already in the Penguins system.

Patrick's efforts to bring in experienced talent with a winning pedigree didn't stop with the management staff. Later in the summer, he signed free agent Joey Mullen, a 33-year-old sniper who had scored 36 or more goals in each of his past seven seasons and had won a Stanley Cup with Calgary, and Bryan Trottier, the seventh-highest scorer in NHL history and owner of four Stanley Cup rings from his days as a cornerstone of the Islanders dynasty.

Mullen still possessed a quick release and could reasonably be expected to contribute 30 to 40 goals. Trottier, however, was no longer the elite point producer he was on Long Island. His role would center on winning key faceoffs and sound defensive hockey. Perhaps most importantly, Trottier's immense knowledge of what was required to become a champion could be imparted to the Pens' young nucleus.

"He can add tremendous amounts of character and help in the attitude areas," said Patrick.[8]

Meanwhile, Mario Lemieux was diligently following his back rehabilitation program to hopefully be ready for training camp. In early July, however, the pain returned and it was decided to move ahead with surgery that would remove the herniated portion of one of Lemieux's disks and a small amount of bone from his spinal canal. The 80-minute procedure was conducted July 9 and was deemed a success by Dr. Peter Sheptak, the neurologist who performed the surgery. Lemieux noticed an immediate reduction in the pain he'd felt in his buttocks and legs.

"I think I can be a better player now that I will be 100 percent," he said as he left the hospital three days after the surgery. "Hopefully, I can come back and have my best season in the NHL."[9]

Mario's back, however, had different ideas.

While Lemieux was traveling with the team as an observer on a preseason road trip in September, his back pain returned. He reluctantly returned to Pittsburgh to have the doctors investigate. They found an inflammation in the disk area of his back. The condition was identified as vertebral osteomyelitis, an infection that attacks the bony portion of the spine. It seemed to be completely unrelated to the earlier issue that prompted the surgery.

"There's no connection we've been able to find. It's just a case of bad luck," said team physician Dr. Charles Burke. "This is a very uncommon thing, especially in a healthy individual."[10]

The good news was that the new ailment was entirely treatable. The bad news was that the treatment would sideline Lemieux for at least two months, possibly three.

The news cast a pall through the Penguin organization. "There's no doubt we're going to miss Mario," said new assistant coach Barry Smith. "I'd be lying if I didn't say that."[11]

In typical fashion, Bob Johnson tried to take a more positive view. "We'll try to get a good start, and then if things start to slide, we've got a big bonus coming. Sometime, we're going to get the best player in the world back."[12]

John Cullen may not have been the best player in the world, but as the puck dropped on the new season, he was doing a fine impersonation of him. Having scored 92 points the previous year, the 5'10", 180-pound center was a natural choice to assume Mario's spot on the top line. He exploded out of the gate with nine points in his first two games. By the end of the month, to the surprise of even himself, Cullen was sitting atop the NHL scoring race with 26 points in 13 games.

"As far as getting off to a great start like this, I didn't know I could go this good," Cullen said.[13]

Not far behind him were his left wing, Kevin Stevens, who scored an incredible six points against Washington in the season opener and added 16 more throughout October, and occasional right wing Mark Recchi, who racked up 21 points in the season's first month. Together, they formed what came to be known as the Option Line, so named because each player was playing out the option year of their respective contracts.

"The chemistry, as a line, is pretty darned good," observed Bob Johnson. "You've got someone who can shoot off the pass who's quick [Recchi], a center who can pass and is clever at making plays, and then you've got a left winger who is big and strong and can skate."[14]

The line powered the Penguins to the fifth-best goal total in the league by the season's 25-game mark, but the team still found itself in a familiar position: fifth place in the Patrick Division. The culprit was a familiar one: poor team defense. Despite Johnson's best efforts to instill a more defensive attitude amongst his players, the forwards still seemed to backcheck only when the mood struck them and the defense often fed the puck to opposing forwards as often as they did their own.

"It all boils down to bearing down in our own end and taking our responsibilities seriously," said defenseman Jim Johnson. "Until we start doing that, we're never going to pull out of this."[15]

As it turned out, Johnson would never get the chance. In a blockbuster swap of defensemen on December 11, Patrick shipped him and Chris Dahlquist to Minnesota for the offensively gifted Larry Murphy and rugged crease-clearer Peter Taglianetti. It was Patrick's hope that Murphy, who had scored 60 points or more in seven of his 10 NHL seasons, would represent a significant upgrade in a few key areas that had hindered the Penguins throughout the young season.

"Larry can help us move the puck out of our own zone with a little more ease than the people we're letting go," he said. "And being right-handed helps with picking the puck off the boards, with getting it out. We've got to get the puck to our forwards a lot quicker."[16]

The move paid immediate dividends. Shortly after it was made, the Pens reeled off six straight wins, one short of the club record.

The deal was but one in a series Patrick had made in his quest to find the right team chemistry. In late October he had added ruggedness to the defense corps by dealing a late-round draft pick to St. Louis for veteran Gordie Roberts. He later dealt flashy but defense-deficient winger Rob Brown to Hartford for a more complete, two-way forward in the form of winger Scott Young. He also acquired veteran Jiri Hrdina from Calgary for spare part Jim Kyte, not only for what the 32-year-old had left in his on-ice tank but also to help first-round draft pick Jaromir Jagr adjust to life in the NHL and North America. The Penguins had taken the talented Czechoslovakian right winger fifth overall in the 1990 draft—their reward for the heart-wrenching season-ending loss to Buffalo—and watched him get off to a respectable start. But learning English and communicating with his coaches and teammates was proving difficult for the 18-year-old and was affecting his game. On December 13, with Jagr mired in a slump that had seen him score only one point in 13

Paul Coffey's 93 points from the blueline helped offset the absence of Mario Lemieux for 54 games in the 1990–91 regular season (courtesy Ron Kerrigan).

games, Patrick made the move to get Hrdina. The payoff was immediate, with Jagr regaining his aggressive edge and piecing together a seven-game scoring streak before the month was out.

"He's a young guy, so I want to help him when the coaches explain tactics and what they expect from him," said Hrdina. "He didn't understand it before."[17]

As Jagr and the Penguins kept scoring enough goals to give them the NHL lead in that category, Mario Lemieux continued his rehab program. In January, he resumed skating with the team at practice and, after much speculation as to when his return would take place, Lemieux stepped back into game action for the first time since March 31, 1990, when he hopped over the boards against the Nordiques at Le Colisee on January 26. If there were any doubts about whether the Penguins captain would be able to capture the form that had earned him the unofficial title of the game's best player, they were erased in the second period when Number 66 racked up two assists.

He added another in the third to help build a 6–2 Penguin lead, which they almost blew but hung on for a 6–5 win.

"I felt pretty good," he said after the game. "I'm just a little sore, but that's muscle soreness."[18]

Lemieux's return, however, did not bring about any sustained team success, and the problems were entirely in their own end of the rink. A wretched five-game road trip in late February that saw them give up 28 goals and collect just one point left them only seven points up on fifth-place Washington. The team was in free-fall, and unless they somehow started tightening things up defensively, another playoff-less season was becoming a distinct possibility.

Johnson was an astute enough observer of the game to realize that a big reason for his team's poor defense was actually its high-octane offense.

"This team wants to skate; it wants to go. You can't restrain this team. If your personnel includes players like Ray Bourque, you can teach defense effectively, and you can play it. But if you've got Lemieux and Coffey and players with those kinds of inclinations, it's different."[19]

The porous Penguin defense caused Johnson, usually able to see a silver lining in the darkest of storm clouds, to describe the team's chief ill with uncharacteristic bluntness. "We're hurting on defense. It doesn't take a genius to figure that out.... We need a couple more pieces of the puzzle."[20]

Craig Patrick could certainly figure it out. With the NHL trade deadline fast approaching, he began working the phones with feverish intensity to find those missing pieces. His hard work paid off on March 4, when he completed the most important and most shocking trade in the history of the franchise—a trade deadline deal that is still recognized as one of the most successful in league history.

Patrick sent John Cullen, then the fifth-highest scorer in the league with 94 points, Zarley Zalapski and minor-league winger Jeff Parker to Hartford for Whaler legend and all-time franchise leading scorer Ron Francis, hard-hitting defenseman Ulf Samuelsson, and 6'3", 200-pound defenseman Grant Jennings.

The shock and sadness that came with losing two important and popular contributors was offset by the knowledge that the Penguins had added two players who excelled at the part of the game with which they needed help so urgently—on defense. Aside from being an elite scorer, Francis prided himself on playing a dedicated two-way game. He had unfathomably fallen into coach Rick Ley's doghouse, however, and been stripped of his captaincy, leading to an ugly situation in which he was deemed expendable by the organization.

Samuelsson was a vicious hitter and eager shot-blocker who would do whatever it took to clear the Whaler crease, be it brute-force physicality or the occasional high stick to the face or a slash to the shins. "Ulfie" was no mere goon, however, possessing a smooth-skating stride and a talent for reading the play. He could also deliver hard, accurate passes onto the sticks of his breaking forwards.

Jennings was, quite simply, an intimidating physical mass who was more than adept at keeping opposing forwards honest in his own zone.

"We gave up two excellent players, but we got back two all-stars, and we think we're going to help our hockey club," said coach Bob Johnson.[21]

The trade sent a charge of energy through the team. Not only did the three newcomers bring about an immediate improvement in their defensive play, their arrival seemed to send a clear message to the rest of the dressing room that any further lack of effort while the opposition possessed the puck would most likely result in a one-way ticket to another city. The preachings of Johnson about the need for sound defense finally seemed to be soaking in.

The effect was a 6–0–1 record after the trade. Combined with a perfectly timed slump by the New York Rangers, who had been sitting atop the Patrick Division since late October, the surge pushed the Pens into first place on March 17. The franchise's first championship of any kind was square in their sights. They headed into Detroit for the third-last game of the season needing a win to clinch the division title.

With Mario Lemieux standing behind the Penguin bench in a suit thanks to a swollen eye he'd picked up the night before in Philadelphia when a puck struck him in the face, the Pens spotted the Wings a 1–0 lead before exploding for three goals before the first period was done. Detroit tied it in the second, but a Kevin Stevens power play marker with 32 seconds left lifted the team's spirits as they headed to the second intermission. Goals by Ron Francis and Jaromir Jagr early in the third put the Pens ahead for good and they skated to a 7–4 win.

"We can finally put a banner up in Pittsburgh," said Mark Recchi. "And it's going to be a great feeling when we do."[22]

Added Troy Loney, who had suffered longer than anyone in Pittsburgh, "All those years when things went wrong are behind us now. We're looking forward."[23]

The first obstacle on that road forward was the fourth-place New Jersey Devils, who had finished only nine points back of the Penguins and were playing inspired hockey under new coach Tom McVie, who had replaced the fired John Cunniff on March 4. New Jersey was playing a tight-checking, never-say-die brand of hockey, which had resulted in seven come-from-behind victories in the season's final three weeks.

They displayed that spirit in game one of the best-of-seven series in Pittsburgh, erasing a 1–0 Penguin lead late in the second and dominating the game throughout the third, outshooting Pittsburgh 15–7 and outscoring them 2–0 to claim the first game by a final score of 3–1.

"We better open our eyes," said Paul Coffey in a quiet post-game dressing room. "We're playing a good hockey club. It's not like there were 15 or 20 points separating us this year."[24]

A pair of dramatic Pittsburgh wins followed to put the Penguins up 2–1 in the series. The first came on a spectacular individual effort from rookie Jaromir Jagr in overtime of game two, in which he burst down the right wing in the Devils zone, cut in front of the net and held the puck with his long reach long enough to get goalie Chris Terreri to go down, before flipping the puck over him into the yawning cage. The second came courtesy of Mark Recchi in game three in New Jersey, when he knocked home a loose puck in the final minute of the third to give the Penguins a 4–3 win.

Just when the Pens had seemed to have grabbed hold of the series, however, the resilient Devils showed they had no intention of going away easily. They outhustled Pittsburgh for much of game four and Terreri withstood a third-period charge to secure a 4–1 win and even the series at two. Back at home for the crucial fifth game, the Penguins skated for the first two periods like it was just another game in November and fell behind 2–0. Ron Francis brought them back to life with a goal and an assist in the third, but Claude Lemieux answered for New Jersey on a power play. It proved to be the winner in a 4–2 Devil triumph. To stay alive, the Penguins would have to win Game Six in the Meadowlands Arena.

"It's survival now, guys," Johnson told his troops. "It's the law of the jungle. We've got to survive over there."[25]

As was becoming the norm, the Badger's positive attitude was infectious.

"It doesn't even have to be a pretty one," said defenseman Larry Murphy about the upcoming game six. "We've just got to go in there and find a way."[26]

They'd have to do it without two key pieces of their puzzle, however: Paul Coffey, who had been out since game four after being high-sticked in the face, and Tom Barrasso, who had injured his shoulder in game five. The Penguins would have to rely on backup goalie Frank Pietrangelo, who would be making his first career playoff appearance. His debut got off to a shaky start when a pass from behind his net by Devils winger John MacLean caromed off defenseman Larry Murphy's skate and into his net only 3:29 in. Fortunately for the Pens, Mario Lemieux was clearly on his game this night, controlling the play whenever he stepped on to the ice. The Penguins kept their composure and tied things up on a Kevin Stevens snap shot at 10:49. Stevens then added a power play marker to give Pittsburgh the lead.

Later in the period, with the Devils pressing on a power play, Peter Stastny looked ready to fire home the tying goal, with the puck on his stick and an empty net staring him in the face from 10 feet out.

Well, almost empty.

Stastny shot and Pietrangelo, in desperation, reached back with a stretched glove hand to cover a minute part of the gaping cage—the exact part where the puck was headed.

The Devils had their sticks in the air. The Meadowlands crowd was already cheering. But there was no goal to celebrate, thanks to the backup's incredible grab, which has come to be known in Penguin lore simply as "The Save."

"He hit my glove," said a humble Pietrangelo later. "It's not a matter of a skill save. It's a lucky save," He added, though, that "lucky or not, a save like that is a big lift for the team."[27]

From there, the Penguins built a 4–1 lead, only to have the Devils battle back to get within one at 4–3. Late in the third, New Jersey looked to have tied it when the puck hit Laurie Boschman in front of the Pens' net and went in. Referee Bill McCreary, however, ruled Boschman directed it in deliberately with his skate and waved the goal off. Replays showed the puck hit Boschman's stick after hitting his skate, which would make for a legal goal. At the time, however, the NHL did not utilize replays to help determine calls and the apparent goal stayed off the scoreboard. The Penguins had caught a major break. They held on for a 4–3 win to send the series back to Pittsburgh for a winner-take-all game seven.

The Penguins finally put it all together in the decisive contest, dominating the Devils from the opening faceoff to the final whistle. Paul Coffey was a surprise starter after getting clearance from medical staff on his injured eye. Feeding off the boost "The Doctor's" return gave them, the Pens built a 2–0 lead after one and rode another fine performance from Pietrangelo to move on to the second round and a date with the Washington Capitals. And they did it without Mario Lemieux for the final 40 minutes, who had to leave with back spasms.

"It shows a lot of heart, a lot of character, the way we came back," winger Phil Bourque told the *Pittsburgh Press* in the post-game locker room. "It's probably uncharacteristic of the Penguins in the past, but this is a whole different team."[28]

The Capitals had taken out the Rangers in six games in their opening-round series. After dropping the first game 4–2 at home, the Pens rebounded in a good old-fashioned shootout that resembled anything but playoff hockey. Kevin Stevens got the winner at 8:10 of overtime to cap a wild 7–6 win, in which Pittsburgh blew a 5–3 lead and had to tie it late on a Randy Gilhen marker to send it to the extra frame.

Aside from the Caps, the Pens were also battling a rash of injuries to their defensive corps. Paul Coffey had suffered a broken jaw and underwent surgery that was expected to keep him out for at least two weeks. Ulf Samuelsson was sidelined with a broken hand, and Peter Taglianetti was out with a bruised ankle. Bob Johnson was forced to insert rookie Jim Paek into the lineup for game three in Washington to help fill the void.

Sensing that the team needed help protecting their own zone, the forwards buckled down just as Johnson had been pleading with them to all season. With Tom Barrasso back between the pipes, the Pens played a simple yet solid game that resulted in a solid 3–1 win and a 2–1 series lead.

After losing three players as the Penguins had, "you need good goaltending and we needed good backchecking. I think the team rallied around that," said Johnson.[29]

The emphasis on defense continued in game four. Although the Penguins surrendered 39 shots, many were from the perimeter, making them easier for Barrasso to see—and stop. "Tommy B" was clearly in a groove, turning aside 38 of them en route to another 3–1 win. The Penguins were now one victory away from advancing past the second round of the playoffs for the first time in franchise history.

Back at the Igloo before a raucous sellout crowd waving signs with shark fins on them—a nod to longtime Penguin organist Vince Lascheid's rendition of the theme from *Jaws* every time the home team went on a power play—the Caps and Pens played more than 15 minutes of tight scoreless hockey before Joey Mullen scored at 15:38. After killing a 5-on-3 Washington advantage for 1:34 at the beginning of the second, Ron Francis put the Pens up 2–0 by stuffing a Kevin Stevens pass by Don Beaupre.

Dave Tippett got one back for the Capitals before the second period ended, but Jaromir Jagr provided some much-needed insurance at 7:53 of the third when he scored on a highlight-reel rush from center ice. Mark Recchi added an empty-netter and the party was on. Whether their long-suffering fans could believe it or not, the Penguins would be playing in May for the first time ever, in the Wales Conference final.

"We've really put things together and made a tremendous turnaround from last year. And we've got a chance to go far," said goalie Tom Barrasso, who turned in another brick-wall performance, stopping 33 of 34 Washington shots.[30]

"We've climbed two mountains already," said coach Bob Johnson. "But we've got two more mountains to climb."[31]

The next one came in the form of the Boston Bruins, who had dominated the tough Adams Division, finishing with a Wales Conference-best 100 points. The series would open with two games in the tiny Boston Garden, traditionally a house of horrors to Penguin teams since the club's inception in 1967. Their all-time regular-season record at Boston was an embarrassing 6–38–6. The smaller Garden ice surface would do nothing to help the Pens' play their speed- and passing-based game. To get past Boston and make their first appearance in a Stanley Cup final, the Penguins would have to beat the Bruins in the trenches.

"We have to control Ray Bourque, Craig Janney and Cam Neely," said Kevin Stevens. "If we outwork them on the boards, we win."[32]

The Garden, however, would prove as formidable a foe as ever in the series opener. Sloppy turnovers cost the Pens as Boston rolled to a 6–3 win. In the second game, they entered the third period trailing 3–2 but goals less than two minutes apart by Mark Recchi and Mario Lemieux gave Pittsburgh their first lead of the night. With only 3:11 left, however, Janney converted a pass from Vladimir Ruzicka—his fourth assist of the night—during a 5-on-3-man advantage to send it to overtime.

And "Rosie" wasn't done yet. At 8:14 of the extra period he found himself alone with the puck in the Penguins crease. He fired it over a fallen Tom Barrasso to give the Bruins the win and a 2–0 series stranglehold.

In the dressing room, the Penguins weren't disheartened. They knew they had outshot the Bruins (34–30) and felt they had outplayed them but simply hadn't got the end result they wanted. If anything, the loss hardened their resolve to take control of the series.

"We all have our highs and our lows, and right now the Bruins are living a high," defenseman Gordie Roberts told the *Pittsburgh Press*. "But hopefully we'll bring them back down to Earth the next game."[33]

Left wing Kevin Stevens went even further, issuing what would become the most famous guarantee in Penguins history.

"We're confident we can beat this team," he said. "And we will beat this team…. We'll beat this team. I'll say it right now, we'll beat them."[34]

Facing the specter of going down three games to none, the Pens played a tight-checking first period of game three and came away with a 1–0 lead after 20 minutes. By the midway point of the second, they had increased the margin to 3–1 and were controlling the play at both ends of the rink, not giving the Bruins' stars any room to move. In particular, Ulf Samuelsson was getting in the way of Boston's star winger Cam Neely, standing him up every chance he got. With 7:50 left in the second period, Samuelsson met Neely once again, this time near center ice. The big defenseman's right knee crashed into Neely's left one, sending the Bruin to the ice in a heap of pain. Boston coach Mike Milbury flew into a rage, leaping in front of his players, pounding the boards and hollering at referee Kerry Fraser for a penalty. He grabbed a stick and hit it against the glass, but to no avail. Mario Lemieux soon after beat Andy Moog on a breakaway to make it 4–1, which held up as the final score.

The next day, Milbury accused Bob Johnson of encouraging his team to take cheap shots and late hits whenever they had the chance. "The professor of hockey, as he so often projects himself, is subtly becoming a professor of goonism," Milbury stated.[35]

If Milbury's claim was true, he was doing a fine job of acting as the professor's apprentice. For game four, the former Bruins defenseman-turned-coach inserted tough guy Lyndon Byers into the lineup and let the likes of accomplished pugilists Chris Nilan and Bob Sweeney loose on the Penguins' stars. The Pens, however, dominated play again and tied the series up with another 4–1 win.

"They can cheap-shot us all they want," said Mark Recchi after the game. "We just want to win."[36]

Back in Boston for game five, the Bruins opened the scoring only 40 seconds in, but the Penguins stayed poised and answered with three goals from Stevens, Lemieux and Trottier. The game became a wide-open affair and the Bruins simply had no hope of keeping up with the high-flying Penguins.

"It takes a lot from you when they're coming at you 100 miles per hour," said Bruin defenseman Glen Wesley. "It's tough to stop a team like that."[37]

Samuelsson had knocked Neely off his game. Clearly frustrated, the Bruins' main offensive threat took two retaliatory penalties away from the play, the second of which resulted in one of the Penguins' three power play goals on the night. When the final buzzer sounded, the scoreboard read Pittsburgh 7, Boston 2. The Penguins were in complete control of the series and but one win away from advancing to their first ever Stanley Cup final.

Playing at home in game six before a wild home crowd anxious for a big win, the Pens came out tense and found themselves trailing 2–0 midway through the second period. But a power play goal by Larry Murphy at 11:45 got them back in the game, and a pair of tallies from two unlikely sources— Phil Bourque and Gordie Roberts—pushed the Penguins ahead by the midway point of the third period.

The Bruins' Don Sweeney quieted the crowd with less than eight minutes to play when he corralled a loose puck in a scramble in front of the Pittsburgh net and fired it home to tie things at three. The Bruins' successful tight checking of the first 30 minutes had disappeared, however. With a little over four minutes to play, Mark Recchi picked up a loose puck outside the Bruin blue line with a huge expanse of open ice before him. The "Wreckin' Ball" sped toward the Boston net and fired a pin-point wrist shot past Moog on the far side. The crowd exploded in joy, and erupted even louder when Mario Lemieux hit a long empty-net shot at 19:32 to seal the Bruins' fate. Pittsburgh fans may have had to repeat it a few times to believe it, but after 24 years of trying, their Penguins were actually going to the Stanley Cup final. They let it all soak in as Lemieux accepted the Prince of Wales trophy at center ice and invited his teammates to join him before going for a skate and raising it high in triumph.

"When I saw Mario carrying that cup around the ice, I choked up," said Bourque. "It was ... an unbelievable feeling. You had to be here with all of those bad teams and through all of the bad years to understand."[38]

The Penguins' opponent in the finals was an even more unexpected participant than themselves: the Cinderella Minnesota North Stars, who had finished 16th overall with a mere 68 points, but who had gelled once the playoffs started. Led by veterans Bobby Smith and Brian Bellows and young scoring sensation Mike Modano, the Stars knocked off both the Norris Division champion Chicago Blackhawks and the St. Louis Blues in six games before dispatching the defending Stanley Cup champion Edmonton Oilers in five. Minnesota had got to the final by playing hard, tough hockey, receiving stellar goaltending from Jon Casey and timely scoring from what seemed to be a different hero every night.

As game one at the Civic Arena approached, Penguin Fever gripped the city like never before. Core die-hard fans, some who had stuck with the team through all of its travails since the franchise's beginning, rejoiced at their club finally reaching hockey's ultimate stage. Casual fans and others who did not know an offside from an icing were suddenly donning Penguins Wales Conference Champions t-shirts and adding their voices to the roar of support that erupted throughout Western Pennsylvania.

"Our faith in this team has paid off in a big way," said Mayor Sophie Masloff. "It's going to be a very exciting time for both the Penguins and the city, and we're looking forward to another world championship [for Pittsburgh]."[39]

The Penguins, however, looked more like chumps than champs in game one, letting the Minnesota forwards camp out in front of Tom Barrasso as long as they pleased and failing to capitalize on seven of eight power play opportunities. The net result was a 5–4 loss, the fourth time in a row they'd dropped the opening game of a series.

"This team seems to play better when it has problems," mumbled Paul Stanton.[40]

The Penguins brought a greater intensity to game two, finishing checks and working hard in the corners. Barrasso was back in form after letting some less-than-challenging North Star shots get by him in the opener. The effort translated to a 2–1 Pittsburgh lead deep into the second period, but the Stars were pushing back, taking control of the game and looking ready to tie it up at any point. The crowd grew tense, sensing the worst. What they got was the best—as in, the biggest and perhaps the prettiest—goal Mario Lemieux had ever scored in a Penguin uniform.

Gathering in a Phil Bourque outlet pass just inside his own blueline, Lemieux took off in full stride and flew through the neutral zone like a soaring bird of prey, bearing down on retreating Minnesota defensemen Neil Wilkinson on his right and Shawn Chambers on his left. He went to go wide around Chambers but at the last second, with his silky-smooth hands, pulled the puck back toward him through Chambers' skates. The startled defenseman had to pause in an attempt to adjust, but Lemieux was already by him. Wilkinson seemed stunned by Lemieux's approach from the start, simply watching in awe as Number 66 made his jaw-dropping move around his hapless defense partner.

Having split the defense, Lemieux was now one-on-one with Casey, who came out to poke-check the puck off his stick. But Mario was too quick for him, pulling the puck to his backhand and directing it into the empty cage while falling toward the left post. He sprang to his feet, skated to the side boards, pierced the steamy air with a mighty uppercut of celebration, and let out a primal yell that added to the deafening cheers filling the Igloo.

Everyone in the building seemed unable to comprehend what they'd just seen. It was the type of goal that can turn a series

Mario Lemieux follows the play during the 1991 Stanley Cup final. Lemieux would win the Conn Smythe trophy as playoff MVP with 44 points in 23 games (courtesy Ron Kerrigan).

around, and it came at just the right time for the reeling Penguins. Up 3–1, they held the Stars at bay the rest of the way and evened the series with a 4–1 victory.

"[Lemieux's goal] was a great play by a great player," said Bob Johnson. "To handle the puck like that, going that fast … that's hard to do. He was really accelerating."[41]

Added Paul Coffey, who had returned to the lineup after his broken jaw had forced him out of the previous four games, "It was one of the best goals I've ever seen—and I played with Wayne Gretzky."[42]

Even the North Stars were in awe. "I've *never* seen something like that," said forward Mike Modano.[43]

As pumped up as they were by their captain's spectacular goal, the Penguins were just as soundly deflated when they learned, 15 minutes before the puck was to drop on game three at the Met Center in Minneapolis, that Lemieux would not be playing that night. He'd experienced severe back spasms after warmup while trying to take his skates off. The Stars, knowing they would not have to contend with any magical Mario moves on this night, came out with an extra spring in their step. After Barrasso stood up perfectly to the home team's attack in the first period, Dave Gagner and Bobby Smith broke through in the second to put Minnesota up 2–0, en route to a 3–1 win and a 2–1 series lead.

Lemieux was given a firmer mattress at their Minneapolis hotel, took anti-inflammatory medication, and received ice treatments to relieve his back pain. It all worked well enough for him to rejoin his teammates for game four. Inspired, they assaulted the North Star net right off the opening faceoff and didn't let up until they had pumped three pucks into it before the game was even three minutes old. It marked the fastest a team had built a 3–0 lead in Stanley Cup final history.

Part of the Pens' motivation had been fueled by reports in local papers about the North Stars organization planning Stanley Cup parade routes and White House visits once the Penguins had been dispatched. Others described Stanley Cup ring-fittings for some players, while some suggested the Pens were intimidated by the loud Met Center crowd.

"We've read a lot of things in the papers here," said Kevin Stevens. "Not too many people like it, including me."[44]

The Pens maintained their three-goal lead mid-way through the second period but then ran into penalty trouble. Power play goals from Brian Propp and Mike Modano brought the Stars to within one before the middle period was done. Pittsburgh nursed its 4–3 lead through much of the third, riding the rock-solid goaltending of Tom Barrasso. But a five-minute major penalty to Troy Loney at 13:03 for high-sticking Mark Tinordi in the face gave Minnesota a glorious opportunity to draw even. The Penguin penalty killers bore down, however, and frustrated the North Star power play time and again, not even yielding a shot on goal. A Phil Bourque empty-netter in the last minute cemented the Penguin win and sent the series back to Pittsburgh tied at two.

The Penguins again exploded right after the opening faceoff when game five got underway back at the Civic Arena, with Lemieux and Stevens scoring power play goals by the period's halfway point. Regular-season team scoring leader Mark Recchi, scoreless to that point in the finals, broke out in a big way with two goals before the first frame ended. As in game four, though, the Pens didn't know what to do with all their prosperity, and promptly blew most of their enormous lead. Dave Gagner scored twice for the spirited Stars to help bring them back to within one. Ron Francis answered late in the second to restore the two-goal Penguin lead, but Ulf Dahlen beat Frank Pietrangelo at 1:36 of the third to make it 5–4 Penguins. Pietrangelo was forced into the game when Tom Barrasso suffered a slightly pulled groin muscle in the first period. After Dahlen's goal, he flashed the same spectacular level of play he showed in games six and seven against New Jersey in the first round, stymieing the North Stars at every turn. An ugly goal by Loney with less than two minutes to play, in which the low-scoring winger crashed the net and wreaked enough havoc in front of goalie Bryan Hayward to enable a Larry Murphy shot to carom in off a skate, put the Pens up 6–4. The score remained that way until the final horn sounded, and the Pittsburgh Penguins—for so many years the league's laughable losers—were, incredibly, now only one win away from hosting the Stanley Cup.

• • •

The Penguins flew to Minnesota with an opportunity to wash away 24 years filled mainly with ineptitude and embarrassment. With one win, they could help every fan forget about the many missteps and misplays that had defined the franchise from its inception in 1967. One more win would put them on top of the hockey world, making it impossible for anyone to laugh at them anymore. One more win could help erase the painful memory of missing the playoffs in their first two seasons. Of the directionless years in the aftermath of Michel Brière's tragic death. Of the excruciating loss to the Islanders in 1975, and the bankruptcy and padlocked team offices that followed. Of all the humiliating beatdowns in the Philadelphia Spectrum and their 42-game winless streak in that building. Of the last-place league finishes in 1983 and 1984. Of all the subpar coaches and all the general managers who practically gave away those countless first-round draft choices. Of the heartbreaking collapse against Philly in the 1989 playoffs. Of Uwe Krupp and his gut-wrenching overtime goal that ended their 1989–90 season.

All of that pain and misery could be swept away with one, single victory.

"It seems like it's right there," said Kevin Stevens. "I want to reach out there and grab it."[45]

• • •

For the first time in their history, the Penguins would be playing a game with the Stanley Cup in the building. It was theirs for the taking, too. But first they'd have to win another game in the resilient Stars' raucous home rink.

The mood amongst the players was a good, positive one, recalled Troy Loney. While driving to the rink with Joe Mullen that morning for a team skate, he asked his teammate, Can you feel this? "Joey said, 'Yeah. We don't usually get really nervous, but we're pretty nervous here.' And then we both said, 'Yeah but it's a good nervous.' We we're just on fire at that point, and we knew there was no way we could lose that game."[46]

According to assistant coach Rick Kehoe, Mario Lemieux was feeling just as confident in the dressing room before the game. "[Defenseman] Grant

Jennings was kind of injured and he was on the edge of going or not going that night," recalled Kehoe. "He said, 'Well, I should be good for the seventh game.' And Mario just looked at him and said, 'Nope. There's not going to be a seventh game.'"[47]

No one, however, was getting ahead of themselves. They knew how big the task was that lay before them. "Every guy's got to have the game of his life," said Phil Bourque. "If everybody does that, it's going to be worth it."[48]

Only two minutes after the puck dropped that Saturday night, Ulf Samuelsson's innocuous-looking shot from just inside the blueline at the end of a power play found its way past Jon Casey, helping to take some of the buzz out of the building early. Later, with the Stars on a four-on-three power play, Mario Lemieux took a long outlet pass from Larry Murphy off the boards in full stride and swept through a swath of open ice toward the Minnesota zone. Big Number 66 blew past Brian Bellows and put another beautiful right-left deke on Casey before slipping the puck into a wide-open net.

As the stunned Stars were trying to catch their collective breath, Mullen fired a rebound past Casey only 55 seconds after Lemieux's marker. The Penguins bench erupted in celebration as the Met Centre crowd deflated. The Stars, sensing their time was finally up, would mount no comeback like the ones they had put together in games four and five. Bob Errey knocked in a loose puck at 13:15 of the second and breakaway goals by Ron Francis and Mullen before the second period was done left absolutely no doubt about the night's outcome.

The Pens added two more in the third to make it 8–0. All that was left to do was watch the clock slowly tick down. "The last 10 minutes on the bench was a long, long 10 minutes," said Loney. "You're up that much and you could see Minnesota just wants to end it. They're in their own rink. Every offside was kind of painful. You're kind of giddy on the bench. Guys like Trottier are all fired up because they know, they've been there before."[49]

When the clock finally did reach zero, the Penguins poured off the bench and mobbed Tom Barrasso, who had earned his first career playoff shutout on the game's biggest stage.

After accepting the Conn Smythe trophy for playoff MVP—which he earned by scoring 44 points, the second-highest total in NHL post-season history—Lemieux skated to center ice and accepted Lord Stanley's glittering silver Cup from NHL president John Ziegler, hoisting it high above his head before leading his ecstatic band of teammates in a victory skate around the Met Center ice.

The day that many thought they'd never see had arrived. The Pittsburgh Penguins were Stanley Cup Champions.

"It's a great thrill to reach the top of the mountain," said coach Bob Johnson. "A dream come true for all our players."[50]

"I'm so proud right now for the City of Pittsburgh," exclaimed Loney in the crowded Penguin dressing room. "It's been a 20-year struggle for our fans, but they stuck with us. This is the reward. For all of us."[51]

Especially for Lemieux, who had saved a franchise that was on its last legs with his arrival in 1984, and then with his consistently spectacular play over the seven years he'd been a Penguin.

"You dream of this, but it's even better in real life than it is in your dreams," he said. "This is the ultimate."[52]

• • •

Three days later the Penguins and about 80,000 fans gathered at the city's Point State Park for a party 24 years in the making. Fans danced and sang in a sunny, sweaty, 78-degree celebration that honored their conquering hockey heroes. With the Stanley Cup sitting center stage, the players were introduced one by one to the adoring crowd. Mario Lemieux hoisted the Cup high above his head once again and told the crowd, "This Cup is for you!"

He, like all his teammates, had to handle the Cup carefully that day. During a team party at Lemieux's house the day before, it had been thrown into Mario's swimming pool, where it cracked near the middle and quickly filled with water. "It went to the bottom and it was very, very heavy," said Loney. "It took five of us to get it out of the pool."[53]

After hoisting the battered Cup at the city celebration, Larry Murphy pulled out a camera and snapped some pictures of the scene before him. "Stick your hands up and say 'Pittsburgh is Number One!" he instructed the crowd with a wide smile. However, it was the never-at-a-loss-for-words Phil Bour-

Seven years after he arrived in Pittsburgh, Mario Lemieux hoists the Stanley Cup during the team's 1991 victory rally at the tip of the city's "Golden Triangle" (courtesy Ron Kerrigan).

que who best captured the feeling of the day when he grabbed the Cup, hoisted it over his head and bellowed out an idea to the delirious mob:

"What do you say we take this out on the river and party all summer?"

The fans roared their approval. At long last, their hockey team had given them a reason to celebrate. The Penguins' long road, filled as it had been with so much heartbreak, embarrassment and frustration, had finally led to hockey's ultimate peak: the Stanley Cup.

27

Repeat Performance: 1991–92

Bob Johnson was reflecting on the Penguins' championship season a few days after they'd returned from Minnesota with Lord Stanley's mug in tow. He was describing what a thrill it was to finally reach "the top of the mountain" and marveling at how well his players had performed in the games of their lives. The perpetually forward-thinking Johnson, however, was soon talking about the future and, in particular, the great days ahead for Mario Lemieux.

"With his skills and the experience he gained from playing in the finals this year, there's no doubt he's going to be a playoff force in the years to come. I can't wait to see it happen."[1]

Unfortunately, Johnson's ability to do so was thrown into grave doubt on the night of August 29. While dining at a Pittsburgh restaurant, he suffered what appeared to be a stroke. Paramedics arrived and rushed him to Mercy Hospital, where doctors discovered the cause was actually a tumor on the right side of his brain. They performed emergency surgery to remove part of it, but the prognosis was not good. Doctors were almost certain the tumor was cancerous, a belief that was soon proven to be accurate.

"His condition is very, very serious. So many bad things can happen with something like this," said Penguins doctor Chip Burke.[2]

"I'm devastated," said a shocked and emotional Craig Patrick.[3]

Johnson was transferred to his home in Colorado Springs, Colorado, where he underwent 14 days of radiation treatment. Unable to speak, Badger was still able to watch the Penguins play on a newly installed satellite dish. Ever the coach, he wrote out strategy suggestions and other observations, which were sent to the team.

Just before the season got underway, Scotty Bowman accepted Patrick's request to step in as interim coach. The winningest coach in NHL history, Bowman was a natural choice for the role. But his taskmaster-style approach would mark a significant change for the players after a year under the upbeat and perpetually positive Johnson.

"Scotty's more of an old-school type," said Tom Barrasso, who had Bowman as a coach in Buffalo. "You better show up every day, or it's not going to be rah-rah to get you going. It's going to be some yelling and screaming."[4]

As the organization did its best to forge ahead amidst the gloom of Johnson's illness, a big change was taking place at its highest levels. After 14 years of ownership, Edward J. DeBartolo was looking to sell off his hockey team. A downturn in the real estate market had created a cash-flow crisis in the DeBartolo empire, and unloading the Penguins could help keep creditors at bay. After initially coming on board to help DeBartolo broker a deal, long-time hockey executive and former World Hockey Association president Howard Baldwin emerged as the leader of a three-person group that would eventually buy the team. The sale was completed November 18. The price tag came to $63 million, which included $23 million for Spectacor Management Group to assume the lease on the Civic Arena.[5] DeBartolo wasn't completely out of the Penguin picture, maintaining a "special limited partnership" in exchange for his underwriting of some of the team's operating losses.

Baldwin assumed command amidst fears he and his partners would sell off much of the Penguins' top—and increasingly expensive—talent in order to finance the club. Much of the concern amongst fans and the media began after a leak to the press of a letter from Baldwin to Paul Martha written in August in which Baldwin tossed around the idea of dumping $7 million in player salaries to help finance his purchase of the Penguins. At the press conference introducing Baldwin and his partners, Morris Belzberg and Thomas V. Ruta, as the new owners, Baldwin reiterated that such fire sales were not in his plans.

"Craig Patrick is the general manager of the Pittsburgh Penguins. All player transactions will be done by Craig Patrick, not Howard Baldwin or Morris Belzberg."[6]

Only eight days after that press conference, the Penguin organization received the news they had been dreading since Bob Johnson entered hospital in late August: the Badger had passed away, at his home in Colorado in the early morning hours of November 26. The entire Penguin organization was left stunned and saddened. In the midst of their grief, players, coaches and staff members reflected on all that Johnson had meant to them.

"What he's done for this city and this hockey club in one year is pretty incredible," said Mario Lemieux. "Nobody would have thought we'd win the Cup last year, but with Bob Johnson, everything was possible."[7]

Tom Barrasso spoke of the road ahead for the team: "Bob wanted us to go on and win another Cup. If we go out and do anything but play hard for him, it will be a disservice to Bob."[8]

A tearful Craig Patrick added, "We will have Bob's memory in the back of our minds at all times."[9]

In a game the very next night at the Civic Arena, the team paid tribute to Johnson in a touching 10-minute pre-game tribute, the overall vision of which was contributed by Patrick. The Penguin players, wearing special patches on their left shoulders that read "Badger 1931–1991," gathered in a circle around center ice. The arena lights dimmed as fans held up battery-operated candles and Linda Ronstadt's "Goodbye, My Friend" played throughout the hushed arena. Stenciled renderings of the Badger's famous saying, "It's a Great Day for Hockey," were unveiled just outside both blue lines.

"It was really tough. It was very emotional for all of us," said Ron Francis. "But that would have been him, saying it's a great day for hockey, saying we have to move on."[10]

Somehow, Francis and his teammates overcame their emotions well enough to beat the New Jersey Devils that night, 8–4.

As the season wore on, however, the Penguins found it extremely difficult to put the tragedy behind them, and their record reflected their struggles. By mid–February they were barely above the .500 mark, sitting in fourth place in the Patrick and a mere five points up on the fifth-place Islanders. Hardly the stuff of defending Stanley Cup champions.

The Penguins wore three special patches during the 1991–92 season: one for the team's 25th anniversary, another for the NHL's 75th anniversary, and one honoring the late "Badger" Bob Johnson. A Stanley Cup Final patch replaced the NHL 75 one when they reached the final round of the playoffs (courtesy Ron Kerrigan).

Many of the contributing factors to the lackluster showing were all too familiar: lack of commitment to team defense; Lemieux's wonky back that made his appearance in the lineup any given night anything but a certainty; and a parade of injuries to other key players like Ulf Samuelsson and Paul Coffey. The absence of Jaromir Jagr for 10 games thanks to a suspension for deliberately skating into referee Ron Hogarth during a game against the Washington Capitals didn't help matters. Add in the lingering disillusionment caused by the death of their old coach and the 180-degree turn in coaching style under Bowman, and the result was a season that was going off the rails.

By February 18, with his club mired in a six-game winless streak, GM Craig Patrick decided it was time to once again shake things up with a major late-season, multi-player deal. This one involved three teams and began with Pittsburgh sending Paul Coffey, who had earlier in the season eclipsed Denis Potvin's career records for goals (310), assists (742) and points (1,052) by a defenseman, to Los Angeles for defensemen Brian Benning and Jeff Chychrun and L.A.'s first-round pick in the 1992 draft. Patrick then sent Benning, the draft pick and Mark Recchi to Philadelphia for right wing Rick Tocchet, monstrous defenseman Kjell Samuelsson and goalie Ken Wregget. In losing considerable scoring power in the form of Recchi and Coffey, the trade netted the Penguins some sorely needed defensive ability. Tocchet was one of the finest two-way forwards in the game, a talented offensive threat who was also more than willing to pay any physical price to get the puck in the other team's net. He had also proven himself to be a responsible two-way player, something Recchi had not done consistently enough to the management's liking.

Gone also was the smooth stride and electrifying rushes of Coffey, whose arrival in 1987 had added a bona fide superstar to the Penguin lineup and helped to put the team on the NHL map after so many years in the wilderness. In Samuelsson, the blueline was suddenly injected with one of the most intimidating presences in the league. His 6'6", 235-pound frame was enough of an impediment for opposing forwards, but a mean streak that helped clear his goalie's crease was also part of the big Swede's resume.

Wregget, who had almost single-handedly eliminated the Penguins from the 1989 playoffs with dazzling performances for the Flyers in games six and seven of that year's Patrick Division final, would add a solid backup option for starter Tom Barrasso.

The move was a bold gamble by Patrick. In trading two players who were immensely popular and respected in the Pens' dressing room, he risked upsetting the club's chemistry. It wasn't hard to find critics of the deal within that dressing room. Kevin Stevens was the loudest. "To not have Mark here, to not have Paul … it's going to be tough. We won the Cup together. Coff is one of the greatest players to ever put on skates. Recchs is going to get 40 or 50 goals for the next 10 years. To give up a guy of that caliber.… I don't know."[11]

Backup goalies Frank Pietrangelo and Wendell Young were also less than elated, realizing they had been supplanted by the incoming Wregget. With four goalies on the roster, a trade or two was clearly on the horizon. "It's a slap in the face to me and Wendell Young to bring another goaltender here," said Pietrangelo. "If they were not happy with me ... maybe somebody else will be."[12]

Patrick, whose trade received endorsements from Mario Lemieux, Ulf Samuelsson and many other players, maintained that the moves, although perhaps tough to absorb at first from an emotional standpoint, had put the Penguins in a much stronger position to defend their Stanley Cup title.

"We feel we've improved our hockey club, and everyone in our organization will realize that, whether it's today or tomorrow or next week or next month."[13]

There was certainly no evidence of improvement in the days after the trade. The Penguins tied Quebec in the revamped lineup's first game, then lost in Montreal and Washington. The season's low point came in their next contest, however, at home against a Hartford Whaler squad that had gone 0-11-2 in its past 13 games on the road. They looked quite comfortable in their road green uniforms on this night, though, chasing Tom Barrasso after two periods and leaving the Igloo with an 8-4 win. All the Penguins were left with was a feeling of devastation in their locker room. The loss dropped them to the .500 mark at 27-27-8.

"This is the worst game I've played as a Penguin and the worst game I've seen the team play," said Ulf Samuelsson. "I don't know if you can get any worse."[14]

It seemed the players had truly realized there was no time left for excuses. It was either put up or shut up.

"Something's got to change in the way we're playing, and it needs to change pretty quick. Otherwise, we're going to be in a lot of trouble," said Barrasso.[15]

Two nights later, things did start to change. The Penguins rebounded with a solid 5-2 win against Buffalo, and then followed that up with victories on the road against Calgary and San Jose. Finally having heeded the wakeup call, the Pens proceeded to win eight of their next 10 games following the Hartford debacle. The defensive abilities of the newcomers were beginning to have an effect, helping to curtail the deluge of pucks that had been filling the Penguin net all year.

Tocchet in particular was proving himself to be every bit the player Patrick had hoped he would be when he acquired him. Unburdened by the pressure of having to be the cornerstone of the rebuilding Flyers, number 92 was flourishing amidst the plethora of talent suddenly surrounding him. He turned in one of the gutsiest performances by any player wearing the skating penguin during a game in Chicago on March 15. After absorbing an errant puck to the jaw off the stick of Mario Lemieux that opened a gash late in the second period, Tocchet headed to the dressing room, where he convinced the team's trainers to forego an X-ray and simply stitch him up, allowing him to get back to the action as quickly as possible. That occurred less than three minutes into the final period, with the Blackhawks holding a 2–1 lead. Steven Larmer made it 3–1 at 6:53, seemingly putting the game out of reach.

Tocchet had other ideas.

Thirty-four seconds later he banged his own rebound past Dominik Hasek to make it 3–2. With just over five minutes to play, Tocchet was credited with the tying goal when a Ron Francis knuckleball hit him and went in. Only 30 seconds later, Ulf Samuelsson goaded the Hawks' Dirk Graham into a roughing minor, which Larry Murphy converted into a go-ahead power play goal with less than four minutes left to go. The Pens held on for a 4–3 win, their most important victory of the season, one driven by Tocchet's refusal to let his team lose. Further exams by doctors later revealed that he'd performed his heroics with a hairline fracture of his jaw.

"To come back like we did is a big thing for us," said Ron Francis. "Hopefully, we can build on this and really turn it around down the stretch."[16]

Build on it they did, losing only one more game in March. Just as they seemed to be hitting their stride, however, the resurgent Pens were suddenly faced with an obstacle that threatened to not only end their season early, but the entire NHL campaign as well. On April 1, NHL players went on strike, grinding the schedule to a halt and leaving arenas dark. Among their demands was a request for fewer restrictions on those who wished to change teams as free agents; an increase in playoff bonus money; and changes to the waiver process, which allowed teams to place players on waivers simply to determine trade interest among other GMs. The owners had a demand, too, centered around, of all things, hockey cards. No longer the near-exclusive domain of grade school kids, trading cards had become big business thanks to a suddenly booming collectors' market. Players collected about $11 million of the $16 million the trade generated, with the owners getting the remainder. For them, that was simply not enough.

The impasse dragged on for 10 agonizing days before both sides reached an agreement that saw the players' playoff money increased and an agreement on hockey card and other licensing revenues, among other compromises. Most importantly for the Penguins and their fans, the team would get a chance to defend their Stanley Cup title in 1992.

The Pens' strong play during the March stretch run landed them in third place in the Patrick and a first-round date with the Washington Capitals, who had finished 11 points better than Pittsburgh. In games one and two in Landover, Maryland, the Penguins looked more like the Penguins of November than those of March, losing 3–1 and 6–2. Mario Lemieux, who had missed game one with a shoulder injury, came to the rescue with a dazzling three-goal, three-assist performance in a 6–4 game three Penguin win back at the Igloo.

Any inspiration the latest offensive outburst from Lemieux may have provided dried up with the game's final buzzer, however. In game four, the Capitals came out storming with 19 shots in the first period and racked up a 3–0 lead. They cruised to an all-too-easy 7–2 win in the Penguins' own barn, pushing the defending champs to the brink of elimination.

Playing without two of their key additions from the blockbuster March trade—Rick Tocchet and Kjell Samuelsson, who were both injured—the Penguins turned in a more determined effort in game five in Washington. The difference was mainly in the Pens' sudden attention to defense. In the previous four games, Washington's forwards had skated nearly unimpeded through the neutral zone, allowing them to enter the Penguins' end with speed and generate quality chance after quality chance. Not so on this night.

"For game five, we called a meeting and came up with trying to go with the one-four delay [strategy] and try to contain their defensemen," recalled Mario Lemieux. "We knew right away that if we could play that type of game and wait for our chances that we had the better team, that we could win."[17]

The one-four delay involved a lone forechecker harassing and delaying the opposing defenseman who had the puck in his own zone. The other four skaters would line up near their own blueline and form a near impenetrable wall.

It worked. The entire team bought into the new strategy, standing up the likes of Dino Ciccarelli and Peter Bondra at the blue line, gobbling up the sudden bonanza of loose pucks, and applying their quick transition game the other way. The Capitals were suddenly confused. The final score read 5–2, and the Penguins had survived to fight another day.

Lemieux added to the Caps' addled state in game six back in Pittsburgh, turning in another performance that showed the world why he was on another plane of talent and ability. He assisted on two Kevin Stevens goals before the game was barely five minutes old. Later, after the Pens had squandered that fine start and fallen behind 4–3, Lemieux set up Phil Bourque to tie it and then netted two power play goals to make the final 6–4.

"He loves the big games," said Stevens afterward. "We're just lucky to have him here, so we don't have to try to stop him."[18]

Game seven began with both teams playing strong defensively and goalies Tom Barrasso and Don Beaupre clearly showing that they were "on." Lemieux, proving his big-game ability once again, broke the ice with a short-handed goal with just under six minutes to go in the first. Al Iafrate tied it early in the second for Washington. With the Caps' Todd Krygier in the box for interference later in the middle frame, Lemieux fed a quick pass to Jaromir Jagr in the slot, who put it past Beaupre for a 2–1 lead. Tom Barrasso and the suddenly solid Pens defense corps held the fort until Joey Mullen deposited a long shot into an empty net with 33 seconds left to seal the game and the series. The Penguins had become just the ninth team in NHL history to come back from a 3–1 series deficit. Lemieux finished with an incredible 17 points in the series, and that total was attained without even having played in game one, and playing injured in game two.

"We were beaten by one guy. Lemieux was just too good," said Capitals coach Terry Murray. Added Iafrate, "I give all the credit to Mario Lemieux. Period. Exclamation point."[19]

Having dispatched the league's second-best team in the regular-season standings, the Penguins' reward was a matchup against the number one club, the New York Rangers. The Broadway Blueshirts had risen to the top of the hockey heap on the outstanding play and leadership qualities of captain Mark Messier, acquired from Edmonton in October.

The Pens picked up right where they had left off against Washington by winning game one in Madison Square Garden, 4–2, to steal home ice advantage. The shutdown defense on display in the last three games against the Caps was once again deployed as Pittsburgh protected its two-goal lead throughout the game's final 28 minutes. The brick-wall approach caught the Rangers off-guard.

"They're a different hockey club once the playoffs start," said Messier. "Definitely, they play defense better than I've seen them play before." Added Mike Gartner, "[Defense] is a different philosophy for the Pittsburgh Penguins. That's not a characteristic Penguin trait."[20]

Ranger coach Roger Nielson was dismayed at the lack of toughness his troops displayed in game one. It was a key part of his philosophy to knocking out the defending Cup champs: hit their stars hard, and hit them often. In game two, one Ranger certainly took the "hitting hard" directive to heart— with disastrous consequences for the Penguins' hopes of capturing a second straight Stanley Cup.

With the Penguins leading 1–0 early in the first and setting up shop in the Rangers zone on a power play, Mario Lemieux gathered the puck in at the right point. Ranger forward Adam Graves closed in on him and unleashed a vicious two-hand slash on Lemieux's wrists, sending number 66 to the ice in a crumpled heap of pain. He was gone from the game and the foreseeable future with what would later be diagnosed as a broken metacarpal bone in his left hand. Graves received only a two-minute slashing penalty. Later, Joey Mullen was knocked out of the game by a Kris King forearm to the head, after Mullen had been forced to step over the outstretched leg of Ranger Paul Broten. The high-scoring sharpshooter would be lost for the rest of the season with a leg injury he suffered while falling to the ice.

Despite the shocking turn of events, the Penguins kept their poise and built a 2–1 lead. They locked into their new defensive shell, but did so a bit too thoroughly, sitting back and letting the talented Rangers tee off on Barrasso. New York scored two goals in two minutes late in the third period and added an empty-netter to take the game 4–2 and send the series back to Pittsburgh tied at one.

Revenge was on the minds of Penguin fans and players, but the guys in black and gold knew that restraining their emotions would be crucial if they had any hope of getting past the Rangers.

"You just have to pick your spots and, hopefully, there's a time and a place in the series where we can do something about it," said winger Phil Bourque. "I think the best revenge would be just to beat them in the series."[21]

Much to the chagrin of Pens fans, Graves—who had not received any suspension for his hack job—opened the scoring at 3:45 of the first period, beating Barrasso with a slapshot from the left faceoff circle. It was the first goal of a wide-open, see-saw affair that saw Kris King win it in overtime for the Rangers on a shot he banked off Barrasso's right pad from behind the goal line.

Things continued to look bleak for the Pens through two and-a-half periods of game 4, as the Rangers built a 4–2 lead and seemed to have grabbed a stranglehold of the series. With less than 10 minutes to go, Ron Francis stepped over the red line and fired a routine drive toward the goal. Somehow, Ranger goalie Mike Richter missed it. The puck slid over the goal line and the Igloo exploded.

But Francis wasn't done. After Troy Loney had tied the game to send it to overtime, Francis put the capper on one of the greatest games of his Hall of Fame career. After a pinching Larry Murphy knocked the puck off Messier's stick in the slot and fired it toward the goal, Francis deftly deflected it past replacement goalie John Vanbiesbrouck to hand the Rangers a stunning defeat and tie the series at two.

"This team never quits," said Kevin Stevens. "It's got more guts than any team I've ever seen. It seems like we never do things the easy way, but we always get the job done."[22]

In game five in New York, it was Jaromir Jagr's turn to fill the role of game-breaking scoring hero in the absence of Lemieux. Leading 1–0 on a goal by the returning Rick Tocchet, who was finally healthy, Jagr was hauled down on a breakaway by Brian Leetch, resulting in a penalty shot. With the Garden crowd raining boos and jeers on him, Jagr made a wide circle in his own zone, gathering speed before he swooped in on the puck and bore down full-speed on Vanbiesbrouck, looking like a 747 jetliner hurling down a LaGuardia runway. He fired a pinpoint laser shot into the far side over the Beezer's stick to give the Penguins a 2–0 lead.

The Rangers fought back to tie the game at two, but late in the third it was Jagr to the rescue with what would become one of the most important, and prettiest, goals of his career. Swooping into the Ranger zone along the right boards, Jagr cut suddenly toward the goal. Big defenseman Jeff Beukeboom loomed right in front of him, but Jagr deftly got around him by faking left and quickly pulling the puck back to his right. He was now one-on-one with Vanbiesbrouck, who came out hard to try to poke-check the puck off his stick. The 20-year-old phenom was having none of it, however, reading the move early, stickhandling around the prone netminder and easily sliding the puck into the open cage. It was the type of breathtaking goal that can lift a team sky high and deflate an opponent just as thoroughly. It stood up as the winner in a 3–2 Penguin win.

"He's a dynamite kid," said Bryan Trottier. "He showed a lot of composure on the penalty shot, and for him to come through like that with the game-winner is really something."[23]

After a scoreless first period in game six in Pittsburgh, Rick Tocchet opened the scoring six minutes into the second when he muscled the puck in through a crowded crease. The Rangers answered with a Doug Weight tally two minutes later, but Jagr scored another pretty "puck-on-a-string"-type goal at 11:22, deking Vanbiesbrouck in close and putting a backhander in to make it 2–1. It would turn out to be the winner as the Rangers, out of answers to the Penguins' powerful offense—even without Lemieux and Mullen—watched Pittsburgh add two late empty-netters in the third and cruise to a 5–1 win, extending the Blueshirts' Stanley Cup drought to 52 years. Considering they'd won the series despite the Rangers being 18 points better than them in the regular season and forced to play without Lemieux, Mullen and the also-injured Bob Errey for most of it, the series win was easily one of the franchise's finest achievements.

"I don't know if it's equal to lugging that Cup around the ice, but this ranks right up there with anything," said Stevens.[24]

Along with Francis and Jagr doing fine Mario Lemieux impersonations, another key factor in the win was the inspired performances of fringe players like rookie Shaun McEachern and the "Muskegon Line" of Jock Callander, Mike Needham and Dave Michayluk, all of whom had spent most of the season toiling for the Pens' top minor-league team and had been summoned to fill the suddenly gaping holes in the Penguin roster. There was also the stellar goaltending of Tom Barrasso. The big goalie proved once again he could come up big when the pressure was on, making key saves when they were needed and turning aside 33 of 34 New York shots in the decisive sixth game.

"They had great opportunities and Tommy made some fantastic saves and gave us the opportunity to win," said Larry Murphy.[25]

Now it was on to a return date with the Boston Bruins in the Wales Conference final, which opened in Pittsburgh. Jagr once again proved that he enjoyed the big stage as much as his mentor Mario Lemieux, scoring another dazzling goal in overtime to help the Pens take a 1–0 series lead. Jagr entered the Bruin zone with speed but twice put the brakes on to elude confused Boston defenders before beating Andy Moog between the legs.

"He's a human highlights film," said Tocchet. "Every move gets better."[26]

Things got even brighter for the Pens when Mario Lemieux made an earlier-than-expected return for game two. He turned in a performance that made it look like he hadn't been out of the lineup at all. Lemieux set up Tocchet for a second-period goal that gave the Pens a 3–1 lead. Gaining confidence in his healing wrist as the game wore on, Lemieux asked Bowman to play him more. Mario restored the Penguins' two-goal lead with a goal at 12:47 of the third and capped his inspiring return with an empty-netter with one second left.

The series shifted to the Boston Garden, where hometown boy Kevin Stevens always seemed to get up for a game. Game three was no different. The 6'3", 230-pounder from nearby Brockton, Massachusetts, pumped in a natural hat trick before the game was barely 15 minutes old, effectively draining the Bruins of any fight they may have had left in them. A modest Stevens deflected the praise showered on him to his teammates.

"Tonight was probably the easiest four goals. Guys made great plays, and when you play with guys like that, it's pretty easy."[27]

Said Bruins defenseman Don Sweeney of Stevens' performance, "He has a sense of smell to move in for the kill. And, obviously, he wants to perform—especially here [in Boston]."[28]

Stevens talked about a different kind of scent wafting through the Penguins' dressing room. "I think our team has shown we have a lot of character…. We can smell that Cup."[29]

That smell was just as strong in game four after Jagr used his massive wingspan to score a nifty backhand goal five minutes in. Later in the first, the Bruins looked to even things up on a four-on-three power play. Lemieux, however, picked off a pass intended for Raymond Bourque at the point and headed up ice with a full head of steam. Bourque turned and tried to keep up with Lemieux but to no avail. Big number 66 turned the all-star defenseman into a big ball of confusion by putting the puck in Bourque's skates and plucking it back out of them as he moved past him. All Bourque could do was hook Lemieux just like so many lesser players had done in a desperate attempt to thwart his attack. And like all those others, his efforts were in vain. Lemieux bore down on Moog, made a couple of quick fakes and flicked a hard, quick wrist shot over the goalie's left hand and into the top corner. There was no looking back from there. The Bruins were finished. The Penguins handed them another 5–1 defeat to win their second consecutive Wales Conference championship.

Lemieux's goal was scored in the exact same spot where he had scored his very first NHL goal eight long years earlier, against the same elite Boston defenseman. How times had changed. Lemieux was now universally acknowledged as the game's greatest player and his team, back then still living in the dark shadows of the pitiful 1983–1984 era, was the defending Stanley Cup champion, and now knocking on the door of a repeat performance.

The Penguins would meet the Chicago Blackhawks in the final, a team that had earned the same shoulder-shrugging number of points as Pittsburgh in the regular season (87) but had done so with three fewer wins, meaning home-ice advantage would go to the Pens. The Hawks had steamrolled their way to the final, having swept both the Detroit Red Wings and Edmonton Oilers along the way. In fact, they hadn't lost since the first round, reeling off an NHL record 11 consecutive playoff victories as they entered the Igloo for game one. Their success was based on a deep commitment to coach Mike Keenan's game plan that involved lots of hitting, few dumb penalties, and a ferocious work ethic that generated quality scoring chances for dangerous for-

The Penguins face off against the Chicago Blackhawks in the 1992 Stanley Cup final (courtesy Ron Kerrigan).

wards like young Jeremy Roenick, Steve Larmer and reliable veterans Brent Sutter, Michel Goulet and Dirk Graham. Chris Chelios anchored the defense, while goalie Ed Belfour seemed impenetrable. The Penguins came in on a seven-game winning streak themselves. Something had to give, and no one truly knew which way the series would go.

Things went decidedly Chicago's way for most of the first period of game one as the Hawks came out playing their brawny, opportunistic style to a T, frustrating the Penguins' big guns at every turn and putting three behind Tom Barrasso in the first 14 minutes. A late Phil Bourque wraparound kept the Pens within hailing distance. Brent Sutter made it 4–1 midway through the second, but the Penguins once again proved that, with their elite firepower up front, no lead was safe against them. Rick Tocchet and Mario Lemieux—on a clever bank shot off Belfour from behind the goal line—struck late in the period to make it 4–3. Things stayed that way until, with less than five minutes remaining and the Hawks desperately clinging to their tenuous lead, Jaromir Jagr put on a display of artistry that outdid any of his previous stickhandling masterpieces.

Holding the puck near the boards on his off-wing deep in Chicago territory, Jagr first sidestepped a Sutter check and slipped the puck between his legs. Gathering the puck in with his long reach, Jagr then danced around Brian Noonan and skated into the slot. With Shaun McEachern containing Igor Kravchuk in front of Belfour, Jagr slid a hard backhand that eluded a shocked Belfour and sent the Civic Arena into a frenzy.

"That was probably the greatest goal I've ever seen," said no less an authority than Mario Lemieux afterward.[30]

Now, as regulation time wound down, the revved-up Penguins started coming at the Hawks with full force. With only 18 seconds left, Lemieux burst through the neutral zone toward a loose puck with nothing but open ice and Belfour ahead. Slow-footed defenseman Steve Smith tried to catch Lemieux, but could only hook him and bring him to the ice, earning him a two-minute trip to the sin bin. On the ensuing faceoff to the left of Belfour, Ron Francis won the draw back to Larry Murphy, who stepped into a low, hard slap shot that Belfour kicked out with his right pad. From his spot at the right point, Lemieux, with the poise of a riverboat gambler, had read the play and bore down on the big rebound, which had fortuitously landed right on his stick. Unchecked, Lemieux slammed the puck past a prone Belfour for an electrifying goal that completed the Penguins' stunning comeback and effectively broke the backs of the Blackhawks.

"I just wanted to get in the dressing room and get ready for overtime," said coach Scotty Bowman, as shocked as anyone by the dramatic finish. "But you always have time left with guys like Jagr and Lemieux."[31]

Said the Penguin captain afterward, "I cheated a little on it. The puck got back to Larry and I figured I'd head for the net. If he doesn't get it, it's a breakaway for them. He got it, and I was the only guy uncovered."[32]

A despondent Keenan had no mercy for his troops in post-game interviews. "There is no excuse to give up a three-goal lead in the playoffs. We weren't disciplined.... They get the winning goal when no one picked up the most dangerous player in hockey. We didn't deserve to win."[33]

In an attempt to slow down Lemieux, Jagr and Co. in game two, Keenan opted for a couple of extra doses of toughness in the forms of Mike Peluso and Stu Grimson. Their ice time, however, came at the expense of scorers like Roenick, Graham and Larmer, all of whom spent much of the second period on the Blackhawk bench. As a result, the Chicago attack looked no more fearsome than a litter of kittens, generating only four shots at Barrasso in both the second and third periods. Another two-goal effort from Lemieux was more than enough to outdistance the Hawks on the scoreboard. The Penguins won 3–1 to take a 2–0 stranglehold on the series.

The Hawks hoped to get back in the series as things shifted to their legendary Chicago Stadium, filled as it was with the sounds of its famous pipe organ and crazy fans that had helped the old barn earn its "Madhouse on Madison" nickname. Chicago fed off the atmosphere and came out with more jump, firing 13 shots at the Penguin goal in the first period. Their problem was the man guarding that goal. Tom Barrasso, despite suffering from a headache for most of the day, stopped every one of them. He also stopped the 13

Mario Lemieux celebrates a goal in the 1992 Stanley Cup final with Ron Francis. The duo formed one of the greatest one-two punches at the center position in NHL history (courtesy Ron Kerrigan).

others the Hawks fired at him over the next two periods, allowing Kevin Stevens' marker in the first to stand up as the winner in an atypical 1–0 Penguin triumph.

"The big thing the entire game was that there were no rebounds," said Barrasso. "Late in the third period, we always seemed to get the puck at the right time and get it out of the zone."[34]

The Penguins now stood on the cusp of an accomplishment that seemed next to impossible at countless points throughout the season. But here they were, ready to prove to the hockey world that their first Cup was no fluke, and to realize Bob Johnson's goal, stated so eloquently by GM Craig Patrick on the day of Badger's passing, of winning more Stanley Cups.

Pittsburgh's big three guns showed how determined they were to make that goal a reality when the puck dropped on game four. Jaromir Jagr, Kevin Stevens and Mario Lemieux each bulged the twine behind Belfour in that first frame. The only problem was that Chicago's Dirk Graham returned the favor each time with a goal of his own. Thanks to the 32-year-old's Herculean performance, the teams went into the first intermission tied at three. Rick Tocchet gave the Pens another one-goal lead when he notched his sixth of the playoffs only 58 seconds into the second. The Hawks answered back again, though, this time thanks to a Jeremy Roenick shot from close in.

The Penguins' offense was in high-gear, looking more than comfortable in the familiar setting of a good old-fashioned shootout. They took control and began swarming the Chicago end, but were continually foiled by the spectacular relief performance of a young Domink Hasek, with whom Keenan had replaced Belfour back in the first period. Hasek foiled Lemieux on a clear-cut breakaway and robbed the other Penguin shooters time and again with a number of acrobatic saves. But he couldn't stop everything. Five minutes into the third period, Larry Murphy's harmless looking shot from the top of the left faceoff circle found its way through a maze of bodies in front of Hasek and into the back of the net. Ron Francis then finally broke the Blackhawks' serve at 7:59 when he came in on a two-on-one with Shawn McEachern, paused for a split second to keep Hasek guessing, then blasted a pinpoint slapshot over Hasek's stick on the short side to put the Pens up 6–4.

Roenick scored again at 11:18 to make it 6–5, but Barrasso and the bend-but-don't-break Pittsburgh D held off a late Chicago charge to kill the clock and help the Penguins capture their second consecutive Stanley Cup. Barrasso raised his arms and danced triumphantly in his crease as the final buzzer sounded and the Penguins poured off the bench to mob him and begin the celebration. Mario Lemieux, who finished with 34 points in only 15 games, again won the Conn Smythe trophy as playoff MVP, joining Philadelphia's Bernie Parent as the only player to win it two years in a row.

"He was unbelievable," said Stevens of Lemieux. "He was under a ton of pressure, with people all over him, and he just seemed to get better and better. He's the best player in the world, by far."[35]

Barrasso, whom Lemieux felt should have won the Conn Smythe, said of his team: "We never lost our focus. We always stuck together and we went through a lot with the death of our coach." He later spoke of the significance of winning back-to-back titles: "I think you can win one Stanley Cup and people might say you got the breaks. But two in a row, that really says something. It says something about your character."[36]

After the traditional handshakes were completed, Mario Lemieux accepted the Stanley Cup from NHL president John Ziegler and went for a victory lap around the Chicago Stadium ice, once again hoisting the gleaming silver prize high over his head. Later, he and his teammates gathered at center ice for a joyous team picture with the Cup. The Pittsburgh Penguins had climbed the mountain yet again, leaving no doubt in anyone's mind: they were the best team in hockey.

Epilogue

Like their first 25 years, the Penguins' second quarter-century had no shortage of twists and turns. In January 1993, Mario Lemieux began the biggest battle of his life when he underwent treatment for Hodgkin's Lymphoma, a form of cancer. Like so many goalies he faced on the ice, Lemieux beat the disease. His comeback later that season is one of the greatest in sports history. Le Magnifique resumed his scoring ways and, along with heir apparent Jaromir Jagr, kept the Penguins near the top of the NHL until his retirement after the 1996–97 season.

Lemieux's Penguin story was hardly finished, however. Under the financial mismanagement of owners Howard Baldwin and Morris Belzberg, the Penguins were forced to declare bankruptcy for a second time in November 1998. Lemieux, not wanting to see the club he had led to a pair of Stanley Cup championships move to a new city, offered to convert the $32.5 million the club owed him in deferred salary into an ownership stake. With partner Ron Burkle, Lemieux's plan succeeded, and in September 1999, the franchise's former superstar became its primary owner. To the delight of Penguin fans everywhere, Lemieux came out of retirement in December 2000 and played 170 more games over five seasons before hanging his skates up for good in December 2005.

As had their Pittsburgh predecessors of 1983 and 1984, the Penguins of the mid–2000s struggled mightily on the ice. Also similar to that era, their low finishes in the standings eventually resulted in high draft picks that infused much-needed talent into the lineup. With the likes of goalie Marc-Andre Fleury, defenseman Kris Letang and superstar centers Evgeni Malkin and Sidney Crosby, the Pens became winners again, capturing Stanley Cups in 2009, 2016 and 2017.

Today, the Penguins have a sparkling new home arena, located right across the street from where the old Igloo stood. It's a modern-era facility that Lemieux ensured got built in the face of significant political wrangling and the renewed possibility of the team leaving town. Its existence means the club

The Penguins' Stanley Cup championships of 1991, 1992, 2009, 2016 and 2017 are celebrated in a display at their primary training facility just north of Pittsburgh (author's collection).

will remain in Pittsburgh for years to come. In its rafters hang five Stanley Cup banners—three more than cross-state rival Philadelphia and one more than both the Islanders and Rangers. Such accomplishments were unfathomable during the team's early years of struggle. Somehow, though, the franchise that waddled out of the gate in 1967 has survived—and thrived.

During the 2016–17 season, the Penguins helped celebrate their 50th anniversary with four theme nights celebrating different eras of the franchise's history. Former players were invited back to catch up with their former teammates, spend some time with Mario Lemieux and the current squad of Penguins, and catch a game, before which they were honored with a ceremony.

A mural in downtown Pittsburgh celebrates the Penguins' history (author's collection).

"When you have your picture on a post in downtown Pittsburgh, it is an honour," said Jean Pronovost. "It was a great time. I appreciated them having me back and to be introduced to the crowd again. Some of them I'm sure were saying, 'Who is this?'" he said with a laugh, "but that's OK. Time goes by and people forget about you. You're only as good as your last game. I'd like to live in the past but I can't, so you just have to go on and say to those that are shining, well, 'Let them shine.'"[1]

For Ron Stackhouse, the 2017 event and an earlier ceremony in 2010 he had attended when the Penguins played their final game in the Civic Arena helped to "heal up a bunch of old wounds that I'd had from Pittsburgh." Thanks to the constant home-crowd booing he'd endured throughout most of his time as a Penguin, Stackhouse had left the city with a bitter taste in his mouth. The warm reception he got from the Penguin organization and the fans at the reunion events, however, went a long way to changing his perspective.

"Outside the hotel and around the arena they had these posts with pennants on them, and guess whose face is front and center on one of these pennants? It was unbelievable."

Inside the arena, Stackhouse recalled, "they had us out on the ice and introduced us all. I got cheered. No boos."

Earlier, club executives had spoken to Stackhouse and his fellow retirees who had worn the blue Penguin uniforms. "They said, 'For you guys who were here during the lean years when the club was going bankrupt and whatnot, we consider you to be every bit as much a part of this franchise and history as these guys who are here today.' It was just amazing. It totally changed my perspective on my career [in Pittsburgh]."[2]

A statue of Mario Lemieux graces the outside of the Penguins' current arena. It stands right across the street from the site of the old Civic Arena, home to so many of his magnificent plays (author's collection).

Troy Loney was fortunate enough to stick around with the Penguins from the absolute worst of times in 1983–84 to the rise to the very top. While the journey was exciting on the ice, witnessing the sport of hockey truly take hold in the city of Pittsburgh is what sticks out in his memory today.

"It was so fun to be part of a city embracing a sport that was not embraced fully because the team didn't win. The expectations in the city were to win, and to see that come full circle was really, really exciting."[3]

What will the future hold? We'll all just have to sit back and watch to find out. Regardless of what twists and turns lie ahead on the Penguins' road, every day the team takes to the ice will truly be, in "Badger" Bob Johnson's immortal words, "A great day for hockey."

Chapter Notes

Chapter 1

1. *Pittsburgh Press*, February 11, 1966.
2. Interview with author, November 2018.
3. *Pittsburgh Post-Gazette*, February 10, 1966.
4. Interview with author, November 2018.
5. *PG*, February 10, 1966.
6. Interview with author, November 2018.
7. *Ibid.*
8. *PP*, May 17, 1966.
9. Interview with author, November 2018.
10. *Ibid.*
11. *PP*, May 17, 1966.
12. *PG*, November 3, 1982.
13. Interview with author, December 2018.
14. *PP*, September 7, 1967.
15. PittsburghHockey.net.
16. Interview with author, November 2018.
17. Interview with author, December 2018.
18. *PP*, September 7, 1967.
19. Interview with author, January 2019.
20. Interview with author, November 2018.
21. *Ibid.*
22. Interview with author, January 2019.
23. *Ibid.*
24. *Ibid.*

3. *Montreal Gazette*, October 12, 1967.
4. Interview with author, December 2018.
5. *PP*, October 30, 1967.
6. Interview with author, November 23, 2018.
7. *Ibid.*
8. *Ibid.*
9. *PP*, November 9, 1967.
10. *Ibid.*
11. *PP*, November 14, 1967.
12. *PP*, November 9, 1967.
13. Interview with author, November 2018.
14. *Ibid.*
15. *PP*, December 14, 1967.
16. Interview with author, January 2019.
17. *PP*, February 16, 1968.
18. *PP*, January 29, 1968.
19. *PP*, February 2, 1968.
20. *MG*, January 10, 1968.
21. *PP*, January 5, 1968.
22. *Ibid.*
23. *Ibid.*
24. *PP*, January 26, 1968.
25. *PP*, February 28, 1968
26. *PP*, March 22, 1968.
27. *PP*, November 9, 1967.
28. Interview with author, December 2018.
29. *PG*, March 22, 1968.
30. *PP*, March 21, 1968.
31. Interview with author, December 2018.
32. *Ibid.*

Chapter 2

1. *PP*, October 9, 1967.
2. Interview with author, December 2018.

Chapter 3

1. Interview with author, January 2019.
2. *PPG*, November 18, 1968.

3. *PP*, November 21, 1968.
4. Interview with author, January 2019.
5. Interview with author, March 2019.
6. *PP*, December 19, 1968.
7. *PP*, December 11, 1968.
8. *PP*, December 13, 1968.
9. *PP*, January 24, 1969.
10. *PG*, January 31, 1969.
11. Interview with author, January 2019.
12. *PP*, February 16, 1969.
13. *PP*, September 15, 1969.
14. *PP*, October 9, 1969.
15. *PP*, April 20, 1987.
16. *PP*, January 10, 1969.
17. *PP*, January 17, 1969.
18. *Ibid.*

Chapter 4

1. *PG*, July 3, 1969.
2. *Ibid.*
3. *PP*, July 3, 1969.
4. *PP*, September 25, 1969.
5. *PP*, November 9, 1969.
6. *PP*, January 17, 1970.
7. *PP*, February 20, 1970.
8. *The Hockey News*, March 6, 1970.
9. Interview with author, March 2019.
10. *Ibid.*
11. *PP*, April 2, 1970.
12. *PP*, April 8, 1970.
13. *San Francisco Examiner*, April 9, 1970.
14. *PP*, April 10, 1970.
15. *PP*, April 13, 1970.
16. *THN*, April 24, 1970.
17. *PP*, April 19, 1970.
18. *PP*, April 22, 1970.
19. *Ibid.*
20. *PP*, April 24, 1970.
21. Interview with author, March 2019.
22. Interview with author, December 2018.
23. *PP*, April 24, 1970.
24. *PP*, April 25, 1970.
25. *PP*, April 27, 1970.
26. *Ibid.*
27. *PG*, May 1, 1970.
28. *Ibid.*
29. *PP*, May 17, 1970.
30. *PP*, May 17, 1970.

Chapter 5

1. *PG*, May 22, 1970.
2. Interview with author, January 2019.

3. Interview with author, November 2018.
4. *THN*, November 20, 1970.
5. *PG*, October 27, 1970.
6. *PP*, October 16, 1970.
7. *PP*, November 7, 1970.
8. Interview with author, January 2019.
9. *PP*, December 29, 1970.
10. *Montreal Gazette*, January 19, 1971.
11. *PP*, January 28, 1971.
12. *PP*, March 21, 1971.
13. *PP*, April 14, 1971.
14. *Ibid.*
15. Interview with author, March 2019.
16. *Ibid.*
17. Interview with author, November 2018.
18. Interview with author, December 2018.
19. Interview with author, January 2019.

Chapter 6

1. *PP*, February 20, 1971.
2. *PG*, April 24, 1971.
3. *PP*, September 23, 1971.
4. Interview with author, December 2018.
5. *PP*, October 21, 1971.
6. *PP*, January 20, 1972.
7. *Ibid.*
8. *PP*, January 30, 1972.
9. *PG*, April 8, 1972.
10. *Ibid.*
11. *Washington (PA) Observer-Reporter*, April 8, 1972.
12. *Chicago Tribune*, April 10, 1972.
13. *Ibid.*

Chapter 7

1. *PP*, October 18, 1972.
2. *PG*, November 24, 1972.
3. *Toronto Star*, November 30, 1972.
4. *PG*, January 13, 1973.
5. *PP*, January 14, 1973.
6. *Ibid.*
7. *Ibid.*
8. Jim Proudfoot, *Pro Hockey 73–74*, p. 155.

Chapter 8

1. *PP*, April 3, 1973.
2. Jim Proudfoot, *Pro Hockey 73–74*, p. 155.

3. *PP*, November 5, 1973.
4. *PP*, November 30, 1973.
5. *PG*, December 29, 1973.
6. *PP*, January 15, 1974.
7. *Ibid.*
8. Interview with author, January 2019.
9. *PP*, January 24, 1974.
10. *PG*, February 12, 1974.
11. *PP*, March 19, 1974.
12. *PP*, February 13, 1974.

Chapter 9

1. Interview with author, January 2019.
2. *PG*, September 19, 1974.
3. *PP* November 21, 1974.
4. *PG*, December 2, 1974.
5. *PP*, January 23, 1975.
6. *PG*, February 4, 1975.
7. Interview with author, January 2019.
8. *Ibid.*
9. *MG*, April 3, 1975.
10. *PP*, April 9, 1975.
11. *PP*, April 11, 1975.
12. Interview with author, January 2019.
13. *PG*, April 16, 1975.
14. *Ibid.*
15. *PG*, April 19, 1975.
16. *PG*, April 18, 1975.
17. *PP*, April 18, 1975.
18. Interview with author, March 2019.
19. *PP*, April 21, 1975.
20. *PP*, April 22, 1975.
21. *PP*, April 23, 1975.
22. *PG*, April 23, 1975.
23. *PP*, April 25, 1975.
24. *PP*, April 26, 1975.
25. *PP*, April 27, 1975.
26. Interview with author, January 2019.
27. *PP*, April 27, 1975.
28. *Ibid.*
29. Interview with author, March 2019.
30. *Ibid.*
31. *Ibid.*

Chapter 10

1. *PG*, June 14, 1975.
2. *PP*, June 18, 1975.
3. Interview with author, January 2019.
4. *THN*, August 1975.
5. *Ibid.*
6. *Beaver County (PA) Times*, July 24, 1975.

Chapter 11

1. *PG*, October 8, 1975.
2. *PG*, October 10, 1975.
3. *PP*, October 11, 1975.
4. *PP*, November 12, 1975.
5. *PP*, November 4, 1975.
6. *PP*, November 8, 1975.
7. Interview with author, March 2019.
8. *PG*, January 15, 1976.
9. *PG*, January 20, 1976.
10. *PP*, January 18, 1976.
11. *PG*, January 19, 1976.
12. *BCT*, March 25, 1976.
13. *Ibid.*
14. *Ibid.*
15. Interview with author, March 2019.
16. *PP*, March 22, 1976.
17. *PG*, March 11, 1976.
18. *PP*, April 7, 1976.
19. *PP*, April 9, 1976.
20. *PG*, April 10, 1976.
21. *PP*, April 10, 1976.
22. Interview with author, March 2019.

Chapter 12

1. *PP*, October 7, 1976.
2. *PG*, October 30, 1976.
3. *Ibid.*
4. *PP*, November 5, 1976.
5. *THN*, November 19, 1976.
6. *PG*, December 4, 1976.
7. *PG*, December 13, 1976.
8. *PG*, January 15, 1977.
9. *PG*, December 23, 1976.
10. *Ibid.*
11. *PG*, December 17, 1976.
12. *PG*, December 23, 1976.
13. *PG*, January 5, 1977.
14. *Ibid.*
15. *PG*, January 7, 1977.
16. *PG*, January 26, 1977.
17. *PG*, January 25, 1977.
18. *PP*, April 6, 1977.
19. *PG*, April 8, 1977.
20. *PP*, April 10, 1977.
21. *Ibid.*
22. Interview with author, March 2019.
23. *PP*, April 12, 1977.

Chapter 13

1. *PG*, April 20, 1977.
2. *PG*, June 14, 1977.

3. *PG*, October 19, 1977.
4. *Hockey News*, March 10, 1978
5. *PG*, October 14, 1977.
6. *BCT*, October 12, 1977.
7. *PG*, November 3, 1977.
8. Interview with author, March 2019.
9. *PP*, December 2, 1977.
10. *PG*, January 31, 1978.
11. *PG*, April 11, 1978.
12. *PG*, April 6, 1978.

Chapter 14

1. Jim Proudfoot, *Pro Hockey* 78–79.
2. Penguins legend has it that Bastien didn't think the swap was lopsided at all because he believed he had acquired Montreal's *other* Shutt (minus the "c"): scoring superstar Steve, a 60-goal man in 1976–77 and key cog in the Habs' vaunted top line. Years later, Rod Schutt said there was nothing to the story.
3. *PG*, March 31, 1979.
4. Interview with author, March 2019.
5. *Ibid.*
6. *Ibid.*
7. *Ibid.*
8. Interview with author, January 2019.
9. *PG*, November 3, 1978.
10. *PG*, December 14, 1978.
11. *PG*, March 23, 1979.
12. *PP*, April 13, 1979.
13. Interview with author, March 2019.
14. *PP*, April 15, 1979.
15. Interview with author, March 2019.
16. *Ibid.*
17. *PG*, April 18, 1979.
18. *PP* April 23, 1979.
19. Interview with author, March 2019.
20. *PP*, November 12, 1980.
21. *PG*, April 18, 1979.
22. *PP*, April 24, 1979.

Chapter 15

1. *PP*, October 15, 1979.
2. *PP*, January 3, 1980.
3. *PG*, January 4, 1980.
4. *PG*, January 23, 1980.
5. *PP*, January 29, 1980.
6. *Ibid.*
7. *PG*, February 18, 1980.
8. Interview with author, January 2019.
9. *PG*, April 9, 1980.
10. *PG*, April 10, 1980.

11. *New London (CT) Day*, April 9, 1980.
12. *BCT*, April 11, 1980.
13. *Millville (NJ) Daily*, April 15, 1980.
14. *Ibid.*
15. *PG*, May 9, 1980.
16. *PP*, July 16, 1980.
17. *Ibid.*
18. *Ibid.*

Chapter 16

1. *PG*, October 1, 1980.
2. *PP*, September 30, 1980.
3. *Ibid.*
4. *Toronto Star*, December 3, 1980.
5. *PP*, December 3, 1980.
6. *THN*, November 7, 1980.
7. *PP*, November 26, 1980.
8. *PP*, January 3, 1981.
9. *PG*, December 1, 1980.
10. *PP*, December 29, 1980.
11. *PP*, December 30, 1980.
12. *PG*, January 17, 1981.
13. *PG*, December 15, 1980.
14. *PG*, December 5, 1980.
15. *BCT*, January 15, 1981.
16. *Ibid.*
17. *PG*, January 31, 1981.
18. *PP*, April 10, 1981.
19. *PP*, April 13, 1981.
20. *PG*, April 11, 1981.
21. *Latrobe (PA) Bulletin*, April 10, 1981.
22. *PG*, April 16, 1981.
23. *Ibid.*
24. *PP*, April 15, 1981.
25. *Philadelphia Daily News*, April 15, 1981.
26. *PG*, April 16, 1981.
27. *Ottawa Citizen*, April 15, 1981.
28. Interview with author, January 2019.
29. THN, December 4, 1981.

Chapter 17

1. *PP*, November 27, 1981.
2. *PP*, November 30, 1981.
3. *PP*, October 30, 1981.
4. *PG*, October 30, 1981.
5. *PG*, January 13, 1982.
6. *PG*, February 4, 1982.
7. Interview with author, January 2019.
8. *PP*, April 7, 1982.
9. *PG*, April 8, 1982.
10. *Ibid.*
11. *PP*, April 10, 1982.

12. *PG*, April 10, 1982.
13. *PP*, April 12, 1982.
14. *PP*, April 11, 1982.
15. *BCT*, April 12, 1982.
16. *Windsor (Ontario) Star*, April 12, 1982.
17. Interview with author, December 2018.
18. *PP*, April 13, 1982.
19. *New York Daily News*, April 13, 1982.
20. Interview with author, December 2018.
21. *Ibid.*
22. *OR*, April 15, 1982.

Chapter 18

1. *PP*, October 19, 1982.
2. Interview with author, January 2019.
3. *Ibid.*
4. Interview with author, January 2019.
5. *PP*, December 16, 1982.
6. *PP*, December 31, 1982.
7. *PP*, January 13, 1983.
8. Interview with author, March 2019.
9. *PP*, February 14, 1983.
10. *THN*, April 1, 1983.
11. *Ibid.*
12. *PP*, April 4, 1983.

Chapter 19

1. *PG*, May 28, 1983.
2. *PG*, October 4, 1983.
3. *PG*, November 24, 1983.
4. *PP*, December 21, 1983.
5. McElhanney, *TSN Presents: Playing to Lose*, 3:30–4:07.
6. *PG*, January 20, 1984.
7. *PG*, January 25, 1984.
8. *PP*, November 8, 1983.
9. *PP*, March 21, 1984.
10. *PG*, April 2, 1984.
11. *PP*, March 7, 1984.
12. *Ibid.*
13. McElhanney, *TSN Presents: Playing to Lose*, 5:57–6:12.
14. Interview with author, January 2019.
15. *Ibid.*
16. *Ibid.*
17. *PG*, June 8, 1984.
18. Interview with author, January 2019.
19. *PG*, June 20, 1984.
20. *BCT*, June 20, 1984.
21. *Danville (PA) News*, June 20, 1984.

Chapter 20

1. Interview with author, March 2019.
2. *PG*, October 12, 1984.
3. *PG*, November 7, 1984.
4. *PP*, October 31, 1984.
5. *PP*, November 14, 1984.
6. *PG*, February 19, 1985.
7. *Ibid.*
8. Interview with author, March 2019.
9. *PP*, March 14, 1985.
10. *PP*, March 18, 1985.
11. *THN*, April 26, 1985.
12. *PP*, March 29, 1985.
13. *THN*, September 20, 1985.

Chapter 21

1. *PG*, April 26, 1985.
2. *PG*, November 25, 1985.
3. *PG*, April 26, 1985.
4. *PG*, July 26, 1985.
5. *PG*, September 25, 1985.
6. *PG*, January 24, 1986.
7. Interview with author, March 2019.
8. *PG*, January 8, 1986.
9. *PG*, January 25, 1986.
10. *PG*, January 1, 1986.
11. *Hockey Digest*, March 1986.
12. *PG*, April 7, 1986.
13. *PG*, January 8, 1986.
14. *Danville (PA) News*, January 8, 1986.
15. *PG*, April 7, 1986.
16. *PP*, March 29, 1986.

Chapter 22

1. *PG*, October 13, 1986.
2. *PP*, October 23, 1986.
3. *PG*, October 24, 1986.
4. *PG*, December 10, 1986.
5. *PP*, November 13, 1986.
6. *Ibid.*
7. *PG*, November 20, 1986.
8. Interview with author, November 2018.
9. *PG*, November 20, 1986.
10. *PG*, March 28, 1985.
11. *PP*, February 22, 1987.
12. *PP*, January 27, 1987.
13. *PP*, March 6, 1987.
14. *Latrobe (PA) Bulletin*, March 16, 1987.
15. *PP*, March 30, 1987.
16. Interview with author, November 2018.

17. Interview with author, January 2019.
18. *PP*, April 13, 1987.

Chapter 23

1. *Hockey News*, October 2, 1987.
2. *PP*, September 22, 1987.
3. *Ibid.*
4. *PG*, June 4, 1987.
5. *PP*, November 25, 1987.
6. *PG*, November 25, 1987.
7. *PG*, November 26, 1987.
8. Interview with author, November 2018.
9. *PP*, February 6, 1988.
10. *PP*, March 2, 1988.
11. Interview with author, January 2019.
12. *PG*, March 9, 1988.
13. *Indiana (PA) Gazette*, March 10, 1988.
14. *Ibid.*
15. *PP*, March 30, 1988.
16. Interview with author, January 2019.

Chapter 24

1. *PG*, June 29, 1988.
2. *PP*, October 16, 1988.
3. Interview with author, January 2019.
4. *PP*, January 15, 1989.
5. *PP*, November 6, 1988.
6. Interview with author, November 2018.
7. *PP*, February 3, 1989.
8. *Ibid.*
9. Interview with author, November 2018.
10. *PP*, February 3, 1989.
11. Interview with author, March 2019.
12. Lemieux's "5 goals, 5 ways" feat would be recognized in a 2017 NHL fan vote as the greatest moment in NHL history.
13. Interview with author, November 2018.
14. *PP*, April 6, 1989.
15. *PP*, April 9, 1989.
16. *PP*, April 10, 1989.
17. *PP*, April 22, 1989.
18. *Ibid.*
19. *PG*, April 22, 1989.
20. *PP*, April 20, 1989.
21. *PP*, April 26, 1989.
22. *Philadelphia Inquirer*, April 26, 1989.
23. *PI*, April 30, 1989.
24. *PG*, May 1, 1989.

25. Interview with author, November 2018.
26. *PG*, May 1, 1989.

Chapter 25

1. *PP*, October 25, 1989.
2. *PP*, October 31, 1989.
3. *PP*, October 26, 1989.
4. *PG*, December 6, 1989.
5. *PP*, December 6, 1989.
6. *Ibid.*
7. *PP*, January 22, 1990.
8. *PG*, January 22, 1990.
9. *PP*, February 15, 1990.
10. *PP*, February 10, 1990.
11. *MG*, February 25, 1990.
12. *Ibid.*
13. *PP*, March 31, 1990.
14. *White Plains (NY) Journal News*, April 1, 1990.
15. *Indiana (PA) Gazette*, April 2, 1990.
16. *PG*, April 2, 1990.
17. *Latrobe (PA) Bulletin*, April 2, 1990.

Chapter 26

1. *PP*, April 8, 1990.
2. *PP*, June 12, 1990.
3. *PP*, June 13, 1990.
4. *PP*, June 12, 1990.
5. *PG*, June 12, 1990.
6. *PP*, June 13, 1990.
7. *PG*, June 13, 1990.
8. *PP*, July 21, 1990.
9. *PP*, July 13, 1990.
10. *PP*, September 28, 1990.
11. *Ibid.*
12. *PP*, September 28, 1990.
13. *PP*, October 30, 1990.
14. *PP*, November 21, 1990.
15. *PP*, December 3, 1990.
16. *PPG*, December 12, 1990.
17. *PP*, December 30, 1990.
18. *PP*, January 27, 1991.
19. *PP*, February 22, 1991.
20. *PP*, March 2, 1991.
21. *PG*, March 5, 1991.
22. *PP*, March 28, 1991.
23. *PG*, March 28, 1991.
24. *PG*, April 4, 1991.
25. *PG*, April 12, 1991.
26. *Ibid.*
27. *PP*, April 14, 1991.
28. *PP*, April 16, 1991.

29. *PP*, April 22, 1991.
30. *PG*, April 26, 1991.
31. *Ibid.*
32. *PP*, May 1, 1991.
33. *PP*, May 4, 1991.
34. *Ibid.*
35. *PP*, May 7, 1991.
36. *PG*, May 8, 1991.
37. *PP*, May 10, 1991.
38. *PG*, May 13, 1991.
39. *PG*, May 15, 1991.
40. *PP*, May 16, 1991.
41. *Detroit Free Press*, May 18, 1991.
42. *PG*, May 18, 1991.
43. *Ibid.*
44. *PP*, May 22, 1991.
45. *PP*, May 25, 1991.
46. Interview with author, March 2019.
47. *Ibid.*
48. *PG*, May 25, 1991.
49. *Ibid.*
50. *PP*, May 26, 1991.
51. *PG*, May 27, 1991.
52. *Ibid.*
53. Interview with author, March 2019.

Chapter 27

1. *PP*, June 2, 1991.
2. *PG*, August 31, 1991.
3. *Ibid.*
4. *PG*, October 2, 1991.
5. *PP*, November 19, 1991.
6. *Ibid.*
7. *PP*, November 27, 1991.
8. *BCT*, November 27, 1991.

9. *PG*, November 27, 1991.
10. *PG*, November 28, 1991.
11. *PG*, February 20, 1992.
12. *Ibid.*
13. *Ibid.*
14. *PP*, February 28, 1992.
15. *Ibid.*
16. *PP*, March 16, 1992.
17. Ross, *Against the Odds: Pittsburgh Penguins 1991–92*, 19:14–19:32.
18. *PP*, April 30, 1992.
19. *PP*, May 2, 1992.
20. *PP*, May 4, 1992.
21. *PP*, May 7, 1992.
22. *PP*, May 10, 1992.
23. *PP*, May 12, 1992.
24. *PP*, May 14, 1992.
25. *Ibid.*
26. AP, May 19, 1992.
27. *Boston Globe*, May 22, 1992.
28. *Ibid.*
29. *Ibid.*
30. *MG*, May 27, 1992.
31. *Chicago Tribune*, May 27, 1992.
32. *MG*, May 27, 1992.
33. *Chicago Tribune*, May 27, 1992.
34. *Chicago Tribune*, May 31, 1992.
35. *THN*, June 26, 1992.
36. *THN*, June 12, 1992.

Epilogue

1. Interview with author, March 2019.
2. *Ibid.*
3. *Ibid.*

Bibliography

Author Interviews

All interviews conducted between November 2018 and March 2019.

Dave Burrows, former Penguins player.
Joe Gordon, Penguins public relations director, 1966–1969.
Bob Grove, former Penguins beat reporter, *Washington (PA) Observer-Reporter*, radio personality.
Mike Hanczar, long-time Penguins fan.
Dave Hannan, former Penguins player.
Denis Herron, former Penguins player.
Bill Heufelder, former Penguins beat reporter, *Pittsburgh Press*.
Earl Ingarfield, former Penguins player.
Rick Kehoe, former Penguins player.
Troy Loney, former Penguins player.
Dick Mattiussi, former Penguins player.
Bill Peduto, Mayor of Pittsburgh.
Lou Prato, former *Hockey News* Pittsburgh correspondent.
Jean Pronovost, former Penguins player.
Dan Quinn, former Penguins player.
Bob Smizik, former sports reporter/columnist, *Pittsburgh Post-Gazette*.
Ron Stackhouse, former Penguins player.

Newspapers

Beaver County (PA) Times
Boston Globe
Chicago Tribune
The Day (New London, CT)
Montreal Gazette
New York Daily News
Ottawa Citizen

Philadelphia Inquirer
Pittsburgh Post-Gazette
Pittsburgh Press
San Francisco Examiner
Toronto Star
Washington (PA) Observer-Reporter

Periodicals

Hockey Digest
The Hockey News

Books

Jim Proudfoot. *Pro Hockey 73–74*. Richmond Hill, ON: Simon & Schuster, 1973.

Websites

Hockey-reference.com
PittsburghHockey.net

Videos

McElhanney, Jeremy, dir. *TSN Presents: Playing to Lose*. Toronto: TSN/Bell Media, 2014. Running time: 23:29. Accessed via YouTube.
Ross, Stuart R., dir. *Against the Odds: The Story of the 1991–92 Pittsburgh Penguins*. Philadelphia: Ross Sports, 1992. Running time: 66:30. Accessed via YouTube.

Index

Numbers in **bold italics** indicate pages with illustrations

All-Star Game 50, 54, 91, 165, 201
Amarillo Wranglers 23, 60
Anderson, Russ 88, 114
Angotti, Lou 23, 25-26, 30, 148-151, 154-155
Apps, Syl, Jr. 1, 43, 52-53, 55, 59, 66, 68, 72, 80, 86-88, 90; as part of Century Line 81; on Penguins' identity 65; trade to Los Angeles 96-97; trade to Pittsburgh 42
Arbour, Al 35, 68, 72, 136
Arnason, Chuck 61, 66, 68
Atlanta Braves 21
Atlanta Flames 1, 54, 88, 100
attendance 19, 27, 45, 55, 59, 66, 87, 90, 101, 105, 128, 145, 152, 156-157, 165, 170, 172
Awrey, Don 94

Babych, Wayne 122, 124, 162
Badali, Gus 153, 156-157
Baldwin, Howard 225, 240
Baltimore Skipjacks 148, 154-155, 189
bankruptcy (1975) 1, 5, 74-76, 97-98, 220
bankruptcy (1998) 240
Barrasso, Tom 194-198, 212, 214-215, 217, 219, 227-228, 230-233, 236-237; on Bob Johnson 206, 225; and daughter's illness 202; March 1990 return 203; on 1990 Uwe Krupp goal 204; on repeating as Stanley Cup champions 239; on Scotty Bowman 225; trade to Pittsburgh 190; winning 1991 Stanley Cup 221; winning 1992 Stanley Cup 238
Bartimo, Vincent 98, 115
Bassen, Hank 15, 19-20
Bastien, Aldege "Baz" 86, 95-97, 99-101, 108, 110, 119, 121, 126, 140, 143, 147-148, 248 (note); death 146; eye injury 84; hired by Penguins 84; named NHL Executive of the Year 105; named Penguins GM 94
Bathgate, Andy 12-14, 16, 22-24, 41, 46

Baxter, Paul 123, 129-130, 133, 137, **151**, 205
Belanger, Roger 157
Belfour, Ed 236, 238
Beliveau, Jean 15, 19, 153
Belzberg, Morris 225, 240
Berenson, Red 37, 123
Berry, Bob 161-162, 165, 168-169, 171, 173, 175-176, 178, 180; circus performers rant 177
Bignell, Larry 58
Binkley, Les 1, **13**, 18-20, 22, 24, 27, 31, 34, 36, 43, 52, 64
Bladon, Tom 85, 99, 102
Blair, Wren 76-79, 84, 86-87, 93-94
Blaisdell, Mike 168
Block, Peter 8-10, 31, 45, 74-75
Bodger, Doug 157, 162, 171, 173, 178, 190
Boileau, Marc 61-62, 65-66, 71-72, 77-81
Boivin, Leo 13, 22, 26
Bossy, Mike 132-133, 136, 141
Boston Bruins 1, 20, 42, 47, 80, 100, 103-105, 108-109, 111-115, 127, 132, 161, 184, 186, 214-216, 234
Boston Garden 19, 103-104, 109, 111-113, 115, 160, 214-215, 234
Bourne, Bob 78, 110, 135
Bourque, Phil 149, 191, 194-195, 203-204, 213, 216-217, 219, 221-223, 230, 232, 236
Bourque, Ray 114, 160, 172, 201, 210, 215, 234
Boutette, Pat 129, 134
Bowman, Scotty 32, 36, 92, 108, 227, 234, 236; coaching style 225; joins Penguins 205-206; named Penguins interim head coach 224; on Tom Barrasso 190
Boyd, Randy 133
Boyer, Wally 32, 34
Brière, Michel 1, 30-**31**, 34-41, 43-45, 72, 220

Brown, Andy 58-59
Brown, Rob 183, 189-192, 194-195, 198, 208
Buffalo Sabres 46, 48-49, 52, 65, 78-80, 82, 87, 94, 103-104, 108, 111-112, 115, 140-141, 173, 190, 203-204, 206, 209, 225, 228
Bullard, Mike 122-123, 132, 136-137, 141-142, 168-169, 171, 191, 196-197; on 1983-84 Penguins *150*; trade to Calgary 175
Burkle, Ron 240
Burrows, Dave 46, *50*, 52, 58, 68, 71-73, 83, 88, 97, 99-101, 112, 119-120
Buskas, Rod 141, 199
Button, Jack 46, 60-61, 63-64, 66-67, 74-76

California Golden Seals *see* Oakland Seals
Calgary Flames 121, 151, 171, 175-176, 192, 203, 205-206, 209, 228
Caligiuri, Richard 164
Callander, Jock 194, 233
Campbell, Clarence 20, 42, 45, 66, 75, 93
Campbell, Colin 68
Canada Cup (1987) 179-180, 184
Carlyle, Randy *100*, 102, 104, 114, 121-123, 125, 130, 136-137, 143, *144*, 148; Norris Trophy win 124; style of play 118; trade to Pittsburgh 99; trade to Winnipeg *154-155*, 162
Carr, Gene 96
Casey, Jon 217-218, 221
Century Line 80-81
Chabot, John 163, 171
Chapman, Blair 85, 90, 103
Cheevers, Gerry 3, 105, 114-116
Cherry, Don 108, 115, 199
Chicago Blackhawks 9-10, 17, 20, 24, 46, 49-51, 58-60, 79, 94, 99, 115, 120, 122, 157, 162, 167, 188, 217, 229, 235-238
Chorney, Mark 130
Civic Arena (Pittsburgh) 4, 8, 15, 25-26, 28, 30, 36-37, 40, 43-45, 47-49, 53, 61, 66-72, 77-78, 82, 84, 86-87, 97, 102, 109-110, 118, 121, 124, *128*, 131, 133-134, *141*, 142-143, 145-146, 149, 152, 161, 163, 165, 170-173, 176-178, 182, 184, 188, 192-193, 196, 204, 214, 217-219, 226, 228, 230, 232, 235-236, 240, *243*; All-Star Game at 201; DeBartolo lease of 105, 125, 225; design 11; doors padlocked 74; final game ceremony 242, improvements to 167, 191; 1984 draft event at 157; seating capacity *9*, 55, 59
Clarke, Bobby 48, 54, 85, 95, 140-141
Cleveland Barons 96
Coffey, Paul 171-172, 179, 183-185, 190, 197-198, 200-202, *209*-210, 212-213, 218, 227; leadership qualities *193*; trade to Pittsburgh 181-*182*
Colorado Rockies 85, 94, 97, 115, 119, 121

Columbus Owls 76, 88
Corrigan, Mike 144-146
Cossette, Jacques 103
Creamer, Pierre 180, 183-185, 188
Crombeen, Mike 124, 126
Crosby, Sidney 240
Cullen, John 191, 194, 207-208, 210
Cunneyworth, Randy 173, 194-195, 198

Dahlquist, Chris 208
DeBartolo, Edward J., Jr. 163, 183-184, 188, 199-200
DeBartolo, Edward J., Sr. 105, 111, 116, 118, 125, 140, 146, 148, 152, 157, 163-164, 167, 175, 181, 184, 186, 199; assumes majority ownership 98; buys ownership stake 93; estimated net worth 166; playoff refund offer 133-134; sale of Penguins 225
DeMarco, Ab 60
Denver, John 70
Detroit Red Wings 9, 12-13, 26, 30, 40, 42, 46, 53, 60-61, 65, 71, 84, 94, 98, 143, 162, 167, 171, 173, 192, 235; clinch first division title vs. 211; New Year's Eve 1978 comeback vs. 101-102
Dillabough, Bob 13, 18
Dion, Michel *127-128*, 130, 133-137, 143, *144*, 145, 147, 149, 151, *164*
Drouin, Jude 70, 75
Dryden, Ken 3, 67, 96, 108
Duguay, Ron 171, 176, 180
Durbano, Steve 60-61, 77-79

Edestrand, Darryl 48
Edmonton Oilers 108, 145, 152-153, 161, 167-168, 171, 181-182, 184, 206, 217, 231, 235
Esposito, Phil 1, 170, 193
Esposito, Tony 49, 188-192, 198-199
Errey, Bob 149, 189, 191, 193, 196, 221, 233

Faubert, Mario 88-89, 117, 124, 131
Favell, Doug 48-49
Federko, Bernie 122
Feltrin, Tony 130, 141
Ferguson, George 99, 103-104, 109, 119, 123, 140, 147
first division championship 211
Flaherty, Peter 33, 66, 71
Fleury, Marc-Andre 240
Flockhart, Ron 149
Fonteyne, Val 18, 24, 34
Fort Wayne Komets 61
franchise granted 9-10
Francis, Ron 210-212, 214, 219, 221, 226, 229, 232-233, 236-238
Frawley, Dan 168, 176, 183-184
Frenzel, Otto "Nick", III 76, 79, 87, 89, 93, 98

Gagner, Dave 219
Gardner, Paul 119-120, 123, 129, 131, 134, 136, 142
Gartner, Mike 231
Gatzos, Steve 130, 141
Gessner, Bob 12
Gilbert, Gilles 80, 109
Gilbert, Rod 63
Gilbertson, Stan 80, 95
Gilhen, Randy 213
Gillies, Clark 70, 132
Gordon, Joe 9-12, 15, 18, 21-22, 24, 27, 41, 60
Graham, Dirk 229, 236-238
Graves, Adam 231-232
Gretzky, Wayne 152-153, 161, 169-170, 172, 178, 181, 185, 189-190, 192, 195, 201, 218; at Canada Cup 179-180; on Mario Lemieux 162
Guenette, Steve 181, 184

Hadfield, Vic 63-64, 66, 68, 82, 85, 101
Hall, Glenn 32, 35
Hamilton, Jim 103, 110
Hamilton, Ontario 163
Hannan, Dave 141, 145, 155, 177-178, 182, 191, 199
Harbaruk, Nick 33-34, 37, 41, 49
Harrison, Paul 127
Hartford Whalers 108, 126-127, **128-129**, **142**, 147, 149, 151, 175, 186, 203, 208, 228; 1991 trade with Pittsburgh 210-211
Hasek, Dominik 229, 238
Herron, Denis 3, 58-59, 84-85, 88-90, 97, 102-104, **109**-110, 112, 143, 149; on Mario Lemieux 160-161; on Penguins' shortcomings 105; as rookie 52; trade to Montreal 108
Hershey Bears 11, 23, 64, 79, 85, 88, 97
Heufelder, Bill 12-13, 22-23, 40-41, 44, 47, 59
Hextall, Bryan 32, 35, 52
Hextall, Ron 191, 194-197
Holland, Rob 108-111, 119
Holmgren, Paul 196
Horton, Tim 46-47, 50-52
Hotham, Greg 136
Howatt, Garry 69, 71
Howe, Gordie 13, 46
Howe, Mark 174, 194-195, 197
Hrdina, Jiri 209
Hucul, Fred 58
Hughes, Pat 108, 110, 119-120
Hull, Bobby 17, 26, 49-50
Hunter, Dave 182, 184

Iafrate, Al 153, 201, 230-231
"Igloo" *see* Civic Arena

Ingarfield, Earl 11, 13-15, 17, 19, 22, 26-27, 33-34
Inness, Gary 65, 68-70, 72, 77, 79

Jagr, Jaromir 209, 211-212, 214, 227, 231-234, 236-238, 240
Jennings, Grant 210-211, 221
Johnson, Bob (coach) 207-208, 211-212, 214-215, 218, 238, 243; death of 225; hired as coach 205-206; illness 224; on Penguins' playing style 210; tribute to 226; on winning Stanley Cup 221
Johnson, Bob (player) 65, 69
Johnson, Jim 197, 208
Johnson, Mark 111, 113, 123
Johnston, Eddie 116, 118-124, 130-131; 133-135, 140, 143-147, 149-150, 162-163, 165, 167-168, 170, 175, 180-181; attempt to sign Andy Moog 184; and Bobby Orr 117; demoted to assistant GM 188; drafting Mario Lemieux 156-157; hired as head coach 115-116; and Michel Dion 127; named GM 148; and power play tactics 132; signing Mario Lemieux 157; and tanking 154-155
Jones, Ron 78
Joseph, Chris 181-182

Kansas City Scouts 79, 84, 119, 200
Keenan, Larry 36-37
Keenan, Mike 179, 235, 237-238
Keener, Elmore 46-47
Kehoe, Rick 3, 64, 66, 70, 80, 82, 86, 88, 100, 104, **115**, 120-123, 129, 132, 155, 160, 162, 220-221; overtime goal vs. Islanders 134; on Penguins' financial problems 67, 75; trade to Pittsburgh 63; wins Lady Byng Trophy 124
Kelly, Bob "Battleship" 60-61, 66, 69, 89-90
Kelly, Leonard "Red" 30-33, 35-37, 39-44, 46-48, 51, 53-54, 63
Kindrachuk, Orest 99, 103-106, 111, **112**, 118
Krupp, Uwe 204, 220

Labre, Yvon 58
Lafleur, Guy 120, **141**, 152
Lange, Mike 176-177
Larouche, Pierre 1, 65-68, 71-72, 80, 82, 88-89, 122, **129**, **142**, 152; junior career **64**; requests trade 87; suspension 85; trade to Montreal 96
Lascheid, Vince 214
Laxton, Gord 77, 79, 84, 108
Leach, Reggie 95
Lee, Peter 96, 102, 108-109, 113, 121, 146
Legace, Jean-Guy 58
Leiter, Bob 48-50

Lemieux, Mario 1, 5-6, 154-155, 162, 167-173, 175-178, 181, 183-185, *189*-191, 193-195, 197-199, 203-205, 209-212, 215-216, 220, 224-225, 228-230, 233-236, *237*, 241, *243*; Adam Graves slash 231-232; adopts number 66 153; back injuries of 201-202, 207, 213, *218*-219, 227; becomes Penguins owner 240; on Bob Johnson 206, 225; drafting of 156-157; eight-point game in 1989 playoffs 196; first NHL game 160-*161*; first NHL goal 160-*161*; five-goals-five-ways game 192, 250 (note); 46-game scoring streak 200-202; and Hodgkin's Lymphoma 240; junior career 152-153; Minnesota goal, 1991 finals 217-*218*; and 1987 Canada Cup 179-180; 1990 All-Star Game (Pittsburgh) 201; signs with Penguins 157-158; wins Conn Smythe Trophy 221, 238; wins first scoring title 186; wins first Stanley Cup 221-*222*; wins 1985 All-Star Game MVP 165; wins second Stanley Cup 238-239

Letang, Kris 240
Libbett, Nick 119
Lindstrom, Willie 167
Liut, Mike 122-124
logo 3-4, 12, 24, 117
Loney, Troy 146, 149, 163, 168-169, 191, 194, 201, 211, 219-222, 232, 243
Lonsberry, Ross 48, 95, 99, 114, 120, 129
Los Angeles Kings 10, 20, 23, 30, 32, 41, 47-48, 53-54, 61, 94, 96, 103, 110, 120, 122, 146, 153, 161, 167, 173, 176, 190, 227
Lynch, Jack 52, 60

MacDonald, Lowell 1, 41, 43, 53-54, 59, 63, 69, 80, 85, 87-88, 124
MacLeish, Rick 136, 140
Mahovlich, Pete 4, 96-97, 102, 105, 108
Malkin, Evgeni 240
Malone, Greg 85, 90, 102-103, 111, 118, 121, 123-124, 130, 145
Mann, Jimmy 131
Mantha, Moe 151, 162, 171, 174, 182
Marshall, Paul 109, 119
Martha, Paul 98, 106, 110-111, 116, 121, 126, 140, 145, 147-148, 152, 157, 166-167, 177, 180, 188, 225
Masloff, Sophie 217
Masterton, Bill (trophy) 54, 124
Mathiasen, Dwight 171, 176
Mattiussi, Dick 10-11, 17-18, 26
McAdam, Gary 103, 105, 113
McBain, Andrew 198
McCallum, Dunc 34
McCammon, Bob 148
McClelland, Kevin 136, 141

McCreary, Keith 26, 28, 32, 34, 37, 43, 50
McDonough, Al 48, 52-53, 55, 59
McEachern, Shaun 233, 236, 238
McEwan, Mike 136
McGregor, Jack 8-11, 19, 21-22, 27, 31-32, 40, 45
McManama, Bob 64
McNab, Peter 105, 114
McVie, Tom 153, 155, 211
Meehan, Gerry 49
Melanson, Roland 136
Meloche, Gilles 168, 171, 181, 183
Messier, Mark 179, 181, 231-232
Michayluk, Dave 233
Middleton, Rick 105, 113-114
Miguay, Rudy 23
Milbury, Mike 104, 215
Millen, Greg 102, 108-112, *113*, 114-115, 119, 122-124, 126-127
Minnesota North Stars 20-22, 26, 32, 35, 41-42, 76, 78, 97, 131, 140, 145, 147, 156, 163, 208; in 1991 Stanley Cup Final 217, 219-221
Modano, Mike 217-219
Monahan, Hartland 94, 96, 99
Montreal Canadiens 3, 5, 17, 19-20, 24, 43, 64, 67, 84-85, 87, 96, 99-100, 103, 108, *109*, 110, 128, *141*, 143, 145, 147, 153, 157, 177, 202, 206, 228, 248 (note); end road winless streak vs. 120; in first Penguins game 15-16
Moog, Andy 184, 215-216, 234
Mullen, Joey 206-207, 214, 220-221, 231, 233
Muller, Kirk 153, 157, 185
Murphy, Larry 180, 208, 212, 216, 220-222, 229, 232-233, 236, 238
Muskegon Line 223

Nassau County Coliseum 69, 110, 132, 136
Needham, Mike 233
Neely, Cam 147, 215-216
New Jersey Devils 145-147, 149-151, 153, 155-157, 163, 173, 175, 177, 183, 185-186, 192, 219, 226; 1991 playoffs vs. 211-213
New York Islanders 1, 52, 75, 78, 82, 85, 122, 126, 128, 130-131, 140, 144, 149, 164, 168-169, 183, 192, 202-203, 206, 220, 226, 241; 1975 playoffs vs. 68-73; 1982 playoffs vs. 132-137
New York Rangers 10, 20, 12-13, 26, 42, 46, 53, 63, 68, 80, 84, 94, 121, 126, 149, 156, 162-163, 168, 171, 173, 176-177, 183, 185-186, 202, 211, 213, 241; Craig Patrick and 199-200; 1989 playoffs vs. 192-194; 1992 playoffs vs. 231-233
nickname 11-12

Nielson, Roger 231
Nystrom, Bob 68, 132, 136-137

Oakland Seals 10, 17, 20, 25-27, 33-35, 42, 59, 66, 168, 200
Olczyk, Ed 153, 157
option line 208
O'Reilly, Terry 113, 115
Orr, Bobby 1, 42, 117, 181
Owchar, Dennis 88, 97

Paek, Jim 214
Paiement, Wilf 181
Paradise, Bob 94
Parise, Jean-Paul 68
Parliament, Marv 65
Parsons, Donald 20-21, 26-28, 40-42, 46, 48, 54
Patrick, Craig 199-202, 204-210, 224-228, 238
Patrick, Lester 199-200
Perno, Bob 153, 157
Perreault, Gilbert 82, 141
Pete the Penguin (mascot) 24
Philadelphia Flyers 10, 18, 22-23, 26, 32-33, 45, 61, 67, 71, 73, 79, 85, 90, 95, 99, 102, 108, 111-112, 114, 120, 126, 128-130, 140, 148-149, 163, 171, 173-174, 176-177, 192-193, 203, 211, 220, 227-228, 241; "Broad Street Bullies" 58-59; end road winless streak vs. 191; miss 1972 playoffs 48-49; 1989 playoffs vs. 194-197
Philadelphia Spectrum 48, 73, 95, 101, 130, 177, 191-192, 196, 220
Pietrangelo, Frank 181, 183-184, 190, 202, 219, 228; "The Save" 212-213
Pittsburgh Hornets 8-9, 11-13, 18, 22, 84
Pittsburgh Pirates (NHL) 10, 111
Plager, Barclay 32, 35
Plager, Bob 32, 35-36
Plante, Jacques 32, 35, 37, 43
Plasse, Michel 69, 82, 127
players' strike (1992) 229
Polis, Greg 41, 43, 48, 52, 54, 60
Pollock, Sam 96
Potter, Thayer (Tad) 45-46, 53-54, 59-60, 66, 74-75, 98
Potvin, Denis 68-69, 71, 132, 140
Poulin, Dave 179, 197
Pratt, Tracy 26, 30
Prentice, Dean 30, 34-36
Price, Noel 18-19, 22, 25
Price, Pat 129-130, 132-133, 143-144
Pronovost, Jean 1-3, 28, 34-36, 49, 52, 63, 65, 68, 71-73, 78-79, 83, 86-91, 196; on Century Line *81*; on Michel Brière 41, 44; at Penguins' 50th anniversary 242; on

Pierre Larouche 96-97; on Red Kelly 32-33; scores 50 goals 80-*81*; trade to Atlanta 100; trade to Pittsburgh 25
proposed move to Norris Division 168
Propp, Brian 195, 197, 219

Quebec Nordiques 108, 121, 127, 145, 156, 177, 182, 186, 192, 209, 228
Quinn, Dan 175, 178, 182-184, 191, 193-195, 197

Ratelle, Jean 63, 105
Recchi, Mark 208, 211-212, 214-216, 219, 227
record for fastest five goals 52-53
Resch, Glenn 70-71, 153
Ricci, Nick 119, 127, 146
Richter, Mike 232
Riggin, Pat 181, 184
Riley, Jack 15, 21-23, 25-28, 30, 32, 34-35, 37, 42-43, 45-46, 53-55, 84; fired 60; hired as GM 10; and Penguins nickname 11-12; promoted to executive director 40; reassumes GM role 48
Rissling, Gary 128-129, 167
Robert, Rene 46, 48-49, 82, 103
Roberts, Gordie 208, 215-216
Roberts, Jimmy 178
Roenick, Jeremy 236-238
Romano, Roberto 154, 171, 173
Rooney, Art 9, 20
Rupp, Duane 26, 37, 78
Ruskowski, Terry 167, 172, 175, 180
Ruta, Thomas 225
Rutherford, Jim 46, 50, 52, 58-60, 64, 102
Ruzicka, Vladimir 215

Saginaw Gears 76, 86
St. Laurent, Andre 134-135, 146
St. Louis Blues 10, *16*, 17, 19-22, 30, 32, 48-49, 54, 60-62, 72, 111, 115, 120, 144, 162, 168-169, 189, 192, 200, 203, 206, 208, 217; fastest five-goals record vs. 52-53; 1970 playoffs vs. 35-37; 1975 playoffs vs. 67-68; 1981 playoffs vs. 122-124
Samuelsson, Kjell 227, 230
Samuelsson, Ulf 210, 213, 215-216, 221, 227-229
San Jose Sharks 228
Sanderson, Derek 97-98
Sather, Glen 30, 32-33, 42, 181, 184, 206
Sauve, Bob 103-104
Savill, Al 76, 79, 86-90, 92-98
Schinkel, Ken 13, 17-19, 28, 34-35, 43, 52-54, 58-60; 83, 85-87, 90, 92; hired as head coach 55; reassumes head coaching duties 79-80; relieved of head coaching duties 61; resigns as head coach 93

Schock, Ron 30, 34, 37, 41, 52-53, 64, 66-68, 72, 85, 94
Schultz, Dave 95-97, 103
Schutt, Rod *100*, 105, 110, 121, 123, 134, 135, 248 (note)
Seattle 66, 76
Shack, Eddie 48-50, 52-53, 129
Shedden, Doug 130, 141
Sheppard, Gregg 100, 102, 104, 113-114, 118, 140
Shero, Fred 59, 92
Simmer, Charlie 181
Simpson, Craig 182
Sinden, Harry 112-113, 184
Sittler, Darryl 82, 89
Smith, Al 31-32, 37, 43, 102
Smith, Barry 207
Smith, Billy 68, 70, 110, 132-134, 136-137
Smith, Bobby 217, 219
Smith, Doug 203
Smith, Gary 25, 33-34, 50
Smith, Steve 236
Solomon, Sid III 60
Spencer, Brian 94
Stackhouse, Ron 3, 61, 70, 73, 90, *91*, 97, 111, 114, 118, 121, 140, 143; on Penguins' financial troubles 67; and Pittsburgh fans 78-79, 242; trade to Pittsburgh 60
Stanley Cup win: (1991) 221-223; (1992) 238-239
Stanton, Paul 217
Stevens, Kevin 194, 208, 211-216, 219-220, 227, 230, 232-234, 238
Stoughton, Blain 63
Stratton, Art 13, 17-18
Sullivan, George "Red" 10-11, 14, 17-20, 22-28
Swarbrick, George 26
Sweeney, Don 216, 234

Taglianetti, Peter 208, 213
Tallon, Dale 99
tanking accusations 154-156
Taylor, Mark 149
Teitelbaum, Hubert 76
Terreri, Chris 212

Thomas, Wayne 82-83, 89, 90
Tocchet, Rick 179, 227-230, 232-234, 236, 238
Tonelli, John 132, 135-137
Toronto Maple Leafs 5, 18, 26, 30, 40, 42-43, 46, 48, 53, 63, 65, 71, 86, 94, 97, 99, 111, 115, 119-120, 124, 153, 168, 177, 197, 199; 1976 playoffs vs. 82-83; 1977 playoffs vs. 88-90
Tremblay, Vincent 154-155
Trottier, Bryan 132, 134, 140-141, 206-207, 216, 221, 233

Ubriaco, Gene 25-26, 189, 191, 196, 199
Unger, Garry 62
uniforms 3, 12, 24, 110-111

Vanbiesbrouck, John 173, 232-233
Vancouver Canucks (NHL team) 47, 52, 61, 65, 84, 87, 199-200
Vancouver Canucks (WHL team) 24, 41
van Impe, Ed 88

Washington Capitals 1, 77-78, 87, 94, 118, 121-122, 126, 145, 173, 176-177, 185, 192, 194, 200, 208, 210, 227-228; 1991 playoffs vs. 213-214; 1992 playoffs vs. 229-231
Watson, Bryan 26, 30, 32, 49, 53, 58, 60
Westfall, Ed 71-72
Wilkins, Barry 68, 83
Williams, Dave "Tiger" 83, 89-90
Wilson, Dunc 84-85, 88, 95, 97
Wilson, Johnny 94-95, 97, 109-110, 115
Winnipeg Jets 108, 118, 121, 127, 130-131, 145, 150-151, 154-155, 162-163, 171, 198
World Hockey Association 52, 64, 94, 108, 121, 127, 225
Woytowich, Bob 28, 32-34, 48
Wregget, Ken 197, 227-228

Young, Scott 209
Young, Warren 161-162, 167, 173, 176, 180
Young, Wendell 190-191, 202, 228

Zalapski, Zarley 181, 195, 200, 210
Ziegler, John 111, 221, 239

www.ingramcontent.com/pod-product-compliance
Ingram Content Group UK Ltd.
Pitfield, Milton Keynes, MK11 3LW, UK
UKHW030938100125
453515UK00018B/229